THE SPACE BETWEEN MEMORIES

PRAISE FOR
The Space Between Memories

"In *The Space Between Memories*, David Joannes shares a captivating journey through his life, moment by moment, story by story. He is vulnerable about the victories and the trials of life as a missionary in China. He learned one of my favorite God lessons: Jesus is the vine, and we are the branches. If we let Him, He will prune us until our lives are hidden in Him, so we can see what He sees and feel what He feels. I pray that as you read this powerful book, you will surrender your heart in a deeper way to the only One who can teach us what love looks like. I pray you will be inspired by David's life to see the poor and the broken as treasures God wants to bring to His banqueting table and invite them home."

HEIDI BAKER, *Co-Founder and CEO, Iris Global*, irisglobal.org

"The caricature of the missionary as some stodgy old plodder swathed in polyester has never had much basis in fact, and anyhow *The Space Between Memories* blows all that to pieces. David's tales of wildfaring and wayfaring, close calls and close encounters, all in the service of the Gospel, unfold like an Indiana Jones plot. Or better: like a sequel to the book of Acts. If your own faith has gotten a bit stodgy of late, here's the antidote."

MARK BUCHANAN, *Author, The Rest of God & Your God Is Too Safe*

"*The Space Between Memories* is a stirring masterpiece of adventure, danger, excitement, and heart-wrenching passion for people. The imagery David paints with words make you feel like you are actually there, wishing you could jump into the story with him!"

RON LUCE, *Founder, Teen Mania Ministries*

"The letters on these pages are inked in blood from a heart for China spilled out on digital cotton, burned in by a passion aflame for the lost. Reading this reminds me why we do what we do—for the sake of the unreached. Be careful—in reading this book, you, too, might catch fire."

JUSTIN LONG, *Director of Global Research, Beyond*, beyond.org

"David Joannes mixes a passionate heart for the nations with a kaleidoscope of transformational experiences and deeply-embedded scriptural truth to produce this delightful, heart-warming, and challenging pilgrimage of the obedient Christian life. Time is precious and you would do well to use it to join him in this journey."

DAVID POPE, *Director of Operations, Issachar Initiative*, issacharinitiative.org

"David Joannes is a man who has clearly said, 'Lord, use my life as You want.' In *The Space Between Memories*, David gives a crystal clear example of a man who heard God's call and obeyed it—an increasing rarity in our world today. The end result is a man who has been used in mighty ways. As you read this book you will be encouraged and challenged, not only by what God has done in David's life, but what He can and will do in your own as you obey His call."

MIKE FALKENSTINE, *President, One Eight Catalyst*, oneeightcatalyst.org

"David Joannes retells his experiences on the mission field with both wit and humor, then peppers his narrative with a healthy dose of humility. In *The Space Between Memories*, David raises critical questions that have long concerned those aspiring to be missionaries. At the same time, he brings comfort to those who have lived on the mission field and experienced failure and disappointment.

"His stories capture the complexities of cross-cultural ministry and gives the reader an impressive assortment of diversified daily situations that any ordinary (or extraordinary) missionary might find themselves in.

"The story is as entertaining as it is enlightening, which is a rare find for books dealing with the harsh realities of missions in the darkest, most unreached areas of the world. Above all, *The Space Between Memories* gives glory to God and rekindles in all of us the child-like excitement on the journey of global missions."

EUGENE BACH, *Back to Jerusalem*, backtojerusalem.com

"I highly recommend *The Space Between Memories*! David uses his God-designed artistic gift to communicate his passion, calling, and how God transformed his life as he journeyed to the unreached world. *The Space Between Memories* will inspire, challenge, and encourage you in ways you may have never experienced. But be warned! You may just find yourself giving up everything to advance God's Kingdom after you read this book! Consider yourself warned!"

STEVE SCHIRMER, *President, Silk Road Catalyst*, silkroadcatalyst.com

"At once a travelogue, a love story, and a profound reflection on the missionary task, David's memoir narrates an intense odyssey of the heart. In the process he captures a pivotal time in China's recent history as paddy fields gave way to skyscrapers and a fledgling persecuted church matured into an outward looking movement with a heart for the nations.

"David's journey, from the streets of Hong Kong to the jungles of Yunnan and beyond, brings you face to face with the unvarnished realities of frontier evangelism as the Gospel breaks through geographical, cultural and political barriers. He relates in poignant detail the joys and struggles of ministry among the Yao, a hitherto unreached people group in which David witnessed God's sovereign work despite many apparent setbacks. David's missiological reflections go beyond textbook theory and probe deep into the question of what it means to have a heart for the unreached and a lifestyle to match.

"*The Space Between Memories* is both inspirational and informative, a personal narrative that speaks to the heart and an in-depth look at God's work among the peoples of China during the past two decades."

BRENT FULTON, *President, ChinaSource*, chinasource.org

"God has a plan for every nation, tribe, people, and language on the earth, and His plan includes you. He is passionate for those without access to the Christian Gospel, unwilling that any should perish without ever having the opportunity to hear about His grace and glory. In *The Space Between Memories*, David Joannes wields words in artistic fashion to reveal the heart of God, the struggle of unreached people groups, and an urgency for the missionary venture. Are you ready to take part in God's epic redemptive plan? This book will help you realize that God wants you to join Him in redeeming the times and ushering in the Kingdom of God."

DAVID HASZ, *Vice President of Leadership Development and Discipleship, Bethany Global University*, bethanygu.edu

THE SPACE BETWEEN MEMORIES

RECOLLECTIONS FROM A 21ˢᵗ CENTURY MISSIONARY

DAVID JOANNES

○ **within reach global**

DEDICATION

To my wife, Lorna.

We have traveled to the highest mountains and the deepest valleys together, and at every juncture along the journey, God's presence has been with us. You are a treasure to me, and you help me find joy in the space between memories.

CONTENTS

ACKNOWLEDGMENTS

If there's one person who has stood by me, inspired me, and encouraged me through thick and thin, it is my wife, Lorna. I am so blessed that God led me to you! Thank you for being a sounding board for my scattered thoughts and helping me articulate these recollections. I look forward to many more years of finding joy along the journey together.

Thank you also to my daughter, Cara, who daily helps me recognize the small wonders of life. I see the world reflected in your eyes and it is a beautiful thing. Never allow your wonderment of life to wane.

I am grateful to my parents who raised me with godly Christian principles. Thank you for supporting my missionary calling. Though it was not an easy task to release me to far-away regions, you gave me wings to fly.

Had it not been for Teen Mania Ministries, I would have never found my way to China. Special thanks to Ron Luce for creating a platform for me to pursue my missional calling. You made it possible for me to enter the world of overseas missions.

The house Church in China has taught me many things about life, faith, and the heart of God. I am especially grateful to Zhang Rong, my close friend and trusted local missionary, who inspires me with faithful persistence in the face of danger. An exquisite crown of glory awaits you, my brother.

Had it not been for the lighthearted mentorship of Chad and Mindy Layman, I never would have learned the practical means of evangelizing and discipling unreached people groups in Southwest China. You generously sowed your life into mine. Much of the fruit that we are experiencing at Within Reach Global will be accredited to you. Thank you for your leadership and friendship.

Thank you, Felecia Killings, for helping me reconstruct my thoughts in this book. I so appreciate your content editing services and input. Your feedback helped me hone my writing skills.

Juliann Itter has taken this book to a whole new level with her cover design and content layout! Thank you so much for all your hard work and effort. I am so proud of you and will always be an avid supporter of your upside-down smiley faces. (:

Thank you also to Joanna Alonzo, Cassandra Smith, and Sarah Ferguson for allowing me to bounce ideas off you. I really appreciate your help.

There are many more people who have helped this book become a reality. Some of you traveled with me to distant villages in China; others shared your life with me throughout Asia. Many more helped me understand the beauty of memories formed along this missional journey. You are too numerous to count, but I am grateful for every one of you.

INTRODUCTION

In the retelling of a story, the lines between truth and fiction grow blurry. Small embellishments here and a dab of forgetfulness there, and the narrative takes on new shapes and forms. Though the recollections in this book are true, I still have questions about the fictitious undertones they carry. At times, these stories feel outlandish, and I debate the reality of my anecdotes. But when I recall the space between memories, a holy hush befalls me, and I realize the magnificent hand of God in every detail.

Sometimes I wonder if I have a faulty hippocampus; if the place my memories are stored is as accurate as I think.

Scientists tell us that our memories are surprisingly malleable, and our recollections cannot be fully trusted. For memories mix with an awareness of each current situation, and whatever is present around us in the environment can interfere with its original content.

For those of us who cherish our memories and like to think they are an accurate record of our history, the idea that memory is fundamentally malleable is more than a little disturbing.

We want our memories to be in reality as they are in our minds. But often our memories are so influenced by the things we experienced at their occurrence that we see them through a dim lens. We look at the past through our worldview and limited perspective, forgetting that God sees these moments outside the dimensions of time and space.

Some have likened a person's memory to one's own collection of private literature. Housed within this vast library are countless pages of nostalgic thoughts and unique perspectives existing within our own heads. But over time, this literature can be edited. What we choose to remember alters the past, affects who we are, and reshapes who we become. Thus, our collection of private literature is not entirely private; there is a communal aspect to memory as well.

Whether I choose to tuck my memories into the bookshelves of my mind or publish them with ink and paper, they will someday be made known nonetheless; for at pivotal junctures along the journey, our lives intersect in mysterious ways.

This story is as much yours as it is mine, for it is a story of divine purpose and God's relentless grace.

God reminds me daily that the infinitesimal details of my life are part of His bigger, more macro plan. He weaves them into the tapestry of His redemptive narrative, crafting a masterpiece from the mundane. The individual threads of your life merge with my own, and every strand of our memories is woven into the glorious tapestry of the Divine.

Masterpieces are hanging on the walls of my mind. They are made from memories painted on textured canvas, matted and framed. And even though the past is the past, there are times when I want to reach out and touch a particular one. I want to caress it, to feel the texture and sensation of the memory on my fingertips. But my hand passes through the frame; I find that it is nothing but mist. It fades into the folds of a fantasy, and vanishes into the corridors of a sepia-toned dream.

One of the great challenges of life is finding the subtle glories in the space between memories. These are the heavenly tinges that fashion our story into eloquent prose; that sprinkle our recollections with effulgent expectation.

For the last twenty years, this journey has taken me to some of the world's most contrasting geographical coordinates. I experienced fascinating missionary travels from the quaint small-town sidewalks of Prescott, Arizona to the chaotic hullabaloo of Manila, Philippines. I pushed through crowds along the jam-packed city streets of Kunming, and eventually made my way to the bucolic village settings in Southwest China.

Most people may find my story unique. But the truth is, each of our callings is intrinsically unique. You might not be called to move to the opposite side of the globe, but I believe Jesus *has* called us to traverse geographic coordinates. He commanded us to be His witnesses "in Jerusalem and all Judea and Samaria, and to the uttermost part of the earth." We are commissioned to minister locally and globally, within our zip codes and beyond; to bring light to those without access to the Gospel message.

There is no sense in emulating what God has done in and through others. You are called to be who God created you to be; to partake in His redemptive plan by fulfilling your unique role. My story is a part of your story because we are one body in Christ. Perhaps I am the boots on the ground. Would you become the hand outstretched?

William Carey, the Father of Modern Missions, responded to his missionary call by saying, "I am willing to be lowered into the darkness, to venture down into the goldmine to dig, but remember, you must hold the ropes!" I pray that through these missionary recollections, you would also be inspired to join the heart of God for every nation, tribe, people, and language.

Chapter 1

INITIAL CALLING

"Little by little, one travels far."

J. R. R. TOLKIEN

Life can only be understood backwards, but it must be lived forwards.

Who I am today has been constructed from my quondam experiences, chiseled by the slap on the cheek I received from a Chinese customs official while smuggling Bibles into China. I have been fashioned by midnight interrogations in sugar cane fields, police stations, and shoddy rural hotels. A metamorphosis took place within me as one-hundred United Wa State Army child soldiers carrying AK-47s caught me sneaking into the Myanmar border while translating for *Time Magazine*. The course of my life was altered by the ethnic Wa grandmother who cradled me like an infant after my back went out in the former headhunting village of Dadong. Her boney fingers lovingly brushed my forehead as we jerked and trembled over rugged, rural pathways in the rear wagon of a handheld tractor. I have been shaped in large part by the pig brains and cat soup and grub worms and homemade moonshine I sampled in unreached Asian villages. I have been fabricated by superfluous tragedy and concrete joy, molded by faith, hope, and love.

Who I am today is arduous for me to define. I am a mixture of courage and fear, compassion and anger, hope and uncertainty. I am a missionary, though that title instills within me negative notions of antipathy. I rather resonate with the anti-hero missionary, fatigued by the façade of Christian pedestals. I call myself, instead, a missional starter and an artistic creative.

Sometimes I am a hero. Most often I am a failure. I am sympathetic toward the poor and marginalized, but would rather be absorbed by a good book in the comfort of a cozy coffee shop. I am experiencing daily grace as God continues to use me, not always because of me, but in spite of me.

I am a trailblazer, a pioneer—shall I be so bold as to say—like the Apostle Paul, passionate about bringing the Christian Gospel to regions where it has not yet been heard. But I am also full of selfish ambition, and I easily tire of bothersome people. I am a homeschooler. I am fluent in Mandarin Chinese. I boast not a single educational degree beside my GED; yet I frequently seek to prove my sophisticated intellect to strangers and acquaintances alike.

I am loved by many. I am disliked by some. I am still learning.

I am a ragamuffin.

———◆———

I didn't mind getting kicked in the ribs by teenagers in black sweat pants and colorful, perspiration-stained t-shirts. It was simple choreography, rhythmic movements to a measured beat, a counting of the tempo in my mind. Two. Three. Four. I stepped back, arms flailing in despair. Six. Seven. Eight. The clashing crescendo of cymbals as I was hurled to the hot pavement, tumbling onto my chest, a crumpled, lifeless heap.

Hong Kong must have been one hundred and ten degrees that day, the stifling humidity around eighty percent. It was just an act by a troop of American teenagers, a colorful production filled with face paint and passion. Even so, the well-practiced routine inevitably generated the occasional cuts and scrapes on the kneecap and palm. These were par for the course, vestiges for a more believable performance.

I was one of the main characters in *The Journeyman* drama, who, after an arduous odyssey, ends up meeting the Miracle Man, only then to encounter the meaning of life.

After one of the teenage actors drove their foot into my abdomen, and I sprawled across the cement, I felt a gentle hand on my shoulder. The Miracle Man had come to my rescue, lifted me to my feet, his right forearm tucked under my armpit, supporting my weight. I was panting heavily, relieved that someone would defend me in the face of my enemies.

My accusers turned their rage toward my defender and began beating the Miracle Man. Two. Three. Four. I stepped back from the tumult and watched as he fell to his knees. Six. Seven. Eight. They whipped him. The rhythmic count began again. Two. Three. Four. They dragged him onto an invisible cross. Six. Seven. Eight. They drove nails into his ankles and wrists. Moments before the exhalation of his final breath, he turned to look at me with eyes of compassion. His head fell forward, his body lifeless, as four teenage actors formed a circle around him, a tomb consuming his inanimate corpse.

One. Two. Three. Four.

Five. Six. Seven. Eight.

The music slowed to a melodramatic hum.

Hong Kongers were inundated with interminable entertainment, but spontaneous live street performances were a rare kind of amusement. The moderate audience of fifty or so locals gawked at the human tomb cocooning the Miracle Man's body. I turned toward the crowd, silently imploring them for help as the rhythmic melody from our traveling sound box ebbed.

The Cantonese narration explained the Messianic portrayal for the audience, as the Miracle Man burst skyward by sudden resurrection force. Two. Three. Four. I ran to him, clasped his shoulders in joyous embrace, and—Six. Seven. Eight.—the drama concluded with our knees bowed and hands raised in adoration, followed by a hurrah from our audience.

After the presentation, we conversed with lingering spectators with the help of local interpreters, speaking about family matters, spiritual issues, the afterlife, God in their midst.

I fell in love with Asia in 1995. There was little magic in the crossing of geographical coordinates by plane from America to the Orient. Still, my initial days spent in the Far East proved to be an enchanting allure I have never been able to shake.

———◆———

I was sixteen-years-old when I first landed on Asian soil for a Teen Mania Ministries short-term mission trip. I was mesmerized by the towering series of stately skyscrapers rising from verdant mountains in Hong Kong. The vibrant hubbub of commotion was incessant with the never-ending deluge of public transportation. The bedazzling luminescence of flashing neon, tech stores, dirty magazine stalls, brash Indian tailors, and Cantonese noodle shops. And the immense population—I had never seen such a sea of humanity, constantly bobbing and weaving, nearly colliding on their way—this way or that—darting in every direction at a startlingly frenetic pace.

For a homeschooled kid from the quaint city of Prescott, Arizona, Hong Kong was a particularly electrifying metropolis of intoxicating pandemonium.

Our American missionary team stayed in the two-story dormitory at Ecclesia Bible College in Shatin, New Territories. Besides fried rice breakfasts and stir fry suppers, group meetings, quiet times, and worship sessions, much of our time during the two-month mission trip was spent in colorful costumes, performing street dramas in the sweltering summer heat.

But there was another ministry dimension that, in retrospect, I am surprised we were allowed to participate in at such a young age. Besides the obvious physical strain caused by hauling overloaded luggage from Hong Kong into China, there were indisputable dangers involved with Bible smuggling.

But we were young, blithe and carefree, giving little consideration to all the possible outcomes of our task at hand.

Once a week, we took to the sidewalks, crossing the footbridge over Shing Mun River, past Shatin Central Park, through New Town Plaza Mall, on our way to Pai Tau Village. Twisting, woody twines coiled themselves around thick banyan trunks, lining the narrow stairway toward Bibleway Ministries. There, we stood panting, nearly breathless under the dense humidity in the courtyard enclosing the gated apartment block.

Opposite the village valley, Ten Thousand Buddhas Monastery rose from the adjacent ridge, an equal number of miniature sacrosanct Buddhist shrines as carried the name of the temple. Lush, green mountains descended spellbound toward the east, enveloping the silent Chinese effigies and ash remains, which lay below the red spires at Po Fook Memorial Hall Crematorium.

It was classic Orient: beautiful and mysterious.

It was fantastical, a dream surreal.

But the humidity was so stifling that I often overlooked the allure of the moment.

Bibleway Ministries was the staging point for international teams smuggling Christian literature into China. The storage room smelled of fresh ink and cardboard, and neatly stacked boxes lined the walls from floor to ceiling.

There was a curious hush that came over us, as if the walls had ears, as if we were under surveillance by snooping professional operatives. We stuffed our backpacks and rolling luggage in a hurried silence, filling every square inch with Bibles, Christian booklets, and tracts.

It was an adventurous enterprise, the stealthy, secret-agent-kind-of stuff I had seen on evening sitcoms in America. But this was not just a game or a carefully constructed narrative by screenplay writers. It was a sort of spiritual warfare, an advancement of the Christian message to regions hostile to its presence. And the divine conduits of spiritual blessing were mere American teenagers, cracked clay jars, unassuming misfits.

In the courtyard outside Bibleway Ministries, our team gathered for a quick debrief, rules and "How To" instructions, and what to expect when crossing the border with contraband. We prayed together. We asked God to go before us; to open the eyes of the blind who were waiting for His word; to blind the eyes of those who would be monitoring x-ray machines.

Down the winding, cement stairway, we lugged our bulging bags past the banyan trees in Pai Tau Village and boarded the KCR train on its way to the border of the People's Republic of China.

In the summer of 1995, I became a Bible smuggler, carrying banned literature into China for the millions of Chinese Christians, hungry for God's word.

———— ◆ ————

What I was doing was dangerous. That's what I wanted to tell my financial supporters back home. It was the bang for their buck, an eerie undertaking. That's what I want you to think now.

There were plainclothes police and government spies trailing our every movement, the thought of which engendered the frivolous notion of heroism.

The reality, though, was that the risk involved was much less perilous than you might think. The danger I faced by carrying Christian literature across the border paled in comparison to the persecution many Chinese Christians were encountering on a daily basis.

I cringe to admit that I subliminally magnified the melodramatic danger tones in my newsletters to financial supporters—less white lies than half truths—exaggerating my valor to come across more heroic than was the actual case.

I was merely a channel chosen by Providence, a default daredevil, just some guy who said yes to God. But oddly enough, God delights in the obedient human response to a divine calling. It is His good pleasure to honor the willing heart, lauding obedience, even glorifying an earthen vessel by infusing it with all-surpassing power.

———◆———

It is impossible to define the exact moment when my initial calling to cross-cultural missions occurred. It seems that the commencement of every narrative carries a hidden backstory, subtle junctures, pivotal moments unnoticed, paramount intersections of divine nature.

We notice the miraculous events in the life of Moses, his encounter with God in the tumult of the storm when holy hands passed to humanity those weighty stone commands. The parting of the Red Sea, when the waters were pulled back, two pulsating, liquid walls and a dry passage for God's people. But even before that, a burning bush and a Heavenly voice, *Ehyeh asher ehyeh, I am who I am*. But Moses' initial calling preceded that moment as well.

I hesitate to say that the commencement of his divine calling was in the crying out to Pharaoh, "Let my people go!" Or in the seven plagues that tormented unsuspecting Egyptians. Was it during his hasty rage when he smashed a stone against the ruthless taskmaster's skull? It must have begun earlier than that, as a boy, perhaps, growing up in palatial surroundings, swinging like a monkey from the golden palace columns.

What we consider being the beginning of a thing seems a surface judgment from dull, human perspective.

Did not the calling of Moses begin much earlier, as a baby floating helpless and unsuspecting along the stream in a bobbing basket, his faint cooing sounds echoing upon gentle waters as his sister sat hidden, watching from distant reeds?

Or perhaps the purpose of his life originated at birth, a God-ordained calling, a storyline in the making. More likely, even farther back in what we understand as time, as God orchestrated unforeseen events where man's watchful eye could not yet penetrate.

"All the days ordained for me were written in Your book before one of them came to be," King David marveled. I am inclined to believe that my understanding of the narrative is much denser than I wish it to be.

Take Jesus, for example. We see His majestic, skyward ascendance, disappearing past the atmosphere, beyond the view of dumbfounded disciples. It was a new beginning for the early Church, but there was a myriad of aspects to the storyline we may have overlooked.

The rolling away of the stone from the musky tomb. The droplets of blood falling from brow and wrist, staining the cross and the ground where it lay. His storytelling under a fig tree, atop a mountain, overlooking rocking boats and rippling sea. The turning of water into wine.

I dare to presume that although the public ministry of Jesus commenced at age thirty, a series of pivotal Providential events led to the climactic scriptures we gravitate to today. When He fled from the company of His parents at age twelve to commune with His Heavenly Father under temple arches. As He sanded smooth the edges of table and chairs in the carpenter's workshop. When infantile murmurs were His only response to gifts of gold, frankincense, and myrrh. And when a star shown in the Eastern night sky, and angels and shepherds danced upon pastoral hills.

The tapestry of life consists of intricately woven strands, a showpiece formed by what some might consider inconsequential fibers. A spool of thread, a tenuous conglomerate of hues and colorful tones that when blended together, comprehensive artistry emerges.

———◆———

My calling to China began long before my initial journey to the East in 1995.

I was three-years-old and terribly cute with plump, rosy cheeks, long eyelashes (for a boy), and lips as red as a Lifesaver. I was the firstborn child of young parents, who bragged to friends and relatives about my artistic genius, placing a crayon in my hand to prove their point.

My art was mostly scribbles, I assume, with occasional flowers and faces emerging on colorful construction paper. My usual canvas of choice was a nearby magazine or Dr. Seuss book.

One particular day, as the afternoon sun cast elongated shadows upon the dining room table in Prescott Valley, Arizona, I was in a notably creative mode, tracing the outline of a blue whale, scribbling artistic masterpieces over descriptive text in a 1982 edition of *National Geographic Magazine*.

My mother was sitting next to me, probably flipping through the pages of *Good Housekeeping*, daydreaming, perhaps gleaning ideas for the evening meal.

My magazine flopped open to its center, and I stared at an image that would change my life forever. The funny thing is, I don't remember the photo but for the memory of it: a barefoot farmer with yellowish, sun-burnt skin, walking along the terraced ridges of his rice fields. The cool mud was squishing between his toes with each step, and the sun was setting behind him. As I sat there, observing his subtle movements, he paused for a moment, the strange awareness that someone was watching him. His head darted left, then right, water buckets dangling precariously from each end of the bamboo pole across his shoulders. Startled, he looked up at me from the magazine, directly into my eyes, and paused. A smile formed on his lips, and he wiped his brow. "Hello, David!" he whispered in Chinese. "Ni hao."

Remember, I was three-years-old, and everything was alive with childlike wonder. It should not be incredulous that images in picture books could walk and talk and smile.

I sat up, flattening the magazine open with my elbows, and with naïve articulations, said, "Mommy, I want to go to China."

I only remember the conversation through the lens of my mother's later recollection to me. Perhaps my childish words were elicited by the many times she told me to finish eating my vegetables, "because," she explained, "there are starving kids in China."

The Chinese would later describe this moment as *yuanfen*, meaning fate or destiny. As if it was the most natural thing for me to be drawn to the East, to move to the exotic landscape of Asia, to someday feel more at home in China than in the country of my birth. As if there was no other course of action, the enormous need of unreached people groups provided sufficient justification for a boy to say, "Yes, Lord. I will go."

Yuanfen.

Some might even be so bold as to translate the Chinese thought into what we refer to in English as Providence.

My mother placed *Good Housekeeping* on the dining room table, lowered her head, perhaps a gesture of realization at the divine moment. She had no idea the future implications involved with my adolescent comment.

"What did you say?"

"When I get bigger, I want to bring bread to all the starving kids in China."

Because bread is what they wanted, right? Not a bowl of rice with collard greens, or deep fried fish, or a steamed dumpling. I was a toddler, learning to share, and American toddlers had plenty of bread. That seemed the obvious possession to give to little Chinese kids, to the sons and daughters of the nice farmer smiling at me from the glossy leaves of the magazine.

———◆———

I swayed with the momentum of the moving crowd, gripping the handrails, as the KCR train swerved along a curving track to the border of China. The Hong Kong landscape was shifting as we zipped northbound through New Territories, less studded with lofty skyscrapers, now a blur of rural countryside, ripe with verdant valleys.

Our team was fidgety, trying to remember all the guidelines and procedures that we were given during our debrief at Bibleway Ministries. I recited the proper responses if caught with Bibles at immigration control.

"I am a tourist."

"I am visiting friends in China."

"I have nothing to declare."

The vaguer, the better. Don't give anything away. Blend into the crowd. Stay calm. If possible, avoid the x-ray machines.

We were told not to have overt Christian conversations during the border crossing. Cut back on the Christianese. Save your "Hallelujahs" for later. Most importantly, never use the words "Bible" or "Christian tract." There were code words for that. We referred to Bibles as "bread," tracts as "crumbs." The safe house, a storage unit where we would deliver our literature for underground Chinese Christians to pick up at a later date, was referred to as "the bakery."

Our team leaders told us to pray under our breath. "Stick with your small group," they said. "See you on the other side."

We came to a slow stop in Lowu, the last station of the KCR train. A final message over the intercom in Cantonese, then English: "Please mind the platform gap when alighting," then the pandemonium began. The pressing and pushing from every side, a human stampede, elbowing and shoving to be first in line at the escalators. Walking was not an option. Pausing to ride the escalator was frowned upon. We were forced to keep a brisk pace, a vigorous scamper.

It was a rush, an excited anticipation. But my backpack was already growing unbearable as the shoulder straps dug into my flesh. I rolled my overloaded luggage over the white tiles at a brisk pace, keeping up with my small group, our team edging toward the customs turnstiles in a staggered formation.

The Hong Kong side of the border was the easy part. Cantonese customs officers eyed us with courtesy, stamped our passports without question, and sent us on our way along the labyrinthine corridors of immigration control.

We followed the crowd up the stairs, through the long hallway, and over the bridge, exiting Hong Kong. Ping Yuen River trickled along the stony banks below, at the edge of sloping greens lined with layers of rusty barbed wire.

My palms were sweaty. I felt the perspiration forming upon my neck, trickling along my arms, creating unflattering blotches around the armpits of my shirt.

Across the bridge, on the China side, a certain stoic impassiveness emerged within the sterile, time-worn hallway, a sobering coldness contrasting the humid summer heat. The sensation lasted but a moment as the shuffling feet of the crowd forced us on, up more stairs, around a curving hallway, back down another staircase and into the wide customs hall.

Our small group queued at the back of a line, the only Americans in a population of hundreds of Chinese travelers.

"Remember to blend into the crowd," one of my team members quipped.

I looked around the room. Businessmen in suits, briefcases, and pointy-toed dress shoes, formal wear. Black hair and slanted eyes, occasional untrimmed moles.

"I'm not doing so well at this point," I retorted nervously.

Immigration control was an expansive white room lit by dim, fluorescent lighting, twenty zigzagging rows of antsy commuters, slowly edging forward. A hushed commotion interrupted by the random thud of stamped-upon passport permeated the anxious ambiance.

Stay calm, I reminded myself, but I struggled to keep my passport from quivering in my trembling hand. Images of me spending the next year in a Chinese prison played upon my imagination. Extreme torture. Bamboo beneath my fingernails. Waterboarding, maybe. They would break me, I knew it. I would crack.

I wondered if I had packed too many Bibles in my backpack and rolling luggage. My bags suddenly seemed much too cumbersome, and I felt suspicious. *Avoid the x-ray machines*, I told myself.

As the line of people in our queue slowly dwindled, I tried to remain invisible, shielding myself behind the Chinese man in front of me. Only a few steps ahead, a stiff customs official sat inside the plexiglass encasement, stamping passports, sliding the travel documents back to commuters through a small opening along the countertop.

After a long, thirty-minute wait, I stepped forward, trying to disguise my nervousness with an awkward smile as I stood in front of the customs officer. I placed my passport through the narrow opening along the countertop, and silently prayed for favor.

His jaw was clenched, statue-like; his forehead lowered. Only his eyebrows moved as he looked up at me dubiously. *He knows,* I thought. I was about to be caught red-handed with contraband Bibles and Christian literature.

His eyes darted back and forth from the photo page of my passport to his computer screen. *American,* I was sure he was thinking. *I don't like Americans.* He scrunched his eyebrows and swiped my passport to retrieve my travel history. His fingers tapped monotonously on the clunky keyboard, entering extra information into the system.

Teen Mania missions trip.

Journeyman drama.

Bible smuggler.

Christian.

Enemy of the state.

I wondered if everyone in immigration control could hear the furious thudding of my heartbeat. I hoisted my backpack slightly upwards, shifting my feet under the immense weight. Beads of glistening perspiration speckled my forehead.

The customs officer glanced up at me one last time before flinging his forearm onto the counter, a sudden violent blow of rubber stamp upon American passport.

I exhaled a momentary sigh of relief, scooped up my travel document, and shuffled around the plexiglass turnstiles toward the exit.

The x-ray machines were larger than I had anticipated, enormous off-white boxes plastered with dirty fingerprints. A group of commuters gathered around the machine, fumbling with their luggage, loading their bags onto the conveyer belt. Three police officers scanned the monitors, carefully examining the contents on the screen.

I made my way slowly, blending into the small group of travelers, waiting for the perfect moment to skirt past the crowd. The three officers were pointing at an object on the screen, and so I darted past the x-ray machine, head down.

"Hello! Hello!" The officials to my left noticed that I had not placed my bags on the conveyer belt. I bolted past a group of businessmen toward the exit. *"Hello!"* I ignored his last-ditch effort to get my attention, turned the corner, and rushed down an adjacent escalator, blending into the crowds outside immigration control.

I was stealth.

I was James Bond.

I was Jason Bourne.

But "secret agent" was the last thing I would admit to if caught with Bibles.

Exhausted from the hour-long transition from Hong Kong to China, I stood motionless under the gray sky in Shenzhen, panting, trying to catch my breath, captivated by the commotion around me. Copious crowds of humanity hauled their luggage in every direction, some in search of a midday bowl of noodles, others purchasing bus tickets, hailing taxis, checking into hotels, strutting nonchalantly along overloaded sidewalks.

To my left was the train station, five stories of weathered blue glass and cracking cement tiles, capped with the gold and red emblem of the People's Republic of China. Opposite the train station to the right, the equally elevated bus depot cast a looming shadow halfway across thick, banyan tree trunks, lining the wide walkway in front of me. Shangri-La Hotel towered beyond footpaths and overpasses, flat onyx black, obsidian absorbing the sun rays, a staggered skyline of high-rises fading into the distance as the hazy air cloaked the horizon.

I stood stationary, spellbound by the sights and sounds and smells as the turbid clouds descended slowly under the weight of impending rain. The empyrean heights were exhausted too, pregnant with vapor; it was easy to see as a reluctant sprinkle began, gradually intensifying until a torrential downpour burst from the sighing skies.

My reveries were interrupted by the deluge, storm waters pounding the cement and soaking my shoes; I sought refuge under the ample banyan branches.

The rain fell heavy that day in June, a cascade of gray mixed with murky sewage as the culverts burst, spewing squalid sludge upon the sidewalks, divulging the dirty secrets of Shenzhen's underworld.

I waded through the foul tide and found my team members huddled together outside the bus station, clutching their bags, rescuing hidden Bibles from the tainted stream.

"Well, no point in hanging around here all day," our team leader quipped. "Since we're already soaked, we might as well make the most of it."

Bus drivers had given up hailing passengers by excessive horn honking, and the traffic came to a halt in the rising waters.

"There's no way we'll get to the 'bakery' at this point. Let's go pass out some tracts."

"You mean crumbs?" someone asked.

"Oops. Yes, crumbs. And maybe some bread, too!"

We separated into our original small groups, wading knee-deep through the rising, slimy tide to the neighborhood apartment complexes tucked along the fringes of the metroplex.

My group of three teenage missionaries and one team leader plodded through narrow alleyways, placing Christian tracts within the dry nooks and crannies we found, up dingy staircases, knocking on metal doors; then down the way we came, maintaining our clandestine presence. It was tract bombing at its best as we littered the neighborhoods with Gospel booklets, praying the Holy Spirit might enlighten those who would discover the small gifts.

We dodged neighborhood watchdogs, unsuspecting security guards who gawked at us, surprised to see a group of Americans in such an obscure part of the city. We prayer walked, seeking divine encounters with unfortunate residents who found themselves stuck in the filthy flood.

As we turned a sharp alley corner in a rundown residential area, I nearly collided with a thin Chinese man in tattered suit pants and an untucked, button-down shirt. He held a rickety, black umbrella with a rusted metal frame, the canopy of which was punctured by the relentless rain.

"Sorry about that," I said, then suddenly realized he had no understanding of the English language. The remainder of our conversation took place in silence, a flurry of raindrops falling in sheets between our umbrellas. Surprised, he bowed his head slightly, apologetically shuffling around me. I reached for his forearm, gripped him with a kind gesture, and held up my forefinger. "Just a second," I motioned with my eyes, and reaching inside my pocket, I pulled out a green Gospel tract, *Help from Above*.

Through the falling rain, I passed the gift from under my umbrella and placed it in his hand where his eyes fell suddenly, examining the Chinese characters, *Shangmian Laide Bangzhu*.

He looked up at me to reveal the most articulate eyes I had ever seen. We stood there, knee deep in flood water, ebbing ripples circling around our legs, rippling away into the city, a divine sort of providence playing upon the surface.

"What is this?" He spoke not a word, his eyes alone inquiring about the flimsy Gospel tract. His gaze fell again upon the title, *Help from Above.* "I need that kind of help, a miracle, perhaps, a truth that has been so terribly elusive all my life."

I nodded in affirmation. "This is truth," I said silently with a smile. "God wants to reveal to you the divine meaning of life."

He nodded back at me with a somber gaze, austerity lacing his brow. A sudden heavenly compassion for this stranger fell over me. He needed not say a word. I would not require thanks. A gift of grace had been shown him, inadequate as I felt it was.

He tucked the booklet into his shirt pocket, turned toward the alleyway, and disappeared around the corner.

It was a moment that would reshape my life for decades, though I did not realize it at the time.

I watched the ripples of his departure recede slowly along the water, curling around the edges of a stairway. They splashed gently against the battered apartment walls, swirling eddies formed by reverse current. The splattering raindrops and flow of flood water through city streets enveloped his wake as if nothing had ever happened, and the storm continued unapologetically. As quickly as the encounter had occurred, so it had passed.

I was left alone, stunned and silent, wondering who the man was, curious about his family, pondering what he did for a living, speculating about the condition of his soul.

Amidst the percussive spatter of raindrops, I thought I heard music. It was a sort of ethereal dissonance, perhaps the hum of celestial song, or in the very least, the feathery whirring of angels' wings. No. It was more of a hushed moan, a divine longing, an ambrosial gasp released from the lips of immortals at the discovery of a secret unveiled.

I stood in the rain with my eyes closed, listening to God whisper about His love for the Chinese.

My mind wandered back to my early childhood, to an image I had seen in a magazine. A barefoot Chinese farmer whose toes squished in the muddy rice terraces. Deep wrinkles were etched upon his weathered brow. A bamboo pole bowed across his shoulders, water buckets suspended on each end. I imagined his children at home in the misty village behind him, and I was sad for them.

"Mommy," I said, "I want to bring bread to the starving kids in China."

A sudden awareness of the weight upon my back seized me, luggage full of Bibles and Christian literature when the Holy Spirit spoke a quiet confirmation.

"David, you're taking bread to the children of China."

Holy emotion gripped my heart, and, as is often the case with the sudden realization of a spiritual encounter, I wept.

"I am calling you to this nation," the Holy Spirit continued. "I want to use you to bring My grace and glory to those who have still never heard of Me. Give Me the pen of your life, and I will write your story better than you could ever imagine it."

I've heard it said that God gives beauty for ashes. So, too, He evokes holy calling from unassuming spots, pulling passion from the profane, wringing vision from vile waters. He is in the business of transformation, of altering atmospheres, taking the squalid and making it exquisite.

I stood swamped in the fetid scent of overflown sewage on Shenzhen's sidewalks, and gave my life for China, believing that God had greater things yet in store.

Chapter 2
LOVE AT FIRST SIGHT

"Through Love, all that is bitter will be sweet. Through Love, all that is copper will be gold. Through Love, all dregs will turn to purest wine. Through Love, all pain will turn to medicine."

RUMI

My quaint little worldview had been altered entirely. A colossal shift had taken place within me, a deviation from normalcy, a sort of transmutation from my small-town perspective and shallow, religious outlook into greater, more transcendent aspirations.

I recognized more clearly the vastness of the world and all its overwhelming need, the triviality of myself and what little I could do about it. I saw now—less through the haze of a clouded mirror—with the clarity that comes with experience.

Still, though, I had few abilities and little more to offer than availability. I threw my life upon the altar of obedience, passionate to do something for the cause of the unreached.

It was obvious that things could not remain as they were and had always been.

During my short-term missions trip to Hong Kong, I had heard testimonies about how life changing the internship at Teen Mania Ministries was. I was intrigued. So, I filled out an application, bought a plane ticket, and six months after my trip to Asia, joined the one-year internship in Tulsa, Oklahoma.

Ministry staff greeted me emphatically at the airport. Their enthusiasm quelled the underlying uncertainty about my decision to attend the internship. I had been wrestling with this decision for months but was relieved to feel so appreciated upon arrival.

"We're so happy you're here! It's going to be an amazing year."

I boarded the ministry van, and we headed to Teen Mania headquarters.

A chorus of blending voices joined the melody of an acoustic guitar on the forty-ninth floor of Cityplex Towers, across the boulevard from Oral Roberts University. Hands raised, swaying back and forth like compliant sails on placid seas. Others fist-pumped toward the ceiling, a sort of jubilant adulation and youthful, godly exuberance.

Ron Luce, the founder of Teen Mania Ministries, thrashed a plastic pick across six bronze strings, less a masterful musical performance than a display of unhindered passion for God. A growing pile of torn picks lay scattered around his feet, loose guitar strings dangling without resonance. He was the same in person as the man I saw on stage at Acquire the Fire Youth Conferences. His eyebrows scrunched, his jaw clenched, and he entered the Holy of Holies with intense passion.

Tens of thousands of young people had been impacted by this man's vision and ministry. From annual missions trips around the world to weekly youth conferences across North America, Teen Mania Ministries was raising up a generation of counter-cultural

Christ followers. "God is calling you to do something great, perhaps even something crazy for Him," Ron often said. "Following the call of God might seem preposterous to the world. It might even seem crazy to you. But the holy pursuit of God is better than the status quo."

Ron's encouragement of radical holiness was less maniacal as it was reasonable obedience. His passion was to raise up an army of maniacs for Jesus who would give witness of God's glory throughout the nations.

The word *mania* within a Christian context has a tendency to evoke outlandishly fantastic imagery: twitching bodies under the influence of the Holy Spirit, charismatic chaos, snake charming.

This was not the case at Teen Mania Ministries. No psychiatric lunacy marked by delusion. The internship recalibrated the definition of mania into an extreme corporate enthusiasm, a pious obsession where the Holy Spirit was given ample space to maneuver.

The room filled with mission-minded young people from all over North America, all of whom passionately sought after God, labored over the future of the Church and interceded for our generation.

Teen Mania was my first glimpse of true Christian community. I grew up in multiple churches, hopping from one to the next as my family struggled to find the perfect fellowship. I learned to breathe at the internship, inhaling the zephyr of my life's abandonment to accomplish the will of God. I exhaled the breeze of His missionary heart for the world.

Our days were spent cold-calling youth pastors and Christian workers around the country, inviting them to bring their youth groups to Acquire the Fire Conferences. Three times a week, we sat under the teaching of ministry staff and renowned guest speakers. We lived together in a nearby apartment complex, breaking bread and delving into the deeper conversations of purpose and the meaning of life. We were of a generation wholly committed to the heart of God to transform our generation. We traveled America together, organizing the logistics of youth conferences, manning merch booths and breakout sessions for young people who were considering short-term overseas mission trips. We worshiped side-by-side, conversed about each other's dreams, and studied our required reading together.

It was community as I had never known it before, the birthing and building of relationships that would last a lifetime.

"Perspectives on the World Christian Movement" was my favorite class. This biblical curriculum outlined strategic methods of contextually bringing a relevant witness of the Gospel to every culture. It examined the mission heart of God, and enamored me with success stories and failed attempts in the missionary endeavor. I logged nuggets of truth for future reference. I knew that my future ministry would benefit from the lessons learned by ministers of the past.

The Teen Mania Ministries internship was my first step to long-term missionary work. It was a diving board into the bubbling surge of blue-black waters, into the unknown of overseas ministry.

Halfway through the year in 1996, the ministry moved from Tulsa to the sprawling grounds of Garden Valley, Texas, to the former location of Keith Green's Last Days Ministries. I was selected as part of the "skeleton crew," a group of young men who prepared the campus for the move.

East Texas became a new environment, no longer the cement sidewalks and paved boulevards of Tulsa. Damp grasslands, seven-foot-tall blades of grass, and red dirt stained everything.

We began work before dawn, watching the aurora wake with dull tinges of pink over a skyline of pines. We cut the tall blades of overgrown grass, often imagining the whisper of Keith Green's voice echoing through the forested landscape—*Jesus rose from the dead / But you couldn't get out of bed!* We fought off swarms of chiggers and red ants, the bites of which would bring a grown man to his knees in pain. We unhinged aged-wooden panels from the exterior of the dormitory with the backs of hammers; covered the cafeteria stains with a new coat of spray paint; soldered electrical wire within the frames of the airplane hangar; and crafted the building into the new office space. Three hundred feet beyond what would become the executive offices, the dirt airstrip that took the life of Keith Green stretched into the arboraceous countryside. At the end of the day, we collapsed in our makeshift sleeping quarters, exhausted yet elated to be part of the ministry's relocation.

During the final two months of my internship, I organized a Bible-smuggling trip to Hong Kong. Three interns expressed interest in the voyage, and so we collaborated, organizing the logistics via multiple faxes from Texas to Southeast Asia. We scheduled to depart a mere two weeks after graduation, hardly enough time to share our internship experience with our families back home and to kiss our crying mothers as we left home once again.

———— ✦ ————

We were bold, reckless, and smart. We were world-wise, whimsical, and silly; but we knew how to get the job done. We were comedians, call-center representatives, and poets. We laughed at ourselves and cried with a stranger.

We had just graduated from the internship at Teen Mania Ministries where our studies of "Perspectives on the World Christian Movement" now became paramount in our cross-cultural setting. We had read about the remaining task of final frontier missions, about unreached people groups, about those who had yet to hear the name of Jesus. But pause for a moment while I define the word "unreached."

I am not talking about unbelievers or unchurched pockets of society. I am not simply talking about people with needs, or individuals considering whether or not they will darken the doors of a church this Sunday.

By "unreached," I mean people who have no access to the Christian Gospel. There are no Christians among them, no witness, no chance to hear about God's grace and glory. An unreached people group is distinguished by a distinct culture, language, or social class who lacks a community of Christians that are able to evangelize the rest of the people group without outside help. Most missiologists consider two percent of the population becoming Christ followers as the "tipping point" at which the group is generally considered "reached" with the Gospel.

Most of these people groups reside within the confines of an invisible rectangle called the 10/40 Window. From ten to forty degrees latitude north of the equator, stretching from West Africa through the Middle East and into Asia, over six-thousand distinct ethnic people groups remain untouched by a Christian presence. The Buddhist, animist, Hindu, Islamic, and unaffiliated blocs of the earth's population are there, waiting at the other end of our obedience.

The unreached people groups of the 10/40 Window are the forgotten ones, people whom we have not prioritized in our evangelistic efforts.

Between us, we had already traveled to Russia, India, China, Thailand, Panama, Canada, Bahamas, Mexico, and Morocco. Now our small band of missionaries embarked upon our next missions venture.

We called ourselves the HK Project, a team of four twenty-somethings, ready to take on the world for Jesus, willing to see the evangelization of the world in our generation. It would start by smuggling Bibles from Hong Kong to China for the next six months.

Kyle Guerrero—the jokester—livened the group. He consistently brought laughter in the midst of mundane and stressful situations. He wore thick, black-rimmed glasses; in essence, legally blind without them. He often sported khaki shorts with deep, button-flap pockets. A self-proclaimed Mestizo—quarter Filipino, quarter Hispanic, the remaining percentage Caucasian. But he acutely resonated with Asian culture. Behind his silly faces and playful jest, his contagious hilarity and animation, he encouraged others. He was a genuine peacemaker, a convivial replica of the less staunch Jesus portrayed in traditional Christian paintings. He emulated a multicultural portrait of Jesus with a colossal smile.

Dawn Breid wore noticeably red, corkscrew curls. Her shy smile captivated us as well. Shakespeare's rich description of Juliet confirmed itself in Dawn: *"The brightness of her cheeks would outshine the stars the way the sun outshines a lamp."* She was thinly built, yet strong, spunky, and tenacious. She never allowed anyone to help her with her heavy bags of Bibles, even in the sweltering Hong Kong heat. She pleasantly dismissed chivalry with a sweet smile, batting whimsical eyelashes, hoisting her backpack more snugly over her shoulders. She was a dreamer, a poet filled with lavish adjectives, ever a medieval fairy princess with a long, white, flowing dress in the stage play of her reveries.

Mandy Kissinger was our Southern belle brunette archetype, easy to spot. She contained a congenial, hospitable spirit, and brimmed with passion. Her aqua-blue eyes sparkled as she shared snippets from her morning devotional. Mandy loved Jesus and America. She always wore blue jeans. She was generous with her use of *ya'll*, and her sing-songy draw was attractive. Her scrunching eyebrows were the windows to her soul, articulating the depth of passion she felt about nearly everything that entered her life. She was sweet Southern summer, fire and ice, weather and noise in the most charming fashion. She was one of the most alive people I had ever met. Mandy encouraged others, yet became easily misunderstood. As an evangelist and seer—a modern-day prophet—she possessed an inferno whose heat lingered long after she left the room.

Kyle, Dawn, Mandy, and I landed in Hong Kong in January 1997, backpacks full of Pepto-Bismol, empty paper leafs of thick journals, and the bare necessities for a six-month stint in Southeast Asia.

We stayed in the dormitory at Bibleway Ministries, up the winding stairway to Pai Tau Village in Shatin. The women's dorms rested on the second floor. Kyle and I lodged in the first-floor men's dorm that also served as a Bible storage room. The acute, inky scent of freshly-printed Christian literature dulled after a week, only to be replaced by the ineffable scent of humidity.

Short-term mission teams arrived from all over the world. We took charge of leading each group across the border from Hong Kong, smuggling Bibles from our bedroom to underground churches throughout China.

———◆———

Day in and day out, we loaded Bibles into our backpacks and strolling luggage, and rode the forty-five-minute train to China. It was exhilarating at first, the sensation of stealthy missionary work. It was a silent defiance, the forceful advancement of an unworldly Kingdom.

But daily Bible courier work began to wear us down. Not because we had grown tired of the task, but because the work was simply exhausting. We loved it, and we hated it.

On nearly every China-bound train ride, I took the opportunity to write daily entries in my journal. I sat on the hard plastic KCR train seat, slumped over my bags of Bibles, penning my thoughts into the blank pages so as not to forget the colors of Hong Kong's blurred landscape streaming past me outside the train window. It was my way of capturing the moments, of gathering the dwindling glimpses, of preserving junctures and instances.

January slipped by quickly, a fading memory. February came and went just as rapidly. Foreign teams arrived from America and Australia, New Zealand and the Philippines, bringing with them new friendships. But after the short visits, each team left, leaving an indelible reminder of the transient lifestyle we lived.

Characters of all kinds came through the ministry doors, representing every part of the Body of Christ. We acquainted with a vast array of personalities, of taciturn introverts and flamboyant extroverts, of pensive poets and stoic philosophers.

The doors of Bibleway Ministries opened to career missionaries who needed a temporary getaway from the missionary task, a rejuvenating sabbatical from China. One of these particular missionaries was a man named Scott Anderson. He was an anomalous character, cogitative and melancholy, shrouded in mystery.

Scott sat sipping hot coffee in the humid men's dormitory, book in hand, deep in thought, mentally elsewhere. He was an American missionary in Southwest China and a teacher at Kunming Television and Radio University. His shaggy, mop-top, silver hair hinted at his long history in the mainland. He had a subtle sadness about him, melancholy merging with the lingering tinge of hope. He was tired but articulate, slightly mad, a few bubbles off plumb. Still, we hung on the commas between his storytelling, as echoes of the inland revealed themselves to us.

Ancient oriental architecture in the City of Eternal Spring.

Chinese college students curious about the notion of divinity.

Pockets of rural China untouched by the Christian Gospel.

"Do you want to come to Kunming with me?" Scott asked Kyle and me. "I need help carrying all my luggage back home, and it would be good to have someone to talk to on the forty-five-hour train ride."

Forty-five hours in a train through China's interior didn't seem that horrific to us at the time, and so we obliged.

———◆———

I had seen the familiar urban portrayal of China, the towering sky-scrapers juxtaposed by ancient Buddhist temples and dragons, apartment complexes ascending high above traffic-jammed grids on narrow boulevards. But these were the outer fringes of a vast land. Verdant landscapes carpeted eighty-five percent of the country, some areas bejeweled with ramshackle residences, while valleys crept into the shadows of alpine mountains.

I had not yet been privy to this. The rural version of China remained but a hypothesis, speculative fiction I brushed up against but knew little about.

But that was all about to change.

In March 1997, Kyle and I joined Scott on a two-day trip from the eastern coast of Guangdong to the southwestern province of Yunnan. Verbose details of our lengthy travel by train is inessential as it has the tendency toward monotony. Apart from long stretches of boredom, there was a certain fascination to these remote regions, a sort of romantic allure.

"The mountains are tall and the emperor is far away," they say of Yunnan Province. At that time, it was off the beaten track, the back-woods, backward and underdeveloped. Scott was one of a handful of missionaries gutsy enough to make a home in the capital city.

This was the antithesis of Hong Kong. The sleepy city of Kunming seemed stuck in a bygone era, drowsy and sluggish, a sort of passive stupor hovering in the air.

Residents wore long green trench coats, fashion suggestive of the Cultural Revolution, of Mao Zedong, of communism. Bicycles emerged everywhere, crisscrossing the streets, swerving in and out of neighborhood alleyways and thoroughfares. A succession of routed city buses and aqua-blue taxis puttered along the potholed roads, picking up commuters. I was told that there were four million residents in Kunming at that time, and it seemed that on any given day, the entire population could be spotted strolling the sidewalks, drifting in and out of street-side stalls, meandering along the spacious urban boulevards.

Every Thursday evening, over one hundred and fifty college students gathered on the sidewalk at the edge of Green Lake to practice their language skills at the weekly English corner. Kyle and I met Thomas Nixon, Jennifer, a girl named Bob, and Michael Jackson—Chinese students who named themselves in English. It was the perfect place to share the Gospel message openly with hungry college students, writing it off as a cultural exchange. Only a handful of students had ever heard of Jesus before. Although we knew the reality of lostness in the 10/40 Window, in this part of the earth where Buddhism, atheism, agnosticism, and animistic worldviews dominated, their ignorance of the Christian message still surprised us.

After exchanging pager numbers with students from the English corner, we now had ample possibilities for translators to show us around the city. We visited the Bird and Flower Market, strolling under the bending canopy of branches, shading a series of vendor stalls selling curious ethnic ornaments, medicinal roots, and erhus. Our new Chinese friends took us to Dongfeng Square, to Jinri Park, to Yunnan Nationalities Village, and to their university campuses. We ate steamed dumplings and Over the Bridge Rice Noodles, chicken feet, and stinky tofu, the students giggling in response to our cultural participation. Kyle and I immersed ourselves in the culture, becoming all things to all men.

After three days in Kunming, and at our friends' recommendation, we took a twelve-hour overnight bus to the ancient city of

Dali. Home to the Bai tribe, and a former Hui Muslim kingdom, the city is set between the ominous cliffs of the Cang Mountain range and the serene waters of Erhai Lake. The cobblestoned city held an infallible charm, its narrow alleys guiding trickling streams from elevated origins, past yellow blooming canola, toward the delta. There, the boats carried tourists across rippling waves with seagulls swirling overhead, to the elaborate temples and Buddhist pavilions.

We stood at the foot of the thousand-year-old Three Pagodas, which rose staunchly and silently at the foot of the mountain. We boated across Erhai Lake at sunset. We bargained with Bai grannies who sold ethnic souvenirs, Chinese chops, Mao's little red book and tie-dyed tablecloths.

Deeper into the inland we went, deeper into China's mysterious rural regions, like pioneer explorers on an excursion through uncharted territory.

The Old Wooden House in Dali served banana pancakes and freshly brewed coffee; and for that fact alone, we enjoyed most of our meals in the Chinese-owned "foreign" café.

Every Saturday, we were told, the owner of the Old Wooden House gathered with his comrades—now grayed by the time—in the back courtyard of the restaurant to perform an ethnic Bai minority orchestra. Here, they strummed tiny mandolins and pulled strained intonations from erhus and hammer dulcimers. Crutches and walkers lined the stage as each elderly gentleman took his place under the spotlight.

The show began. Dim lights glimmered from swaying red lanterns hanging from a shingled roof. The pale moon paused overhead, and the wafting scent of bougainvillea lingered on the breath of the breeze. An inexplicable resonance of Chinese music formed from fingers on strings, from pursed lips through microphones. Kyle and I sat in the center of the audience, more foreign than we had felt in recent days, fascinated with unfamiliar sonance, hypnotized by alien mores.

We watched as one of the restaurant owner's elderly friends, stationed at the bronze gong, closed his eyes for the show's duration. He slept for moments in between musical interludes, when at last he lifted heavy eyelids and brought the performance to a crashing symphonic climax.

The final stroke of musical glory resounded, and the audience cheered. Kyle and I stood to our feet, excited by the chaos, relieved that the lengthy presentation had finally found closure. We cheered for the owner of The Old Wooden House as he stood bowing to the spectators.

The pale moon waned.

The waking stars punctured the celestial canopy.

Secrets from the cavernous caves of Cang Mountain echoed across the valley, lulling the township to sleep under a blanket of chilled whispers.

There is a particular intimacy invoked by recalling my early China experience, the tingling sensation of falling head over heels in first love. The memories seem locked in time, sepia-toned and ecru.

That one week in Yunnan Province changed me forever. It opened my eyes to the reality of who unreached people groups really were, how they lived, and what they cared about.

Part of me was born in Southwest China. Another part died. The experience left deep grooves in who I was becoming: a pioneer, a missional starter, a voice for the voiceless.

After a week of travels, we returned by train to Hong Kong. A deeper understanding of God's heart for China birthed in me, and smuggling Bibles into the mainland made more sense.

———◆———

Though I did not realize it at the time, May 23, 1997 became one of the most important days of my life.

It was another routine trip to the airport to pick up a visiting team, this particular group from the Philippines. They were coming to help us smuggle Bibles. We had already hosted countless teams from the island country, but this one was special, namely because of a single Filipina girl aboard the descending plane.

Kyle and I arrived at the airport early, and so we decided to climb to the roof of the Kai Tak airport in Kowloon. Airplanes on the precarious landing path made sharp turns over skyscrapers, skirting the tops of buildings before skidding to a stop along the Hong Kong harbor. The roar of the engine made the hairs on our arms stand on end. With outstretched arms, we could almost touch the wheels as planes thundered overhead.

"Man! That was close!" Kyle said. We laughed and watched from a distance as the Cathay Pacific plane taxied along the runway. We headed downstairs to greet our arriving Filipino team.

In the arrival hall, interlacing blue text flickered on black monitors. Long, white, incandescent bulbs flooded the building where fathers cradled their daughters and families waited for loved ones. I held a placard that read, "Christ, the Living Stone Fellowship."

From the top of the sloping arrivals ramp, they spotted my sign, waving emphatically. They were all smiles and giddy laughter, like every other affectionate Filipino team we hosted. This particular group comprised of eleven women and one man, but for me that day, there was only one girl.

She wore a pink and white plaid skirt that swayed back and forth as she strolled her roller bag down the ramp. Her olive complexion and beautiful smile vibrated in the sunlight. Innocently attractive, she possessed an alluring piety that caused her to stand out from the crowd.

I leaned over to Kyle and said, "Bro, I think I can marry that girl!" He saw the spark in my eye and laughed. I elbowed him to bite his tongue, afraid he might make a teasing public remark in her presence.

"Welcome to Hong Kong!" We greeted the team, shaking hands, trying to remember everyone's names.

I shook her hand last. "Hello, I'm David."

"I'm Lorna." Her smile made my legs weak. Her soft grip in my hand lasted only a moment, but her charm lingered.

After the greetings and formalities, we gathered the team's luggage and headed to the MTR train.

"Can I help you with your bag?" I asked Lorna.

She smiled at my chivalry. With love-struck infatuation and butterflies in my belly, we led the team through the subway turnstiles.

———— ♦ ————

I loved China. I loved to show her off in all her unique nuances and silly characteristics.

Red qipaos, black suits, and frilly clothing.

Rows of jade jewelry stalls and Chinese seal chops.

Caged puppies barking in their pens outside Cantonese restaurants.

I had been studying Mandarin Chinese, practicing my broken grammar on the streets of Guangdong. The language came quicker than expected because I put myself in situations where I was forced to communicate.

I loved Jesus.

Living and ministering in China was a natural response to the unique call of God upon my life. Though I felt strangely at home in Southeast Asia, the acute clashing of cultural differences brought with it the cognizance of my sheer foreignness. It was a poignant reminder of how I was but a sojourner on the earth, longing for a more permanent eternal home.

I quickly fell in love with a girl.

As we led the visiting Filipino team from Hong Kong to China on daily Bible smuggling runs, I became increasingly enchanted with

Lorna. There was something about her innocent smile, her love of music and art, her love for all things spiritual, and her exotic beauty.

One morning, a few days after she had arrived, I woke up early to watch the sun rising precariously over distant mountains. I sat in the courtyard at Bibleway Ministries, overlooking Pai Tau Village, strumming my guitar, a song developing upon my lips. The morning mist slowly began to dissipate; replaced by prayer, the valley permeated with praise.

Not long after the sun rose defiantly over Shatin's skyline, Lorna joined me outside, drawn by the song. She sat beside me in the courtyard.

"What are you playing?" she asked.

"It's a new song I just wrote," I replied. "It's called 'In Your Arms.'"

I handed her a single sheet of lined paper with my handwritten lyrics and chords.

"Can I hear it?" Lorna requested.

"Of course!"

I played like I had never played before, the resonation of worship flooding the village valley, a singular beautiful audience beside me.

It was awkwardly delightful.

Two hearts beating in unison.

The flicker of love's fledgling flame.

Lorna applauded my composition, and we continued talking about her home in the Philippines, about her dreams, aspirations, and missionary calling. She told me about her ministry among Filipino college students at her church, how she managed twelve discipleship groups in campuses across Manila, raising up new believers in their newfound faith. She told me about her heart for China, how at eleven years of age, she sensed God calling her to someday cross cultures with the Gospel. And as she talked, my mind drifted, inundated with reveries, contemplating possibilities, musing about what could be.

I imagined us traveling to China's forgotten unreached people groups together; of journeys through the rural countryside, hand in hand, making trails where no path had been before. I had only known Lorna for a few days, but there was some sort of providential design to our confluence, like two streams merging between narrow mountain ranges, flowing into one another, becoming singular.

I imagined her as my wife.

We began our relationship, busily concerning ourselves about our Father's business. We were each wholly devoted to the call of God upon our lives, satisfied and in pursuit of God's presence.

Lord, could she be the one for me? I felt myself asking as I sat beside her in the courtyard. Perhaps I was getting ahead of myself. After all, I lived in Hong Kong and she in Manila. She was only visiting for ten days, and would soon leave, like every other short-term team we had hosted at Bibleway Ministries. We would soon be separated by the expanse of the South China Sea, left dangling in limbo, praying to reunite, unsure of what the future might hold.

Still, the more I talked to Lorna, the more I realized how much I loved her.

One week later, after a packed schedule of Bible smuggling, encouraging local believers in China, and sharing the great need for harvest among unreached people groups, Lorna did depart, leaving me in the ebullient wake of first love. Kyle, Mandy, Dawn, and I accompanied them to the airport, said our last goodbyes, and stood in the departure hall, watching the team disappear beyond security checkpoints.

Mixed emotions filled my heart. Infatuation for Lorna grew into something much more than superficial affection; yet the feasibility of future love felt futile in her absence.

Our six-month assignment in Asia was coming to a close, and HK Project would soon disband with little more than shared experience and deepened relationships. But there was more than that.

The divine encounters and missional communities that we created left a permanent impression on all of us, me in particular, as the course of my life would shift toward the East and to China's least reached peoples.

————— ♦ —————

Though the following year in the United States served as a gestation period, preparation for long-term missionary service, I found myself out of sync with the country and culture of my birth. Asia had permanently altered me, had made me ever foreign at every geographical coordinate.

Restless with wanderlust, I could not wait to return to the place of my calling.

Life in Prescott had persisted in my absence. Seasons shifted slightly, but to me, the mundane details admitted little transformation. After all I witnessed, all that I tasted and smelled and sensed, I was frustrated, perhaps even jaded and judgmental, at what I perceived as a lackadaisical Christian response toward the Great Commission.

Autumn passed, followed by a forlorn winter. Green leaves matured into yellows, then oranges and finally reds, slowly descending upon sidewalks, encircling the courthouse square. The bony trees slept for a season, waking to the Spring of a new year. Then came the sweltering heat of another Arizona summer.

For nearly one year, I fixated upon arranging the details of my return to China, focusing on language studies, garnering vision partners and financial supporters. And as the departure date drew near, the underlying conundrum of leaving family to follow the call of God played upon the surface of my emotions.

Journal entry, August 1, 1998: "Not many in this world know of my upcoming departure to China. Fewer still know the depth of my heart's love for the people there. At the same time, I cannot stop thinking about my family, especially my mom."

Leaving my family had always been difficult for me. Short-term mission trips were docile in comparison to the farewells involved in career missionary work.

As the eldest of eight children, the fabric of our family closely knitted together. My father and mother supported my global missionary travels with Teen Mania Ministries, but my upcoming move was a hard pill to swallow. I tried to make every family moment matter.

Journal entry, August 7, 1998: "Before the sun rose this morning, dad and I went on a prayer walk around the downtown square. After praying for half an hour, we found a bench, sat down, and tried to choke back the tears. It was good to spend a quality moment with each other one last time."

I felt the last few granules of sand slipping through the thin center of the hourglass, helplessly grasping at elusive instances, wishing I could cradle the minutes for a moment longer. I was apologetic, particularly to my mother, regretful for causing such heartache. Her firstborn son would soon depart, disappearing beyond her reach; and I knew the pain of my departure would not be so easily quelled. I struggled to articulate the sensations within my spirit; and 19th century missionary to China, Hudson Taylor's recollection of his sorrowful farewell to his mother, terrified me even more.

"My beloved, now sainted, mother, had come to see me off from Liverpool. Never shall I forget that day, nor how she went with me into that little cabin that was to be my home for nearly six months long. With a mother's loving hand, she smoothed the little bed. She sat by my side and

joined me in the last hymn that we should sing together before the long
parting. We knelt down, and she prayed—the last mother's prayer I was to
hear before starting to China. Then notice was given that we must separate,
and we had to say goodbye, never expecting to meet on earth again.

"For my sake, she restrained her feelings as much as possible. We
parted, and she went on shore giving me her blessing. I stood alone on the
deck, and she followed the ship as we moved toward the dock gates. As we
passed through the gates, and the separation really began, I shall never
forget the cry of anguish wrung from my mother's heart. It went through
me like a knife. I never knew so fully, until then, what "God so loved the
world" meant. And I am quite sure that my precious mother learned more
of the love of God to the perishing in that hour than in all her life before."

Leaving family for the sake of the Gospel is easier said than
accomplished. *Are the Chinese really worth it?* I questioned. I was
unsure of the answer. But I was not going to China solely for the
Chinese. I sacrificed things I loved so dearly in obedience to God's
call upon my life. I was going because God said go, and that was
enough.

I took solace in the promise of Jesus, that whoever gives up
houses or brothers or sisters or father or mother or children or
property for His sake would receive a hundred times as much in
return, and would inherit eternal life. Even though the spiritual
mathematics seemed illogical and the equations elusive, I agreed,
surrendering my will to align with the heart of Heaven.

Journal entry, August 9, 1998: "The moment we had for so long con-
sidered, spent so much time in thought about, contemplating how we
imagined it should and should not be, finally arrived. I placed my luggage
in the car, then returned to the house, opened the screen door, and slowly
walked inside. Past the threshold, I turned and met my mother's eyes. We
tried to speak, but the words would not come. Then suddenly, oh, how the

tears flowed. We embraced, weeping together, mourning the moment we had feared for so long. Dad joined us there, and the tears streamed down our cheeks. In our deep anguish, we shared a love that began to comprehend sacrifice and surrender to a higher calling."

On August 9, 1998, I boarded a one-way flight across the Pacific, leaving my family, my birth country and the normalcy of the American life. I flew first to the Philippines, where I would spend time getting to know Lorna more, then on to my destination and new home: Kunming, China.

Chapter 3

CULTURAL MORES

*"What affects men sharply about a foreign nation is not so much finding
or not finding familiar things; it is rather
not finding them in the familiar place."*

G. K. CHESTERTON

Kunming, the capital and largest city in Yunnan Province, also
known affectionately as the City of Eternal Spring, situated in the
fertile basin on the northern shore of Dianchi Lake. Spectacular
steep rockface cliffs towered along a series of mountain ranges,
rising stiff and stalwart from the west. There, the thick mist oft
descended, shrouding giant firs and pines inset above the banks
of the lake near Dragon Gate, laying below the wooded Huating
Temple where the solemnity of Buddhism and the freedom of
Taoism blended into one.

The subtle whispers of warring, bygone kingdoms, of emperors
and their ruthless subjugation of native residents, each made their
way surreptitiously along Tibetan trade routes into Indochina.

They whisked over the back roads of Burma, gliding lightly through treacherous mountain valleys, ascending from Laotian landscapes and skimming up from the Vietnam delta. The historical trade routes around Kunming filled with triumph and tragedy as mountains were quarried out, the opulence of coal, quartz, and copper discovered and plundered.

But now the dust settled, apprehensively no doubt, as the poignant memories of more recent upheavals and insurrections had expired only two decades earlier. The city sighed in relief, exhausted and hopeful. Narrow streets widened; cement and asphalt covered dusty surfaces. Commercial districts and university areas burgeoned. Office buildings and housing projects developed at a frantic pace. The capital of Yunnan Province began its transformation into a special tourist center, a gradual proliferation of high-rises and luxury hotels rising skyward alongside the hearts of its citizens.

Kunming was a unique agglomeration of urbanites, residents representing every reference point along the extensive spectrum of China's polarizing economic classes. There were the local Kunmingers, proud of their southwestern heritage, insouciant and carefree, unhurried and friendly. However, the northerners and Han Chinese, who had migrated from various provinces throughout China, interpreted this calm as apathy and indolence. The *waidiren*, who dressed in swanky suits and upscale dress shoes, viewed the locals with disdain, turning up their noses as they took local jobs from underneath Kunming natives.

Then there were the migrant workers, provincial folks, typically ethnic farmers, who had immigrated to the city in search for a better life. These penurious residents were despised by both Kunmingers and northerners alike, viewed as boorish and unsophisticated, regarded as hillbillies and country bumpkins. And although the urban population contained a rich, cultural diversity, China's subtle yet evident caste system displayed itself at each daily juncture.

———— ◆ ————

I did not know a single person in Kunming prior to my arrival, save the acquaintance I had made via email with a Chinese teacher in Yunnan Nationalities Institute.

I arrived by taxi, and Mister Fan waited under the arched gateway at the college. He greeted me with a wide, toothy smile, and shook my hand with excessive enthusiasm. He was a jovial man, his cheer nearly bordering on giddiness. He stood five-feet, five inches, thin-limbed with wiry glasses, and halitosis so potent, I thought the nearby greenery would wither.

"Welcome to China!" His voice seemed unreasonably squeaky, his accent revealing his modest grasp on the English language.

"Xie xie!" I said, raising my hand over my nostrils to quell the scent of his acidic breath.

"Zou ba." Mister Fan turned, gesturing for me to follow as he gleefully strutted past low-lying, rubber tree branches. A group of Chinese students looked up from their books, gawking at me, shocked at the presence of a foreigner.

My living quarters, I found, would be a four-story building inside the college campus. The cement exterior was cracked; peeling pink paint curled in the arid atmosphere. *God, what a dump,* I thought. I followed Mister Fan up the narrow, dim-lit stairwell to the fourth floor where he jiggled a key in the obstinate doorknob.

A prestigious living space was the last thing I expected in the dingy complex, but still, I was startled by the condition of the room. The meager accommodation was furnished with two twin beds set alongside adjacent walls, barely enough room to stand between them. The covers were stained yellow; the walls smudged with fingerprints and other inscrutable gunk. The room permeated with the reek of mold and perspiration.

Mister Fan made a swooping gesture with his arm, all that was needed for a thorough tour of the room. But cramped living quarters was the least of my concern. The bathroom was frightful, a four-square-foot space, barely enough room to enter, let alone maneuver within. A dangling light bulb swayed over the showerhead, which set directly above the narrow squatty potty hole. Shaving, showering, and squatting will be easy, I thought facetiously to myself. A metal spigot protruded from the wall above the cracked porcelain, apparently the water source for lavatory cleanup. My morning toilet would be immensely simplified, all duties accomplished with one quick motion. The sink screwed into the corner of the washroom, above which was placed a scratched one-foot mirror reflecting my hazy appearance, dumbfounded, staring back at myself in disbelief.

"Ni xihuan ma?" Mister Fan asked.

"Yes. It's perfect," I lied.

Mister Fan delighted that he had been such a sensational host. He shook my hand before closing the door behind him. I sat on the bed, listening to his sprightly whistling echo through the hallway.

For the next week, sleep eluded me, not because of the red vacancy sign blinking outside my window, nor for the incessant bus horns honking on the boulevard below. It was the mold. The moist, musty mildew. It was a living organism, fungi mushrooming from the ceiling, pullulating behind the peeling wallpaper, spreading down where the walls made contact with the bed covers. It was around me, all over me, trying to get inside me.

But this was adventure at its pinnacle, and these were simply minor inconveniences. I was not oblivious to the inordinate discomforts; I just chose to overlook them. I was, after all, in love with China, or at the very least, in love with the thought of her.

Journal entry, September 1, 1998: "I woke up this morning, astonished, marveling that I am here! Never would I had imagined that I would be living on the other side of the world. But now China has become a significant part of my life."

The following day, I awoke moments before the sunrise, smelling like the last ten people who slept in my bed. Reluctantly, I dragged myself to the bathroom where I shaved, showered, and squatted all in one motion. Somehow, I had missed the memo and made the mistake of discarding my toilet paper down the squatty potty hole. After flushing, an opposite effect took place. Instead of draining downward, the water rose, a steady upsurge, flooding the bathroom floor. I scrambled in search of a plunger, but to no avail. The stench permeated the small latrine; fecal sludge rose over the bathroom lip, flowing into my bedroom. I wrapped a t-shirt around my face and began bailing brown sludge water into the sink. I was fighting a losing battle, the water rising from a slow leak in the bathroom spigot.

I ran to the public phone in the hallway outside and dialed Mister Fan's office number.

"Wei?" he answered. I blurted out the first words in Chinese I could think of to describe the situation.

"Bathroom! Crap!"

Mister Fan laughed, amused at my crude depiction of the unfortunate situation. "I come," he assured me. I hung up the phone and continued bailing the fetid flood down the bathroom sink.

Fifteen minutes passed, and the stench had become unbearable. Mister Fan arrived with a plumber and, pinching his nose, assured me that everything would be okay. After tinkering with his tools and snaking the toilet hole, the foul water finally receded. The plumber, Mister Fan, and I exhaled corresponding sighs of relief.

"You no throw paper inside!" Mister Fan reminded me in broken English. I made a mental note, and since that day, I have never erred in toilet judgment.

———◆———

Shortly after my arrival in Kunming, the Chinese population softened then thawed apart, chunk by chunk, like the tip of an iceberg with subaqueous foundation. I was a global explorer on a mission to unearth secrets both for myself and for the world. I was a scuba diver, drifting in the obscure liquid twilight, exploring the unknown depths, diving into a baffling abyss with hopes to gain an understanding of the iceberg's true nature and compound. It was a cultural initiation, an entrance into mysteries that could only be understood by proximity, immersion, and language acquisition.

Generalizations didn't make sense anymore. Instead, they made me cringe and scrunch my eyebrows, seeking to convey proper explanations.

No, they don't all look the same.

Not everyone's a communist.

China is not our enemy.

Details emerged by living from within. Statistical data regarding urban migration and development, cultural values and their underlying belief systems, it all crumbled as I encountered the persons of China. They were individuals, fragments of the whole, integral bits of the perplexing puzzle. Without them, the story could not be fully understood. Each one mattered, somehow. An excess of one billion distinct members became an individual. China, no longer a vast population of nameless, faceless people, had become abbreviated and singular, no longer plural and impersonal.

China was the convivial middle-aged woman at the fruit market, her toothless smile widening at my arrival, jocund and festive. A subtle smacking sound happened as she spoke, squeaky intonations through squishy gums. Her teeth had rotted over time, loosened perhaps by copious cups of green tea or oily, deep-fried dishes; they dangled by gummy threads, each one detached, leaving nothing but uneven depressions within her jaw. Simply speaking was now an ambitious chore for her. However, there was a sweetness about her, a grandmotherly aura, albeit foreign and unfamiliar. I fingered through carefully arranged produce, lychees and mangos, bananas and rambutans, shopping exclusively at her fruit stall for no other reason than her intrinsic jubilance.

And then there was the guard at the entrance of my residential compound. He sat precariously on a flimsy plastic armchair, legs wobbly, seemingly ready to give out at any moment. He greeted me daily with an affable nod. And again, later that day at my return, he bowed his head slightly, a respectful greeting, polite and silent.

Striking up a conversation in inarticulate Chinese with these two proved an obvious dilemma. My foreign accent and brogue vernacular sounded to them like gibberish, and so our salutations remained shallow and superficially cordial.

I so desired to enter into the lives of those around me, to build real relationships, to experience China from within. Language acquisition was the only way to penetrate the unique cultural mores that daily presented themselves. At the onset, I was an outsider. I knew this. Yet I also knew that God was creative enough to use me to reach the Chinese.

I saw language as a key fumbling between forefinger and thumb; my hand probed the doorknob of culture, examining in the dark the indentation of a keyhole. Soon, though, my eyes began to adjust, my pupils dilated, and even in the dimness, I began to grasp my surroundings, sliding the key into the lock to unveil the glowing luminescence beyond the aperture.

However, not every encounter was such a struggle. There were other Chinese individuals, more educated perhaps, more inclined to decipher my hesitant linguistic articulations, to whom I gravitated, befriended, and consorted.

China was Thomas Nixon, an extraordinarily extroverted

atheist student whom I met at the English corner on the sidewalk near Green Lake Park. He had, of course, selected an English name himself, his esteem for Thomas Edison and admiration for Richard Nixon clearly evident.

There was Auntie Zhang, the janitor at Yunnan Nationalities Institute where I studied Chinese. Never do I recall seeing her without a mop and a mirthful smile. She was from a small rural countryside in southern Sichuan, evidently of a lower economic caste in China's growing middle class. But she daily brushed up against the fringes of differing cultures, befriending international students whom she cleaned up after.

And of course, there was Mrs. Ding, my sixty-one-year-old Mandarin teacher with an English vocabulary limited to *hello, okay, I love you* and *bye bye*. Needless to say, our conversations during my first few months of language study lacked a certain acumen and intellectual depth. I was a diligent student, but for sheer complexity of the Chinese language, my communication skills ended up lingering, for too long in my opinion, at a certain bothersome obtuseness.

Chinese class began every weekday at eight o'clock in the morning. Downstairs, below my fourth-floor living space, stretching along the alleyway beside the campus, a row of street vendors lined the sidewalk. Chinese students sat on plastic stools, slurping their bowls of rice noodles, ordering deep-fried fritter sticks and steamed dumplings. I joined the student body on the crowded sidewalk, paid for my noodle soup, and did my best to blend into the environment before heading to my first Chinese lesson.

> *Journal entry, September 2, 1998: "Today is my first day of school in China. Lord, I need Your help. I need You to give me this language supernaturally. Teach me. I am Your student."*

———— ♦ ————

"Good morning, Teacher Ding!" I greeted her in Chinese. "Zao shang hao, Ding Laoshi!"

I arranged my textbooks and notepad side by side, horizontally upon the undersized desk, musing at the adolescence of its inappropriately miniature scale.

"You already eat or not eat?" I asked.

Mrs. Ding scrunched her eyebrows and peaked over her black-rimmed reading glasses. She paused for a moment, considering what level of wit she would allow her retort to entail.

"I already eat," she replied, amused, a subtle parody of which I was unaware hovering upon her intentionally jumbled grammar.

My classmates began to arrive, less punctual than was required in typical Western context, yet reasonably timely by Eastern criterion.

I immediately realized that I was the only Caucasian in the class. All the other students were Asian: two Koreans, one Japanese, three Thai, two of whom had already been living and studying in Kunming for over a year. Then there was me. The lone American. A solitary Western worldview betwixt the unique idiosyncrasies of Eastern mindset. But this did not bother me in the least. It was actually rather exciting.

Our classroom was a healthy heterogeneity of differing thought and culture.

The room chilled. The wintery air seeped through the cracks of skewed window joints. Pivoting metal clasp handles bent awkwardly at perfectly incorrect measurements so that the windows never actually shut out the cold. A thick, pastel-green stripe that screamed Chinese academia was painted horizontally across the walls, kindergarten-like, I reckoned. An excess of antiquated, wooden desks lined the classroom tiles. Atop each occupied desk sat porcelain mugs of steaming, leafy green tea, earthy Pu'er, perfumed Jasmine, or fruity Oolong, depending on the particular preference of each pupil. The foreign students wore thick, wooly coats, cupping their hands around tepid mugs to keep warm. My Thai classmates shivered—accustomed to much more tropical climates—and huddled under their personal quilted blankets.

Mrs. Ding taught in pure Chinese, not a word of English uttered, thoroughly immersing us in the deep waters of language study. Our textbook, *Modern Chinese: Beginner's Course*, was written in symbols and pictograph characters; it too including scant English translation.

Occasionally, when halfway through a complete Mandarin sentence, Mrs. Ding recognized that her students did not comprehend what she said. She turned to the blackboard behind her desk, chalk in hand, and scratched a beautifully penned Chinese character for us. Sudden exclamations of comprehension emitted from the lips of my Asian classmates as they nodded their heads in unison, their *ahas* revealing triumphant, linguistic discovery. They grew up in cultures accustomed to seeing similar pictographs and characters, and Mrs. Ding's sentences now made perfect sense. But not to me. I sat at my desk, encompassed in a haze of confusion, scratching my head and scouring my textbook for clues; I grew ignorant about the content of the day's lesson. I sat there, feeling dumb and befuddled. Hours later, deep into afternoon homework, after frantically thumbing through the pages of my Chinese/English dictionary, I slowly came to understand.

I was like a blind man playing Pictionary with a group of distinguished painters.

"This morning I will teach you *bo po mo fo*," Mrs. Ding told us in Mandarin. "Hanyu Pinyin is the foundation you must learn if you are to master the Chinese language."

An extensive list of vowel-consonant combinations etched across the blackboard: *bo po mo fo de te ne le ge ke he ji qi xi*. Another, longer list of every possible intonation in the Mandarin language followed. Hanyu Pinyin was the official phonetic system for transcribing the Mandarin pronunciations of Chinese characters into the Latin alphabet. The word *Hanyu* meant *"the spoken language of the Han people;"* and *Pinyin* was literally *"spelled-out sounds."*

There it was: every possible pronunciation of this foreign language written on the blackboard in front of me. The task was daunting. *Is it really feasible to master this language?* I questioned. But the Romanized phonetic system was only part of the equation. To the letter combinations on the blackboard were added four basic tones, a glyph above each group of letters, diacritical signs for high-level tone, rising tone, dipping tone, and falling tone.

My head swam; a dull throb loomed at the rear of my cranium and down my back. My jaw ached from arching my tongue along my palate in unfamiliar ways. I clenched a pencil between forefinger and thumb but was unsure what to pen into my notepad.

"Repeat after me," Mrs. Ding said, squinting. She proceeded to pronounce each combination of letters for us to follow. My classmates and I chanted in unison, mimicking the tedious repetition of her sing-song enunciations, pitch rising here, emphasis laid there, modulating without prior notice.

I glanced at the clock above the door, praying for the acceleration of time, anxious for a ten-minute break at nine o'clock.

Even at the outset of my Mandarin studies, *Modern Chinese: Beginner's Course*, our language curriculum quickly became obsolete; its content antiquated; its object lessons outdated. The conversational components in our curriculum felt impractical, even absurd at times; less colloquial than merely historical and academic. I was privy to this pivotal shift. I caught China on the cusp of a new horizon, hanging in limbo between the past, the present, and the undeniably, unpredictable future.

Mrs. Ding, however, hung less in limbo, delighted to disclose the delicate nuances of her cultural upbringing. She taught us formal

Chinese expressions and four character idioms, popular quotes from Confucius, unearthing Ming and Qing dynastic song:

The city's stone path is well-paved and sturdy / The watermelons here are large and sweet / Who is that girl with the long braids? / I wonder if they can reach the ground / If you're ever looking to marry / You don't need to ask anyone else / I insist that you be my bride / I'll bring you the world's riches / And your little sister / On my horse-drawn carriage.

Mrs. Ding taught us Li Bai's romantic, rhythmic poetry from the Golden Age of China:

Before my bed a pool of light / Can it be hoar-frost on the ground? / Looking up, I find the moon bright / Bowing, in homesickness I am drowned.

By chapter nine in our textbook, I was unsure how to order a bowl of noodles, but could confidently ask, "Comrade, would you like to go to the Beijing Opera with me?"

Five minutes before noon, I swooned in and out of misty day-dreams. My brain was mostly mush. Mrs. Ding's voice was now little more than a murmur in the back of my mind, a babbling brook, redundant and incessant. *Is there a test tomorrow?* I tried to recall. *Yes. A test of my fifty new vocabulary words. Or is it a Hanyu Pinyin exam?* I couldn't remember. *I wonder where I should go for lunch,* I pondered. *I have a headache.*

———— ◆ ————

The action was down on Yuanxi Road, a five-minute walk from Yunnan Nationalities Institute. Hawkers and habitués haggled around traveling fruit stands, causing pedestrian traffic jams between the adjacent commercial buildings. Restaurants and pirated DVD shops, a dilapidated cinema, and brazen public adult sex shops lined the streets. My classmates and I swiveled around shuffling mule carts loaded with vegetables and fresh produce; we slithered past a group of young women shopping for dresses at roadside clothing stores; we sidestepped through an impromptu soccer match, dodging the awry ball.

At noon, when classes dismissed for two hours, Yuanxi Road, locally known as Student Street, transformed into a clamoring artery of pandemonium and hullabaloo.

College students packed into the canteens and cafeterias like sardines, jamming the entrances of tea houses and hole-in-the-wall eateries. Bearded Muslim Uyghurs from northwest China yawped raucously, hawking halal lamb kabobs for pennies per stick. Waitresses frantically took orders, barking boisterously toward the backroom kitchens: *One order of this! Two orders of that!* The cooks and clerks perspired profusely in the smoldering, aromatic atmosphere.

We lunched at an ethnic Dai diner—my Thai, Korean, Japanese classmates and I—practicing our broken Chinese with restaurant staff.

After lunch, I stood outside on the edge of Yuanxi Road, my left hand cupping my mouth, a toothpick in my right hand, freeing the remains of the meal between my molars. I stood there, pensive and silent, taking in the ambiance around me. The fruit merchants coaxing their spooked mules. The young women modeling their new dresses in the mirror. The twisting wisps of steam rising from teacups set atop roadside lunch tables. The smoky Uyghur grills and roasting lamb sticks. The Dai waitresses adorned in Siamese silk gowns and ornamental headdresses. A sea of humanity, bustling and alive, ever in movement, darting this way and that.

I stood there, cogitative, foreign, ever in-between mores and folkways, peering through the narrow keyhole of culture, and yet strangely comfortable and contented.

Journal entry, September 16, 1998: "Each ethnic tribe boasts its own uniqueness and individuality, their cultures represented in costume, dance, ornament, and religion. I pause in their presence, pondering the people beyond the veneer. Who are they really? What stirs their souls? From where do they find solace? And, Lord, I wonder, how do You see them from Your vantage point? Father, please tell me that You are watching them with me now."

It was for these precious people that my heart throbbed. The minority nationalities of China, the overlooked and underprivileged—these ones were becoming dear to me. Statistics had been given faces; numbers and data had become real people with real aspirations; they had become individuals who laughed out loud; who were inclined to disdain at the onset of injustice; who wished to provide for their families; who farted and sobbed and drank leafy tea.

It was for these forgotten, unloved, and unreached persons that I raised my voice, advocating for their salvation in my monthly newsletters to churches and vision partners. I sought to illicit missionaries from America by quoting C.T. Studd: "Some wish to live within the sound of a chapel bell; I wish to run a rescue mission within a yard of hell."

I stood there, heavy-hearted, and amidst the tumult, God spoke. He reminded me that He saw, that He cared, that He was ever-present in the loneliness and sense of abandonment that had come at my entrance into the missionary venture. God was not startled at the devastating state of the least reached peoples in this corner of the earth. He understood the conundrum I sensed at present, the intense compassion within my heart contrasted by the sentiment that as a missionary, I, too, was out of sight, out of mind. For He knew that this thought process, though acute, with a tinge of validity, was, in fact, inaccurate and erroneous. For I was not alone in sharing God's heart for those who had never heard the Christian message. True, it was not the focal point from every church pulpit. He was still revealing facets of His heart to His children in my home country, enlarging their hearts that they too might be broken with what His heart broke for. He reminded me that He not only loved the people whom I had begun to care for, but that in fact, He was more concerned for their salvation than I could ever be.

I am not slow to fulfill My promises, I sensed the Holy Spirit tell me. *I am patient, restraining Myself, desiring to include all of My children in this redemptive narrative. David,* He continued, *you do realize that I desire that none should perish, don't you?*

He then began to remind me that I was a sojourner, an alien in a strange land. I closed my eyes and saw Jesus there. And the world dimmed at His advent. *This is not your home,* He seemed to say. *Don't become too comfortable in this temporal dwelling. I am preparing a much better place for you.* The family I missed so dearly, the friends I longed to share my experiences with, the girl I chased, whom I hoped would one day become my wife—God noticed all things precious to me. *David,* He said, *wherever you may roam on this earth, I am your true home.*

———◆———

Within the first two months of my new life in Southwest China, God led me to like-minded individuals from around the world, missionaries who were focused on evangelism, discipleship, and church planting among unreached people groups. God knew that without the help of others, my impact in the country of my calling would be impotent. Only through the partnership of shared vision would grassroots ministry become effective, the unique gifting of each individual combined, blending into a harmonious, Spirit-led medley.

I met Chad and Mindy Layman, who had already lived and ministered in China for many years. Month after month, this American man and his Malaysian wife boarded *Betsy*, their faithful, army-green Beijing Jeep, for expeditions into the rural countryside. They were bold and a speck reckless, courageous enough to dare the impossible. They traveled extensively among unreached ethnic tribes with their two young sons buckled in the back of their vehicle, blazing new trails for the missionary community who would soon follow in their footprints.

While in Kunming, the Layman family hosted a small Christian fellowship for foreign missionaries in their home. There, I met Bret College, Alaskan native, former bad-boy-biker-turned-radical-for-Jesus. His long, gunmetal hair cinched into a ponytail, the wrinkled creases in his brow gathering handsomely as he spoke of his adoration for all things spiritual.

I met Frederik Jensen, a lanky Dane with pale Scandinavian skin, who was filled with the colorful vibrancy of life. He carried a certain ascetic repose in his facial symmetry, an austerity upon his square jaw, juxtaposed by sparkling azure eyes. Superfluous jocularity lay just beneath his thoughtful veneer. His wit and hilarity lightened the atmosphere aboard many a long sleeper bus ride into the backwoods of tribal villages.

I met Glenn and Jeanette Robinson from Ireland, Tim and Julia Meyer from Holland, and Todd and Michelle Rosenwald from America. With this diverse band of pioneer missionaries, I experienced China's subtle cultural mores in urban city centers and the animistic folkways in rural countrysides.

Fellowship in the Layman home gave birth to new missionary dreams. We envisioned the Gospel arriving in the communities of forgotten tribes on the distant horizons of Yunnan Province. Sitting together in a circle one Sunday morning, our hearts united in purpose. We formed an apostolic team, committed to reaching the least reached people groups of Southwest China. It was natural and organic, an alliance of Christian community with no other purpose than to glorify God through willing obedience. Our motto was witty and straightforward: "We have done so much with so little for so long that we can now do anything with nothing!" There was no paperwork, no indentures or contracts; simply a covenant of brothers and sisters that would lead to numerous outreaches and ministries. We cared not for acclaim or tribute so long as God received the glory. And with this spirit of unity, onward we went together into regions untouched by Christian presence.

There, among the minority nationalities of Southwest China, my heart came alive. I loved the awkwardness of entering an unreached village for the first time; the bedazzled grannies riveted at our arrival, the young men timid and ambivalent, wondering why we had strayed so far from the beaten path. I loved the jubilant ruckus that resulted when the children laid eyes on our gifts from afar; they admired our long, twisting balloons from which we sculpted pink puppies, orange swords, and sleek green sombreros. The awkward discomfort turned to wonderment, and we suddenly became the talk of the town, at which point we were routinely invited into the homes of one of the families.

Divine encounters succeeded from these meager moments. The glorious presence of God had come at last to the homes of unsuspecting residents; and inevitably, salvation and revival followed. I began to recognize that the Holy Spirit often moved in the midst of the mundane, through casual encounters and by minuscule means. At most, we were a ragamuffin band of misfit missionaries who had simply arrived at an unreached village; we played with the children, prayed for the sick, and preached about God's grace.

It seemed to me that this was what God was waiting for: willful surrender and pure obedience. Nothing more. He knew all about our weaknesses and inabilities. He was simply requesting our availability. He was aware that our presence was less transformative and life-altering than we cared to admit. But He delighted in including us, in using us to reveal His glory. He joyously allowed us to carry the unhindered light of His Kingdom to regions untouched by Christian presence.

This reality—that God loved to include me in His plan, not because of what I had to offer, but simply because He loved me— was invigorating. It was refreshing and restorative. The great burden of reaching unreached people groups was lifted, replaced by calm compassion; I felt my heart beating a little more in sync with the heart of Heaven.

> *Journal entry, April 26, 1999: "This morning, I am filled with brokenness for those tribes who have never heard of Jesus. A budding burden for souls is growing within me. Who will go to these precious ones? Here I am, Lord. If it is Your will, send me to the hardest places and to the neediest people. May Your love compel me, Father. For if my heart is so filled with sorrow for them, oh, how deeply You must cherish them!"*

After long hours of inhaling the black soot of smoky fire pits in the shoddy homes and dilapidated structures of rural villages, I would sometimes slip away for a moment alone. Outside, I exhaled the hazy fumes I had been breathing for hours. I crossed the narrow foot trail opposite our host's home, found a secluded patch of farmland, and began foraging for flowers. I picked daisies and hibiscus, periwinkles and marigolds, flattening them gently between blank pages in my journal until they dried. Two weeks later, I pasted the pressed, dry blossoms onto the pulpy surface of handmade mulberry paper cards. They became weekly love letters to Lorna, where I described my village journeys and shared with her the cultural nuances of inland China.

> *May 28, 1999: "Atop this mountain, I am taking it all in now. The fading colors of dusk, the looming darkness that slowly shrouds this village in secrets. There seems to be some sort of muted struggle in the realm beyond my eyes, broken suddenly by a ringing exclamation through the valleys below: 'Behold, all souls are Mine' (Ezekiel 18:4)! The elderly gentleman leaning on his hoe. The tiny child with wind-burnt cheeks. The*

elderly woman whose silhouette reflects faintly in the window, her vacant eyes declaring the hopelessness of her experiences. Who remembers them anymore? 'Weep with those who weep,' I am told, and my burden grows heavier every day. Then, there in the silence of the night, I see in the moon your reflection, weeping; but I cannot reach high enough to comfort you. I see your heavy teardrops, nightly dripping at the feet of God. Your burden is heavy because your calling is majestic. When the clouds above you grow dark, and the lurking shadows become elongated, when the sun fades into the blackness of night, you must remember that truth, Lorna. 'Those who sow in tears shall reap in joy' (Psalm 126:5). And you know that 'he who dares not grasp the thorn should never crave the rose.' Please press on. I am weeping in the moon with you."

Rememories

SIDEWALKS

*"Does it not stir up our hearts, to go forth and help them, does it not make
us long to leave our luxury, our exceeding abundant light,
and go to them that sit in darkness?"*
AMY CARMICHAEL

A series of interminable cement sidewalks snaked through
Kunming city, maze-like and labyrinthine. They ran alongside boulevards and thoroughfares. They crisscrossed the metropolitan,
connecting business district to residential suburbia. They weaved
a complex, interconnected web between skyscrapers and tumbledown shanties, joining the rich with the poor.

The sidewalks were impartial. They made no distinction
between opulence and penury. They coupled upper class to lower,
joining society at the shoulder, forming an awkward hodgepodge
from multiple demographic pools.

The pathways were not unlike particular locations of the Great
Wall, chipped and broken at certain points like Mutianyu. At other

spots, they were renovated and rebuilt like the more recent reconstructed brick and mortar at Badaling. Some sidewalks decayed and crumbled like distant peripheries where the Great Wall stretched into the Gobi Desert.

The spiderweb of pathways zigzagged and intersected throughout Kunming. They meandered under the low-lying canopy of branches at Bird and Flower Market; wound around the lip of Green Lake; gridded the matrix of apartment complexes in Northern District.

But not every sidewalk in Southwest China was made for walking.

Thousands of bicycles sat situated within the fenced-off, makeshift parking lots outside noodle shops. Hundreds of cars were parked, bumper to bumper, in unorganized rows. Unruly tree roots ruptured the earth beneath the pavement and pushed through the cracks, fracturing the footpaths. At times, I even came across the protruding red tips of fire hydrants, mostly buried below layers of pavement—reminders of China's rapid development.

It was nearly impossible to stroll unimpeded along the sidewalks.

From between the cracks of each cement slab grew an array of peculiar beauty: weeds and wildflowers, twining vines, bamboo and bougainvillea. But the decorative charm had another, less-desirable companion. Penury rose alongside pulchritude. Poverty was the ever-present partner of prosperity.

The sidewalks of Kunming were occupied by underprivileged residents on the fringes of society. They were tramps and vagabonds, hobos and scroungers. They were beggars and trash pickers, dumpster divers and land clammers. But not by their own choosing. Many of these street people were missing limbs or grossly deformed. Others had boils or swollen warts bulging on their knees and neck. Some had polio or HIV. Even more pitiful were the infants, whose craniums were waterlogged and enlarged, alien-like from the effects of hydrocephalus.

A rusty tin can lay before each of the poor and homeless. They whimpered and cried, bowing their heads incessantly toward the sidewalk, pleading for charity from passersby.

And behind the scenes of each street person lurked a band of pimps, hovering in the shadows, skimming off the top, thriving off their misery and indigence.

I shared the sidewalks with the poor, where sorrow and heartbreak divided among them. I was saddened by my inability to improve their lots; angered at my ineptitude to remedy their hopeless situations.

So, I chose just one of them to serve and bless.

Li Ming was exceptionally streetwise for an eleven-year-old. His father left at an early age and his mother abandoned him soon after. He grew up on the streets, dining on the dregs left in garbage cans behind restaurants, panhandling in public parks. I often noticed him frequenting Jinri Park, begging for small handouts from the crowd.

His hair was matted; his cheeks smeared with dirt from the ground where he made his bed. His shirt was full of holes; his pants torn at the cuffs. He did not own a pair of shoes.

I sat there on a bench, watching orange leaves break from tree branch stems, descend slowly, and spiral downward toward the sidewalk. A sudden, uncanny prompting within my spirit drew me toward Li Ming. I hesitated at first, for what would people think of me associating with a beggar? It was a preposterous contemplation, really, perhaps the same that grip the hearts of good-intentioned men everywhere. But the compassion of God surged inside me and dispelled my insecurities. I stood up from the bench and made my way through the crowd to the beggar boy.

I walked up to him and put my hand on his shoulder. "Are you ready to be blessed?" I skipped the pleasantries, and simply got to the point. "Let's go buy some shoes," I said.

Li Ming cautiously followed me to a nearby shoe store. At first, the owner would not allow the boy to enter. I reprimanded him in Chinese, adamantly pushed past his barred arms, and began browsing branded shoes with Li Ming. His eyes sparkled with delight. I wondered if this was his first time shopping like normal people. After perusing the store, he finally selected knock-off Nike shoes, a new jacket, and dress pants. I threw in a pair of socks and settled the bill.

Li Ming exited the storefront and stepped onto the sidewalk a new person. He smiled so widely, and I thought his face might crack.

He turned to me and bowed. "Xiexie, shushu," he said. "Thank you, uncle."

"Bu yong xie," I replied. "But we're not done yet. Let's go watch a movie!"

We walked to a cinema off Baoshan Street, just north of Jinri Park. I purchased two tickets for *Lord of the Rings* in Mandarin Chinese, with English subtitles. Li Ming sat silently, munching on popcorn, captivated by a world of hobbits and elves, orcs and wizards.

When the movie ended, we stood outside the theater. I laid my hand on the boy and prayed for him. I told him that Jesus loved him, that he was God's prized possession. I told him that he was valued, that I cared, and that he was not alone.

Xiexie, shushu," he said once more. It seemed as if his chin raised ever so slightly as if some small portion of humanity had been returned to him. There was a sparkle in his eyes. Funny that all it took was clean clothing and a new pair of shoes.

Li Ming turned toward the alley, smiled, waved at me one last time, then disappeared.

I lingered there, gazing at the sidewalk. The city pathways were ever telling stories, horrific, haphazard, and beautiful. Between junctures along the journey, joy arose from dejection. I was honored to be included in these quiet stories, to be part of God's redemptive work.

The Kingdom of God was everywhere, all around me, coursing through the city streets; down unfrequented back lanes; up hidden stairways, and into the alcoves and crannies at dead-end alleyways. And I began to understand a deeper truth: that wherever my feet strode, there, too, went the Kingdom.

I recalled a time when Jesus was in the house of a well-known religious man. There, He sat among the elite, watching the guests elbow each other for the best seat in the house. I imagined Jesus being mesmerized by the fatuous jockeying for recognition, a parabolic narrative developing in His mind. He would startle the hypocritical religious with right Kingdom principles. He would challenge the wealthy with the deeper, oft-overlooked, character-istics of God's Kingdom.

So, Jesus told stories of the poor, the crippled, the lame, the blind.

He spoke of the disparity between opulence and poverty. He described the chasmal gap between the renowned and margin-alized. He addressed man's misconceptions of true religion. He talked about who would sit beside the master at the banquet in the Kingdom of God.

Jesus brought His parable to a pinnacle by saying, "Then the master said to the servant, 'Go out into the highways and hedges, and compel them to come in, that my house may be filled.'"

His story culminated with tramps, prostitutes, beggars, and bums, each feasting within palatial walls, awkward at first, perhaps, but before long, merry and ecstatic.

The Kingdom of God has a peculiar way of returning humanity

and honor to the homeless. It raises to glory the disgraced and destitute. The Kingdom of God does not overlook the forgotten. It includes all.

Over the next few weeks, I bused downtown in hopes to bump into Li Ming again. I waited for him on public benches at Jinri Park, but he never came. I strolled through the alleys at Bird and Flower Market. I wandered around the lawn at Dongfeng Square. I thought I might spot him begging on the crowded sidewalks. But the beggar boy was nowhere to be found.

Poverty, like an onion, has many layers. And every layer, from its flaky outer shell to its sweetish center, will make you cry. It was not difficult to encounter poverty along Kunming's sidewalks. Yet, something strange started to take place within me as I spent time among the marginalized. Compassion began to bud and grow inside my heart. The more I focused on the poor, the more I loved them.

I met a young beggar girl with a stub for her left arm and eyes so wide they could contain all the stars in the universe. Each time I arrived, she remembered my foreign face, and would hold a rusty tin can in front of me. "Uncle, gei wo qian," she pleaded. "Give me money." I have never forgotten the dismal, hollow sound that echoed from her tin can as I dropped a few coins inside.

Then there was a man with the most severe effects of polio I had ever seen. His rubbery thighs were thinner than my wrist. His frame warped and deformed with severe scoliosis. One of his limp legs slung over his shoulder to keep it from dragging on the ground. With thick construction gloves covering his hands, he squirmed along the sidewalk, face first, dragging himself forward on a four-wheeled plank. He had the look of an injured animal. The crowd dodged and weaved around him. Some gasped; others whispered. Most people pretended not to notice the man as if his non-existence might make them feel less uncomfortable.

He lifted his head mere inches from the makeshift skateboard. His eyes caught my gaze, and I froze, embarrassed and apologetic. I could not help but stare. Suddenly, a warm smile spread across his face. It startled me. I returned an awkward smile, reached into my wallet, and pulled out a few bills. He thanked me as I dropped the money inside his tin can. I patted him on the shoulder. "Yesu ai ni," I told him. "Jesus loves you."

Not far from Jinri Park, a one-year-old girl laid on a dirty, white sheet in the shade of a fir tree. Her head was grossly misshaped and enlarged by hydrocephalus. She writhed back and forth, whimpering as I passed, forlorn and forgotten. Her abject state was heartbreaking. I did not know how the meager financial donations of passersby actually contributed to her well-being.

The sad stories of these destitute street people seeped between the fissures in the sidewalk, silenced and concealed.

———— ◆ ————

The Kunming World Horticultural Exposition, an A1 category international garden festival, was soon to open. It would draw a massive tourist population from all over China and around the world. With its theme, "Man and Nature, Marching into the 21st Century," the government grew more and more concerned about its image.

Just before the turn of the millennium, the police began forcibly removing the face of poverty from the sidewalks. Chinese newspaper articles referred to the poor as "the scourge of society" and "the dregs of the population." And week after week, the marginalized fringe society began to dwindle.

After two months of searching for Li Ming, I finally chanced upon him at Dongfeng Square, where he stood overlooking the slow-moving Panlong River.

"Li Ming!" I called. "Where have you been? I've been trying to find you."

He was silent and despondent, his head downcast. I looked at his tattered clothing.

"What happened to your new clothes?" I asked.

"I sold them," he responded, embarrassed.

I wrapped my arm around him, and he began to cry. He told me how he had been dropped off in a rural countryside by the police and told not to return to the city. But he had no money and no family to take care of him. As he spoke, his eyes darted back and forth across the park lawn where random police officers patrolled the public square.

"I'm not supposed to be here," he told me. "I don't know what they'll do if they catch me again."

His situation was dismal. The gravity of his lot hit me like a ton of bricks. I reached into my pocket and handed him a handsome amount of Renminbi. "Take this," I told him. "Go get yourself a good meal and some new clothes."

I gave him a Christian booklet and hugged him one last time.

His reply came like clockwork. "Xiexie, shushu," he said. And once again, I watched as he disappeared, this time along the bend of the winding Panlong River.

Though the day was bright and sunny and the sky spotted with heaping cumulus clouds, a certain sorrow filled my heart. I stood where I found the boy, at the edge of the river, and watched the water ripple slowly, descending southbound through the city.

"Lord, take care of Li Ming," I prayed. "Reveal Your heart to him."

Behind me, along the edge of the grass, grew a dense shrub with blooming rouge camellias, Kunming's city flower. Its velvety petals rustled in the gentle breeze, its floral fragrance wafting skyward. The pink hues of the flowers juxtaposed by the drab cement walkways encircling the park.

Beauty and baseness have always lived alongside each other. The sidewalks of Kunming were a striking example of this reality.

But the Kingdom of God pervades every facet of the atmosphere, splashing color on muted canvases, eliciting splendor from somber sites.

Perhaps one day I will sit beside Li Ming at God's great banquet when at last his quandaries will be quelled. And there, among the heavenly hosts, he will have a home.

Chapter 4

THE CHASE

*"I often think that God must have been looking for someone small enough
and weak enough for Him to use, and that He found me."*
HUDSON TAYLOR

One kilometer from Myanmar, just outside Dadong Village, home
to the former headhunting Wa tribe, dusk had died, and darkness
became a punctured canopy of twinkling white stars over the rural
China mountains.

I shuffled along the dusty road, trailing Frederik's hurried pace,
where the swaying bamboo tilted over the road, hovering ominously.

My heart throbbed as I tried to keep up with Frederik.

"Why is this projector battery so freakin' heavy?" I panted.

Frederik ignored me.

"Hurry up!" he said.

The thirty-pound battery jostled in my backpack, digging into
my scapula with every step. It was a two-man job. The rest of the
projector and tangled cords tucked inside Frederik's bag.

"Seriously, why did we take this thing?" I complained

"Forget about it."

"It's slowing me down."

"Hurry up!"

I could barely see the dusty road but for the dull, ghostly moonlight. Frederik was ten feet in front of me, kicking up dust with his shuffling shoes. My teeth were gritty. I felt the sticky beads of sweat tickling my back as it streamed down my vertebrae. My armpits were pungent, and the scent of local moonshine lingered on my breath.

"I'm so out of shape!"

Frederik flung his head around. "Why are you talking so much?" he quipped.

"Sorry."

I brushed away the crusty dust that had formed on the crease of my lips. We were only two miles into our eight-mile hike down the mountain toward Cangyuan city. Like an asylum set in the valley below, the city was our refuge, a safe haven from the conspicuous mountain village we fled from. In Dadong Village, we were simply sitting ducks for the Chinese police.

I squinted, peering into the distance where the curving road disappeared around a bend ahead.

"God, this is gonna take forever!" I panted. "How long have we been running?"

"About twenty minutes."

"We're gonna get into town past midnight, for sure," I reminded him.

"Yea."

The faint murmur of an engine motor echoed across the forested mountains, dissipating down the valley below. Our pace slowed to a halt.

"Did you hear that?" Frederik panted.

"Yea. It's way too late for a car to be driving up this road."

"Not good."

It was nearly eleven o'clock at night. The hutted homes behind us had dimmed as farmers untwisted light bulbs in the sockets that dangled from electrical wire. The yellow glow of dawn would rise early upon these mountains, and the ethnic farmers would awake at first light to tend their fields. The village slept. It was unusual that someone would be driving up the mountain at this hour. We knew immediately that the police were on their way.

"Look!" Frederik pointed straight ahead, directing my attention to two faint headlights beaming around a bend in the distance.

"Not good."

"No."

The police were still a distance away, so our pace quickened as fast as we could manage with the heavy projector in tow. Moments later, the police car lurched around a final bend, engine roaring, advancing toward us at startling velocity.

"C'mon!"

Frederik jumped into the roadside ditch, concealing himself in the thicket. I tumbled headlong into the ditch, scraping my knee on a jagged rock. We threw off our backpacks, ducking below the ridge of the road, camouflaged behind the bamboo. I clutched my knee, nursing the laceration as blood seeped between my fingers, pooling in the mud.

We sat, huffing, trying to slow our breathing.

Two police cars raced past us, spraying our stubby ambush with the dusty wake.

"Two of them," I whispered. "Didn't realize we were that important."

"Yea. I feel like a celebrity!" Frederik quipped.

"Something like that. It's good we're not still in the village signing autographs!"

The dust settled as the flashing red and blue cherry lights disappeared along the narrow road. In a few minutes, the police would arrive in Dadong Village, searching for two foreign missionaries they were notified about.

"We have to go," I said, hoisting my heavy bag around my back. "They'll probably be coming back this way soon."

I rose, stepping gingerly, my leg now a bloody mess.

"Ah, the life of a celebrity!" Frederik joked. "It's not easy!"

"Yea. Not easy at all."

———— ◆ ————

Six hours earlier, the sun set in the Cangyuan valley below, beyond the bending bamboo and distant mountains. Shifting pink hues turned purple before leaking between the thatched walls of poorly constructed bamboo huts. Elongated shadows skewed across our feet as we squatted beside the smoky fire pit in the home of an ethnic Wa family.

We had traveled these mountains before, trekking from village to village, sharing the Gospel, passing out tracts, and showing *The Jesus Film*. We had seen breakthrough and salvation, compelled now to find how our recent converts were growing in their newfound faith.

This particular trip led us to the home of a Wa man in his late fifties who, after seeing us wander through the narrow dirt paths of his village, invited us into his home for handmade moonshine, a Wa specialty.

"Ni jiao shenme mingzi?"

"My name is Ai Xiao. Here, have some mijiu."

To deny such a hospitable gift would be a cultural snub.

"Thank you, Uncle Xiao," Frederik and I said in unison. I reluctantly received the smudged cup he handed me and sipped the clear liquid. The malty, fermented hooch burned my throat as I swallowed. I winced at the acrid bite, trying to conceal my involuntary grimace, then drained the glass in a show of masculinity. Uncle Xiao did the same.

"I'm David. This is Frederik."

"Ni hao."

Uncle Xiao offered us another shot glass of his homegrown liquor. His congenial persistence overcame our polite but adamant refusals, and so we obliged, giving him face. I took the second drink, saluted, and winced as I sipped daintily. Mister Xiao smiled, drained his glass, then turned to fill the second round for Frederik. I doused the remaining contents of my glass furtively between the slats in the floor, wetting the pigs underneath the hut. Frederik saw and snickered. The unexpected shower startled the animals below, and they squealed in agitation. Uncle Xiao's wife lifted her ladle from the stir fried vegetables in her wok, pausing to hush the pigs. Thankfully, no one but Frederik noticed the wet bamboo slats near my feet.

When Jesus sent out seventy-two disciples on evangelistic travels, He instructed them to eat what was offered them without raising questions of conscience. I am unaware of the specific local delicacies they may have partaken of in the homes of unreached communities, but I have often considered the potential similarities I too encountered in my travels: boiled grub worms; bitter greens; furry cat soup; chewy, four-legged mystery meat, most likely dog. And inevitably in this part of the world, the widely consumed fermented beverage of choice, *mijiu*, Chinese rice wine made from glutinous rice. And though these drinks and meals often vexed my stomach, the aching churn was worth getting my foot in the door and access into the homes and hearts of unreached people groups. Still, however, after years of living in China, I would often still default to my juvenile excuse that I had not yet mastered the fine art of chopsticks, intentionally dropping chunks of animal carcasses to the hutted floor for domesticated animals to enjoy.

Uncle Xiao's wife poured her brothy, home-cooked vegetable soup into a porcelain bowl, and placed it in the center of the low table. Kerneled white rice and collard greens, a plate of grisly meat and bones, a bowl of oil-soaked glutinous rice patties. Frederik and I nodded in appreciation, bowing our heads slightly as we squatted awkwardly upon six-inch wooden stools.

Frederik, one of my closest missionary friends in China, wore a short-sleeve, button-down shirt and khaki shorts. His bare, Scandinavian kneecaps were relatively level with his chin as he hunched clumsily over the dinner table, his legs much too lanky to be perched on the short stool. There was a frog-like resemblance about his posture, lumpish and lumbering, offset by his cheery smile.

"These seats are nearly the same height as the ones we use in Denmark," he joked.

"You look right at home!" I replied.

Frederik watched as our host refilled his shot glass to the brim with rice wine. He surveyed the bamboo slats beneath him, considering where he, too, might soon dispel of the fiery, liquid contents.

Uncle Xiao pinched a hunk of meat between his chopsticks, reached across the table and plopped it into my bowl. "Chi ba!" he said gaily, and the evening meal commenced. As we ate, the smoldering haze of the fire pit billowed into our lungs. Frederik's bony kneecaps blackened gradually, spotted with the vaporous soot that mixed with the fragrance of fried wild greens and grub worms wafting through the dilapidated hut.

That night in the home of our new Wa friends, long-kept secrets were revealed to us; horrific stories of methamphetamine production and addiction, of strange unnamed sicknesses befalling little children, of the great demon spirits harassing unlucky families who refused to partake in headhunting practices. Tales of clan rivalry, of human sacrifice, accounts of hopelessness and despair. Narratives that hell was pleased with, the details of which made our stomachs churn more incessantly than the rice wine.

The Wa minority, one of the poorest tribes in Yunnan Province, were former headhunters. To guarantee that their crops would be blessed, they severed human heads from bodies and placed them on a three-pronged bamboo post that towered over their crops. I had read accounts of clan rivalry in historical textbooks but had never heard the stories firsthand. The Wa knew that bloodshed carried a necessary atoning value, but had been duped into believing that salvation and safety from hungry ghosts lay in offering a human sacrifice. These poor people had never heard of the final sacrifice Jesus had made on the cross.

A rusty iron blade hung precariously upon the bamboo wall to my left. I glanced nonchalantly at it, cautious and curious. I placed my bowl against my lower lip and shoveled rice and vegetables into my mouth with my chopsticks, contemplating to what part the nearby blade had perhaps played in the tumultuous history of this people.

"Tell me," I turned to Uncle Xiao, "has this knife ever cut off a human head?"

He looked up from his rice bowl, pausing awkwardly. Even the unleveled, bamboo hutted floor would have carried the resonance of a pin drop in a hushed silence such as this. In normal occasions, such a question would typically be ignored so as to protect the hidden folkways of ethnic tribes. But Mister Xiao's shoulders rose slightly upward, emboldened perhaps from the copious amounts of liquor he had already consumed, and he leaned surreptitiously in toward the dinner table

He began to let the dirty secrets out of the bag.

"Of course," he said. "When I was thirteen-years-old, I cut off someone's head with that very blade."

Frederik reached across the table and scooped a large wad of stringy vegetables from the soup pot, unfazed by the conversation.

"But never the head of a Chinese man," Uncle Xiao continued. "The Hans' vengeance was much too vicious."

"So whose head did you cut off?"

"The Dai. Sometimes the Lahu. Neighboring tribes. Warring clans."

"So, you cut off more than one head in your day?"

"Many," he replied, and I recognized a reticent remorse in his eyes.

Uncle Xiao closed his eyes as he recalled the early days of his youth. The thick wrinkles sagging at the edge of his eyes drooped heavily upon his protruded cheekbones.

"I was thirteen-years-old when I first hid in the bamboo with some men from our village. Some of my friends were there, too. We were scared."

The recollection was still fresh in his memory, so poignant and acute that I thought I saw his lip quiver ever so slightly.

"The sun had set, and darkness had fallen over the valley. We made our way quietly across the fields toward the Lahu tribe. I could hear them laughing from within their huts. They were drinking."

He paused to drain another shot glass of rice wine. His speech progressively began to slur, and his voice cracked.

"We waited there in the darkness outside their homes. Late in the evening, one of the men walked outside to take a piss. That's when we attacked."

Uncle Xiao turned his head toward the fire pit, staring blankly at the red embers. Memories formed around his lips, and he scrunched his eyebrows to recall the details.

"One of the men from my village nudged me. I was scared, but I drew my knife and... and I stabbed the man in the chest."

The pace of his story now began to slow. He lowered his voice to a husky whisper.

"He did not cry out. He was quieter than I expected him to be. Too quiet. I pulled my knife from his body, and we dragged his corpse to the edge of the fields. That's when I hacked off his head."

He pointed at the blade hanging on the bamboo wall. "That's the knife we used."

I sensed a subtle anguish in his intonations, a weight that he had carried his whole life for which he had yet to make penitence.

"We hid his body in a ditch and carried his head back to our village. The hungry ghosts were satisfied. Our crops never failed while a human head hung above our fields."

The crackle of smoldering wood in the fire pit echoed inside the hut. Smoke billowed around the room, creating a dream-like atmosphere that was both terrifying and intriguing.

Frederik and I sat there silently. Uncle Xiao placed his porcelain bowl to his lips and slurped the remaining kernels of rice from his meal.

"But that was a long time ago," he said. "The Wa people don't cut off heads anymore. Now we sacrifice chickens to the hungry ghosts."

———•———

During our meal, Uncle Xiao's neighbors had been gathering at the door, clamoring to catch a glimpse of a foreigner for the first time in their lives. Some hovered outside cautiously. A few brave young boys made their way inside, sat beside me, enamored with my hairy arms. They sat there, stroking my forearm, giggling, making silly faces at me.

After dinner, thirty Wa men and women, and too many children in tattered clothing to count crammed inside the hut. Feet shuffled on the bamboo slats as venomous spiders dangled overhead. The fire pit had nearly burned out, and the lingering scent of black soot and wok-fried vegetables permeated the atmosphere.

We began setting up our bulky, battery-operated projector, unraveling tangled cords and plugging them into the battery we had lugged into the village hours earlier. On the largest curving wall of the room, Frederik directed the glare of our projector upon a hanging, white sheet.

"Are you ready to watch a movie?" Frederik asked the small crowd.

Middle-aged farmers and young men sat on the tiny stools. Children curled in the laps of their mothers. Grannies hovered in the corner of the room. Mister Xiao stood at the dinner table, slightly inebriated, honored to host the special event in his home.

I slid the DVD of the condensed Mandarin Chinese version of *The Jesus Film* into the portable player and pushed play. The voice of the narrator began: *God loved the people of the world so much that He gave His only Son so that everyone who has faith in Him will have eternal life and never really die.* A hush came over the room. It was a rare occasion for the Wa to experience technology like this, and it was their first time to hear the message of the Gospel. The narrator continued: *God did not send His Son into the world to condemn its people. He sent Him to save them!*

For the next thirty minutes, the locals watched the life of Jesus unfold to them for the very first time in their lives. They gasped as He healed the sick. They listened to Him speak of God's Kingdom, of grace and glory and the true meaning of life. They were riveted to the screen as nails were driven into His wrists and feet. As He hung on the cross, I watched the tears stream down the cheeks of Wa mothers.

Jesus spoke Chinese that night. "Bu yao pa. Zhi yao xin," He said. "Don't be afraid. Just believe."

Although there had been a Christian witness among the Wa people over a century earlier, most people knew little to nothing of the Gospel message. The remaining churches still standing after the Cultural Revolution were dead. Now, they were little more than empty, dilapidated buildings where the elderly occasionally met to sing together and where old men sat smoking their water bongs. Young people had no concept of the reality of God's salvation that had been brought to the Wa tribe one hundred years earlier by a missionary named William Young.

But tonight was different. It was intentional Gospel outreach. Frederik and I were prayed up. We were poised for any cross-cultural scenario. We were seasoned veterans, or so we imagined.

The film cast a luminescent glow around that thatched hut, spilling over dark skin, sketching the outlines of the human profiles that gazed at the screen. As I stood there amongst a group of people who had never heard of Jesus before, I thought, *What an incredible calling I have!* Joy filled my heart as I glanced at each individual in the room. *Speak, Lord,* I prayed. *Make Yourself known to these precious ones.*

An enormous, orange, Easter-Sunday sun rose on the screen. The lifeless body of Jesus had been taken from the cross, covered in white linens, and laid gently in the tomb. The operatic music commenced, and moments later, Jesus appeared to His disciples, shining with heavenly luminescence. He had risen from the dead and was alive! I watched Uncle Xiao's neighbors gasp, confused and excited, whispering to each other in Wa dialect.

The bud of new life emerged in the little room, slowly at first, until fresh hope flowered amidst a backdrop of darkness.

Oh, the darkness! This helpless people group had lived for far too long in the haunted shadows where hungry ghosts flitted freely, clasped in the clutches of a dragon, ensnared in the crepuscule of the underworld. Their memories laced with streaks of clotted blood that pooled around headless corpses hanging from bamboo posts. Regret and desperation were their bread as they groped along the blackened stairways of satanic trickery. Animism had been their overlord; shamans and witch doctors their mediators between life and the netherworld.

Oh, the darkness that now fled through the fractured clefts and cracks at the advent of radiant light! Demon hordes dispelled at its onset, retreating into the far-off fringes where shadows gasped and convulsed for their existence. The dragon loosened its grip, wincing in the refulgent glow, vanishing away as a Champion Savior appeared.

When the film ended, Frederik passed out *Help From Above* Gospel tracts, and I stood in front of the group of Wa families.

"Today is the day of salvation!" I said in Mandarin. "It's no accident that we are here. Jesus, the Son of the living God, has come to save you! Tonight, we want to pray with you to receive new life."

Over twenty Wa people gave their lives to Jesus that night. Frederik and I laid hands on old men as their cigarettes burned out, ashes falling through the bamboo floor slats. We gripped the shoulders of young men, rousing within them their divine callings, encouraging them to seek the things of God. We hugged the little children, cupped their faces in our hands, and blessed them with safety and comfort.

"Jesus loves you!" I proclaimed. "Do you know that?"

"Uh-huh," was all that they could muster with their shy, childlike innocence.

Frederik gathered everyone in a circle and closed the night in one final prophetic prayer.

"God, we know that You love the Wa people. We love them, too. That's why we're here. Now, we pray that You would take care of these precious people. Be with them. Send Your Holy Spirit to speak to them. We bless them, in the name of Jesus. Amen."

That night was a pivotal moment in our ministry to the Wa minority. It was a breakthrough. It was one of the greatest hopes a missionary could dream for: to see seeds break through the hard soil and spring into life.

The dim glow of light bulbs dangling from electrical wire cast shadows in the corner of the room as the last of the remaining neighbors stepped down the narrow stairs, returning home, floaty and euphoric.

I stood at the terraced entrance of the raised hut. I looked out at the darkened landscape. The bamboo swayed gently in the warm breeze, silhouetted against the fading midnight blue sky. A million stars spangled the vaulted azure.

"Thank You, God," I whispered. "Thank You for calling me to China. Thank You for including me in the work of bringing Your light to this dark region. I'm amazed how You delight to use me. God, please take care of these new believers."

Below me, one hundred feet to the left, tucked between adjoining huts, a faint blue light illuminated the cheek and eyes of a thin Wa man. I squinted. His muffled whispers into his cell phone carried along the dirt footpath. Something about his crooked stance wasn't right. I squinted and tried to hear what he said.

"They've been here for three hours." He spoke into the phone with a hushed tone. "Yes. They showed a film and passed out booklets."

Immediately, I knew something was wrong. The skinny man had the look of a Judas, the stars reflecting upon his pupils like thirty pieces of silver.

"Yes. They're still here," he whispered. "Hurry. I'll be here when you arrive."

That's when the alarm went off in my head. I felt the beating inside my chest as I spun around. I ducked my head underneath the low threshold and called Frederik.

"We need to go!"

"What's wrong?"

"We've got a Judas outside. He's on the phone with the cops."

Frederik and I had been down this path before. It wasn't our first rodeo. Interrogations and police activity came with the territory for pioneer missionaries.

"Pack the projector!" Frederik said. "I'll see if there are any tracts lying around."

Uncle Xiao's wife laid a comforter on a bed in the adjacent room. She looked up as we quickly packed our bags and belongings. She said something in Wa to her husband.

"My wife is preparing a place for you to sleep tonight," he said in Mandarin. "We are happy to have you stay with us."

"Uncle Xiao, feichang bu hao yi se. We're very sorry," Frederik said. "We need to get back to the city tonight."

"No. It's too far. Besides, there's no one to take you there at this hour."

"Thank you, but we really need to go."

Uncle Xiao was perplexed and offended.

"Don't worry. We'll be back to see you as soon as we can."

After stubborn pleas to stay in his home, Uncle Xiao reluctantly let us go. Frederik and I shuffled down the footpath toward the main road. We turned to wave one last time.

"Don't worry. We'll be back!"

The Wa family disappeared into the night as we began our eight-mile trek back to Cangyuan city in the valley below.

That night was the initial pioneer work that would soon open doors for underground training and discipleship among Wa villages. Years later, it would grow into a thriving children's ministry of over three hundred children, who would pray and prophesy over classmates and neighbors. It was the initial spark that grew into a little revival; that would eventually undergo massive government persecution, police beatings, and the forcible removal of our ministry from the Cangyuan valley.

———•———

The chase was on. But my flight was not only one-sided. The police were not the only ones trailing me.

God was chasing me as well. I could not escape His radar on my life.

Sometimes, it was a whimsical frolic in open fields. I laughed as I fled Him along the grasslands, turning to confirm His pursuit. It was childish and pointless play, frivolous and memorable. But on other occasions, I became the hunted as I fled His calls, like Jonah, turning awry at the sign to Nineveh.

"Anyone who intends to come with Me has to let Me lead," the Holy Spirit reminded me. "You're not in the driver's seat; I am. Don't run from suffering; embrace it. Follow Me, and I'll show you how. Self-help is no help at all. Self-sacrifice is the way, My way, to finding yourself, your true self."

The Hound of Heaven was ever hot on my trail.

Though I fled Him down the nights and down the days; though I fled Him, down the arches of the years; when I fled Him, down the labyrinthine ways of my own mind, and in the midst of tears, those strong feet followed hard after me.

To be certain, there were many times I threatened to give in, to quit, to return to the country of my birth, to flee from my missionary calling.

Life would be so much easier back in America, I reasoned internally. But I knew the fallacy of my reasoning. China had changed me. Or more aptly, God transformed me in the furnace of China's cross-cultural fires. I no longer fit in anywhere. I was foreign in China. I was foreign in America. I was a *laowai*, an old outsider, often mistakenly seeking my identity in the very ministry God had called me to.

As Chinese police chased me through the rural countryside, I questioned why I wanted to live in China. During long, midnight interrogations in sugarcane fields, I simply wanted to throw in the towel. When my phone was tapped, and I felt the presence of plain-clothes police trailing my every step, it was easy to become disenchanted with the missionary life.

It always sounded great on paper, like Indiana Jones, or James Bond—an adventure, a thrilling storyline. My newsletters were epic. *No guts, no glory, no newsletter story*, I thought. But persecution, real or felt, creates a physical and emotional drain.

I threatened to return home. "God, I'm sick of this place, and I can't stand these people."

"But you told Me you loved them."

"I love the idea of them."

"That's not love. It's only a shadow."

I read missionary success stories of Hudson Taylor and James O. Fraser. I wanted to have similar tales written about me. Secretly, I wanted to make a name for myself. Christian celebrity had a strange allure about it. I wanted converts and numbers and success, but I struggled to quantify what that actually meant in spiritual mathematics.

In reality, what was happening to me was a slow death. And from the bowels of death, I would experience the deeper truth of life itself.

"Listen carefully: Unless a grain of wheat is buried in the ground, dead to the world, it is never any more than a grain of wheat. But if it is buried, it sprouts and reproduces itself many times over. In the same way, anyone who holds on to life just as it is destroys that life. But if you let it go, reckless in your love, you'll have it forever, real and eternal."

The deeper my journey took me into the heart of China, the deeper I recognized the heart of God. The missionary venture was not always rainbows and butterflies, flowers and sunsets. More often, it was bloody knees and hiding from the authorities under swaying bamboo. And, of course, crushing loneliness.

19th century career missionary to China, Lottie Moon once said, "I pray that no missionary will ever be as lonely as I have been." Regrettably, many a cross-cultural worker would agree that her wish has yet to actualize. Loneliness as a single man in China was difficult to articulate. I was surrounded by an immense population of people; yet at times, so disconnected.

Being part of a chase, whether it be from the police or the pursuit of God, was exhausting.

Still another pursuit left me fatigued. I had been chasing Lorna from a distance for the last three years. The space between us seemed chasmal—the terrain mountainous, not to mention the breadth of the South China Sea. Add to that the element of time, so slow and methodical, so fast and forgetful. Our long distance relationship was by no means easy.

I wished Lorna was with me, there atop the forested mountain near Dadong Village. I imagined us walking through unreached communities, holding hands, unfazed by the difficulties that came with missionary life.

It was in mountains like these that I routinely paused to pick wildflowers from rural country roads for her. I pressed them between the pages of my journal, and two weeks later, pasted the dried petals on handmade paper notes for her.

While Frederik and I halted our brisk pace down the mountain road for a momentary rest, I wrote a quick letter to Lorna under the light of the moon.

Love letter, March 5, 2000: "I do not doubt that we are perfect for one another, for Asia, and for reaching unreached people groups. God is doing something new in both of our lives, preparing us for His much greater plan. He will do it all in His time. Fear not, my darling. Hold on. I miss you."

———— ◆ ————

Frederik and I had been walking for well over two hours when we finally arrived in Cangyuan city, northeast of Dadong Village. We found a hotel with a flashing, red vacancy sign, flickering in Chinese. We entered, it being past midnight. The guard slept on the lobby couch. We rang the bell at the reception desk, and from underneath the counter, a young Wa girl raised her bed head.

"Sorry to wake you. We need a room."

The girl yawned and cleared her throat.

"Deng yi xia," she said. "Just a minute."

After making xerox copies of our passports, she handed us the key to our room on the third floor.

We were worn out and dirty. The laceration on my knee from my awkward dive into the ditch to dodge the police was a dried, bloody mess. I winced in pain from the sting of soap as I showered. Still, it felt good to clean the village from our skin.

"We need to be out of here early," Frederik reminded me. "I'm sure the police will be checking the hotels for us."

"And we don't blend in very well around here!"

"Nope. I forgot my camo!"

"Bad move. That would have changed the game," I laughed.

"I'm setting my alarm for five o'clock. See you in the morning."

"Goodnight."

But I couldn't sleep just yet. Though my body was exhausted, my mind was alive with thoughts of Uncle Xiao in his hut in Dadong Village; of the twenty people who had just prayed the prayer of salvation. *How are we going to follow up with them?* My mind churned with thoughts of flashing red and blue cherry lights and mud and shadows of swaying bamboo. And of Lorna. She was ever at the forefront of my mind.

I switched my flashlight on and rummaged through my backpack for my journal, which was tucked between dirty clothing and the projector battery. I tore out a page from the back and wrote Lorna a love letter.

March 5, 2000: "They are poor, physically and spiritually. These minorities whom I love are in deep need. My heart aches for them. They have known nothing but misery. The flavor of death is ever upon their lips. Yet, when one of them comes to the throne, freedom consumes them. Heaven rejoices when the impoverished find their Father, for they become rich.

"I consider my life. Mine is one of adventures and joy! I love my calling, as difficult and trying as it is at times. I am blessed in so many ways. I am blessed with you. Just thinking of you warms my heart. I thank God for the treasure He has given me in you. I count the days until we meet again. I am rich now, though, for I know His promises.

"And you... you are rich as well! For how can anyone who is a citizen of heaven be poor? Be glad today. Be uplifted. Yes, lift up your head! Do not worry. He is in control. I speak life and love over you, Lorna. You are a treasure to God. You are a treasure to me, and I cannot wait to see my treasure again.

"When struggle abounds, we are safe. When poverty surrounds us, we are rich! Hallelujah!"

That final hallelujah hovered upon my lips. It was a "yes, Lord" to what was to come in my missionary journeys. It was an agreement to God's purposes, greater than mine, so much larger than my own feeble attempts at bringing salvation to communities that had never heard of Him before. A hallelujah that in my weakness, God was strong; that in my failures, He was able to cause the growth of a handful of seeds scattered on the harsh ground. A hallelujah to relinquish all claims toward glory and Christian pedestals.

I knew that I had done little besides purchase a one-way plane ticket to Asia; to learn Mandarin Chinese; to subject myself to a twenty-four-hour overnight sleeper bus; to hike up narrow trails toward Dadong Village. Sitting for hours around a smoky fire pit, nibbling local delicacies, waiting for pivotal moments in the lulls of conversation to interject an element of the supernatural—these were obvious responses to the missionary calling. I had no claim to be laid for these. I had no stake in the terrain here, no chance to leave an indelible mark of my presence atop a forgotten mountain in Southwest China. It did not matter. This was a story about God's redemptive salvation plan and my often reluctant obedience.

Reluctantly, I went, at times, to urban and rural regions, and somehow, without exception, God chose to use me, chasing me, pursuing me with His profound affection.

Rememories

SMOKE

"Where there is smoke there is fire—that is, that wherever there is the foulest of things, there also is the purest."
G.K. CHESTERTON

The twisting wisps of rose and jasmine-scented joss sticks spiraled upward at Ten Thousand Buddhas Monastery, and the humid Hong Kong air carried hovering ritual afterthoughts to the netherworld. The distinctive smell was enticing and off-putting at the same time. These temple grounds were my first experience with such auspicious ceremonious tokens, and my mind filled with wonderment as I meandered around the monastery.

12,800 miniature golden Buddha statues lined the shelves from floor to ceiling, each carved in individual fashion. Their hands raised in symbolic, sign-based finger patterns—non-verbal modes of communication and self-expression called *mudras*. These symbolic gestures described how the invisible forces were thought to operate in the earthly sphere. Forward-facing palms and upright, joined fingers symbolized protection, reassurance, and blessing; clasped hands at the stomach, palms facing upwards with fingers extended indicated the perfect balance of thought, tranquility, and meditative concentration.

In the center of the courtyard stood a bright nine-story pagoda; fire-engine red, its spires capped in gold. At the foot of the pagoda sat a large bronze basin comprised of flickering embers and fragrant incense. I stared into the basin and watched the smoke ascend toward the sky. Up it went, its curling wisps slowly dissipating until the heavens swallowed up the vaporous mist.

I considered how fleeting and transitory were the works of man; how brief and short-lived our time in this world. Like ghosts on the earth, our spirits were slowly passing from one place to the next until we arrived at a more solid, more real destination.

In *The Great Divorce*, C. S. Lewis paints a picture in which the closer we get to God, the more real everything becomes. "It was the light, the grass, the trees that were different," he says, "made of some different substance, so much solider than things in our country that men were ghosts by comparison."

In the Asian Buddhist context, smoke took on deep symbolic meaning. It symbolized the transition of matter into spirit and represented the ascension of the immortal soul as it leaves the mortal body. But I also recognized the distinct, albeit, oft overlooked and understated Christian similarities.

Our spirits flit about on earth, like ghosts clothed in temporal garments. We were like twisting wisps of misty smoke, here today then gone tomorrow, fragile and forgettable.

I found this evangelical tendency of forgetfulness saddening. We dwell within the dual dimensions of time and space and go about our days within a spiritual atmosphere. But our human density often suffocates important Kingdom truth from our spiritual experience; our jejune nature causes us to overlook that we are sojourners on earth, awaiting our eternal Heavenly home. And so we become overly concerned about the temporal, and our focus draws inward.

Large portions of scripture call us to remember our shadowy existence. "For my days vanish like smoke; my bones burn like glowing embers," mused King David. "For we are strangers before You and sojourners, as all our fathers were," remembered Ezra. "Our days on the earth are like a passing shadow, and there is no abiding."

The smoke permeated the atmosphere at Ten Thousand Buddhas Monastery, and I whispered under my breath, *Oh Lord, make me know my end and what is the measure of my days; let me know how fleeting I am!*

———◆———

From Hong Kong to mainland China, the scent of burning tobacco was everywhere. It seeped out of the cracked side windows of taxis, curled from the lips of ethnic water bongs, and permeated the interwoven fabrics of my clothing. The population of smokers was astounding. Fumes from fire pits in the huts of ethnic people groups billowed around the room, and the verdant landscape of rural China bejeweled with mist as far as the eye could see.

Where there was smoke, there was fire. And where there was fire, there was the indication and auspice of life.

The longer I lived in China, the more I was privy to the subtle ethnic folkways and cultural mores that revolved around the existence of fire and smoke. Of particular notability was the Torch Festival of the Yi minority.

Thomas Nixon and Cynthia Li, Chinese friends who I met at English corner, invited me to join them at Yunnan Nationalities Village. The scenic tourist spot was the location of choice for the celebration.

On the southwest outskirts of Kunming, the jagged shoreline of Dianchi Lake wound along the grassland inlets opposite Western Hills. The blue-black water splashed over the fertile basin banks, dragging discarded plastic bags, cigarette butts and sundry pollution to the shore. The steep, ash gray cliffs of the mountain range towered above the water, casting a dusky shadow toward the east. The sun gradually set over the scarp as Thomas, Cynthia, and I arrived at Yunnan Nationalities Village.

The theme park set in a scenic location on the northeastern banks of Dianchi Lake. It was an ethnographic display, showcasing the architectural styles, religious beliefs, and folk customs of Yunnan's ethnic groups in exquisite detail.

At the lawn near the main gate stood four stone-carved white elephants. They surrounded the raised platform where performances took place. The stage filled with young men and women from around the province, ethnic peoples who showed off their unique cultures to visiting tourists.

The melodious aura of classical folk music filled the park entrance, and the distinct accent of flutes and pipas intermingled with the percussive beat of elephant foot drums and suspended gongs. Dressed in their cultural outfits, the young men stepped to the rhythmic beat as the girls undulated with the music. They sang a warm choral welcome in unison: *Jialing jialing sai! Jialing jialing sai!* A group of Wa minorities twirled and thrust their heads in gyrating motions as they performed their traditional hair dance. Dai ethnic girls garmented in long pink gowns mimicked the twitching, bird-like movements as they performed the peacock dance.

Thomas, Cynthia, and I watched in wonderment as the motions of color and sound intertwined before our eyes. We stood enthralled, gazing at the scene for some time. After a few minutes, we purchased entry tickets and made our way into the park.

Yunnan Nationalities Village occupied over four acres of tailored landscape and was designed with Chinese horticultural traits. A meandering path paved with red sandstones weaved through the park, revealing hidden architectural gems tucked between weeping willow and bamboo. Intermittent ponds surrounded the stilted Dai homes and Burmese-style stupas. Replicas of the Three Pagodas in Dali city rose from a small hilltop across a serene lake. Adjacent to the pagodas, Bai minority homes were painted in white with blue ornamented trimming. The Wa grass huts reminded me of my travels to the actual residences of the people group. But the village was devoid of knives and three-pronged bamboo posts, and so the headhunting practices of the tribe shrouded in secrecy.

Prayer wheels spun at the Tibetan monastery, and a Muslim mosque situated in the center of the Hui village. The Naxi tribe sold their Dongba relics at a souvenir shop; the Mosuo, Mongol, Jingpo, and De'ang villages tucked at the far corners of the theme park. The mellow clarinet-like timbre of a hulusi pipe droned in a nearby teashop, and the chatter of Chinese tourists dissipated in the distance.

"I think it's time to go to the plaza," Thomas Nixon said. "The celebration will begin soon."

As the evening took on darkness, we strolled toward the public arena where an enormous bonfire blazed. Thousands of people came to take part in the festivities, so we pushed through the crowd until we arrived at the flaming altar. We each selected a bundle of tied dry pine and lightwood, lit the tips of our torches, and blended into the pandemonium.

Many legends surrounded the origin of the Torch Festival, yet all of them had the purpose of offering sacrifice to deities and dispelling ghosts. Yi families lit a torch, and with it, illuminated the corners of their homes and fields. The evening culminated with a communal parade so as to drive away bad luck and pray for a harvest.

But the Yi minority Torch Festival at Yunnan Nationalities Village elicited a more festive emotion. The atmosphere bolstered a dizzying spree of wild entertainment, and expelling demon spirits was not at the forefront of the spectators' minds. Thousands of visitors danced clockwise in a large circle, uninformed and uninterested in the history of the spiritual ceremony. Thomas, Cynthia, and I joined in the gambol, torches in hand.

Flaming ash and orange embers showered the assembly. A girl's dress in front of me suddenly caught aflame; a man's hair to my left smoldered from the descending kindling. But the dance continued, accompanied by enthusiastic singing. A small piece of cinder landed on my shirt, and I beat my chest emphatically until the fire burned out.

We danced for what seemed like hours into the evening until at last I slipped away from the circle to purchase a bottle of water.

I stood at the fringe of the activity. Thomas and Cynthia still swayed, burning torches over their heads, marching in circular formation with the crowd. Smoke bellowed from the center of the commotion where the bonfire blazed, ascending skyward in slow motion. A polluted haze permeated the expansive arena, veiling the stars. The ground littered with the ashy sediment of lightwood. The flames slowly faded until the only trace of the dying fire was occasional glimmers of charred ember.

I stood there, quieted with inspired rumination. This land, so steeped in animistic ritual and spiritual darkness became the place of my calling. I thought of the words by Ion Keith-Falconer: "I have but one candle of life to burn, and I would rather burn it in a land filled with darkness than in a land flooded with lights." These shadowlands housed millions of people without access to the Gospel. And I, like a ghost, was passing through the region on my way to a Heavenly home, seeking to take as many souls with me as possible.

But suddenly and without warning, a profound truth befell me.

The intense fire and the dissipating smoke—these symbols spoke of spiritual sacrifice. The Yi ethnic ritual sought to dispel evil spirits and bring blessing to lands and families. But the sacrifice was severely inadequate. Netherworld deities would not be so quickly satiated with flaming torches, and the harassment would continue. But the One True God was more interested in matters of the heart, not merely human rituals. Still, He desired a wholehearted sacrifice.

Though the numerous Old Testament accounts of burnt offerings were relatively foreign to my Western upbringing, I realized that God called humankind toward utter abandonment to His will. In the subtle junctures between waking and sleeping, He whispered to humanity. And at that moment, as the bonfire blazed and the smoke ascended, I heard His still, small voice.

Come up with Me to the altar, I felt the Holy Spirit beckon. *Stay here in the crucible of My fire and be cleansed from all that is not of Me.*

It was a call to complete surrender to the purposes of God, no longer the futility of self-reliance. It was an invitation to die so that Christ might live in me.

I hesitated at first, for who in their right mind would not fear the fiery flame? But the Holy Spirit nudged me gently. *Through the threshold of death, you shall experience true life,* I felt Him say. So I climbed atop the altar and sat there smoldering like a lightwood torch. The smoke was suffocating and brought tears to my eyes. A cheerful flame leapt upward and, crackling and sputtering, it consumed me. It was both painful and cleansing, and I sensed God's delight in my surrender. For as C. S. Lewis boldly stated, "There are only two kinds of people in the end: those who say to God, 'Thy will be done,' and those to who God says in the end, 'Thy will be done.'"

Even in the midst of celebration and festivity, God was ever wooing my heart. He wanted what was best for me. He sought to unearth from within me gems and precious stones, and there was only one way to acquire such treasure. The dross had to be burned away with flames until all that remained was pure gold.

There atop the burning altar, I breathed a final sigh of self-abandonment, and whispered under my breath, "Lord, Thy will be done."

Chapter 5

HARANA

*"After silence, that which comes nearest to expressing
the inexpressible is music."*
ALDOUS HUXLEY

Music is everywhere. But some only hear it as meaningless noise.

Manila, Philippines was noisy. The streets were packed with chrome stretch-jeepneys whose thunderous bass boomed from speaker systems. Emphatic vendors at SM Mall squawked about the latest sales through their megaphones. The music in shopping centers played at absurd volumes.

Evangelical churches were noisy, too. Staccato bursts and blasts of shofars; incessant clapping of hands; soundboard dials sliding upward near ten. It was not your typical Western church. Drum cages were not really a thing, and earplugs would not be passed among the pews.

That's what I often heard during church services: peaking decibels. What God most likely heard, however, was the meaning beyond the melody, the temperament abaft the tumult.

For a soul who finds replenishment in quietness and solitude, Manila would not necessarily be a person's first choice for a restful vacation getaway.

Many would define the bustle of this megacity as a hubbub, a brouhaha, a chaotic cacophony of rowdy racket. Public transportation bereft of admissions control roared along the boulevard as the MTR train rocketed overhead. The blaring reverberation of pop music rang from pulsating sidewalk speakers.

Oddly enough, I often sensed harmonious undertones amidst the babel. "The earth has music for those who listen." Shakespeare was right. And it was correct to include Metro Manila in his depiction.

Perhaps being love struck and mesmerized by a girl brought narrow-minded, puppy-dog fixation; but I found Lorna to be a central source of beautiful euphony. Consonance seemed to dance out from within her, making the world bloom at her presence.

She was to me the epitome of *harana*, Tagalog for serenade.

Lorna evoked poetry and prose within me, which I regularly penned, praying God might choreograph my paragraphs to align with the natural symphonies of life. She made me hum to myself; whistle in the wind; sing instead of speak.

When a lovesick Filipino boy begins to court a young lady, it is only logical that he serenades her either solely with guitar (be he so courageous); or better yet, convince his musically-inclined friends to join him outside her home with an orchestra of bandurria, standup bass, perhaps with percussive gong, and gimbal. He would envision his harana a pivotal deciding factor in the timeline of his triumph in making her his bride.

From the very beginning, I set out to win Lorna by traditional Filipino etiquette.

It was a scorcher that day. The air stood mostly still; the modest breeze lapping at the gentle waves on Manila Bay, gulping up the ocean and misting humanity with moisture. The humidity was upwards of eighty percent, stifling and sticky. The sun's harsh rays burned anyone who wasn't protected by an umbrella.

I had planned an impeccably romantic scenario: a simple picnic on a sunny day. Checkered blanket, a bouquet of roses, packed supper, kite, and guitar—everything was perfect.

We sat side-by-side, staring into the distance where freighters rocked subtly, docked a thousand feet from shore. I leaned closer to Lorna, placing my hand on hers.

"Perfect day for a picnic."

"It's nice," she said, a demure smile elicited by my touch.

Lorna was shy. She was Maria Clara in Jose Rizal's *Noli Me Tángere*, the traditional Filipina feminine ideal, blushingly *pakipot*.

It had been nearly four years since we met in Hong Kong in May 1997, while smuggling Bibles into China together. But our long-distance relationship moved at a pace much slower than I anticipated.

We unpacked our Jollibee burgers—admittedly, not the most romantic choice—and conversed about the twelve discipleship groups she managed in college campuses across Manila. We talked about her family, how she prayed she could start a business to provide for the needs of her parents. I was filled with intense pride for her, lingering upon each syllable, head over heels for this Asian beauty.

We spoke of China, of my travels to unreached people groups, of the rapid development burgeoning in urban settings. Chit chat. Small talk. Banter and pleasantries. We had nowhere to be but with each other and together was best just then and there.

Throughout the years of our courtship, I wrote numerous love letters to her from China. I painted pictures of my missionary life and what our lives together might be like. Between the lines of each affectionate note, deep bonds were created, rooted in *Phileo*. But I had yet to tell her those three special words. Unequivocally, I cherished her with all my heart. Still, I reserved the *"I love you"* for the ideal moment.

We crumpled our used Jollibee wrappers. I stood to discard them in a nearby litter bin.

"Are you ready to fly a kite?" I asked.

"Always!"

Lorna held the spool, and I chased her as she jogged down the steaming boulevard, seeking to create flight with limited wind. At last, our kite caught a gust, and the breeze tugged it skyward. Higher, farther, three-hundred feet it soared; and we stood again, side-by-side—how we've always stood together—watching from the same vantage point. We watched the world around us. The birds in V form, flocking together. The skyline of Manila Bay, Diamond Hotel on Pedro Gil which towered over Robinson's Mall. The clutter of cars clamored to cross the intersection before the lights turned red again. Families on an afternoon vacation strolled slowly across the grass. Street children tapped on the windows of taxis, offering their windshield cleaning services in exchange for a few coins. Street-side beggars looked for a few crumpled bills from commuting passengers.

Lorna and I saw it all. And from my perspective, I realized that this world had become my life. The United States of America was a memory to the east, past the South China Sea, obstructed by the subtle curvature on the globe's horizon. Somewhere, far off in the distance, lay the country of my birth, where tidal waves and ebbing ripples ended at the edge of the Pacific.

I had fond memories buried there in the southwestern state of Arizona, but it was no longer my home. Perhaps it would never again be. My new home was here, not per se in the Philippines, nor necessarily in my temporary residence of China, but here with Lorna. Together with this Filipino beauty, the satisfying sensation of true home realized.

I had not yet told her that I loved her, but I had long anticipated her becoming my wife. I envisioned our future family, our children skipping in front of us as we held hands on a stunning summer day. I foresaw laughter and pillow fights, raking autumn leaves, sledding over white landscapes in subzero climates. I contemplated a small house—it didn't matter where—with a garden of whimsical daisies alongside an array of vegetables and herbs. Maybe papayas and mangos. I imagined our little family on the precipice of a mountaintop, awed and silenced by the majestic allure of sunset hues stretching beyond the horizon.

These reveries, though not yet actualized, were as palpable and absolute as the certain shifting sunset on Manila Bay.

Our kite, a red dot in the blue expanse, was tethered by a string stretched to its limits, tied around the spool in Lorna's slender fingers. Those lovely fingers. I took her hand in mine, our fingers interlocking. Her graceful eyelashes batted as she squinted toward the sky. Her pink lips and collar bones. Her olive skin and jet black hair. She was my girl. I was her boy. We were together now, perhaps for a lifetime, if she would have me.

We reeled our kite in, monotonously looping the string around the spool, tugging the red form from a backdrop of fading empyrean art.

Vibrant colors upon the vaulted canvas overhead gave way to approaching darkness, and the last fated light hovered upon Lorna's cheekbones.

Perfect timing, I thought, and I grabbed my guitar.

Over the last few days, late in the evening, when I found myself alone with my Bible, my journal, and my musical instrument, I had been inspired by a song. I crafted chords and lyrics into what I concluded was the perfect composition to describe our relationship. I called it "The Beauty of Every Season."

I prayed that Beethoven's truth might be realized at this

moment: that "music should strike fire from the heart of man, and bring tears from the eyes of women."

"Can I sing you a song that I composed?"

"Of course."

"I hope you like it."

I tried to veil the quivering of my nervous fingers as I pinched a pick from the folds of my wallet.

"I've been writing this song for you over the last few days."

The simple chords resonated at the edge of the South China Sea from the cement ocean barrier where we sat behind Luneta Grandstand.

All I want to say / Simple though it may seem / I just want to let you know / That being with you I find that the joy of the journey is changing me.

Time paused for a moment then. I found it fascinating that as a little child, Lorna would run along these same city sidewalks, frightening her nervous mother as she skipped ominously close to the water's edge. That her entire upbringing took place not far from this exact location. That I shared an intimate moment with her now, forming fond memories, framing a portrait in slow motion, never to be forgotten.

I continued singing.

In every season I see / The beauty is only beginning / And the beauty of every season is the pleasure of knowing you.

Lorna sat with legs crossed, overhanging the cement barrier. She skimmed the lyrics as I sang. *How is it humanly possible to resist such chivalrous charm!* I thought. The kite. The sunset. The music of love. Harana. Everything was exactly as I had orchestrated it.

Then came the advent of romantic pinnacle, the climactic culmination. The moment of courage had arrived.

I had been planning for days to articulate my true emotions to Lorna. That I adored her. That I wanted to marry her. No, this was not yet a proposal; it was the precursor. I would tell her that regardless of the time, distance, and geographical expanse that sought to keep us from one another, that I loved her. That's what I intended to tell her. *There's no other girl for me. Only you. I love you.*

We would embrace, I thought, perhaps kiss. She would wrap her arms around my shoulders, and I would cup her face in my hands. We would gaze into each other's eyes and actually see one another. She would tell me that she loved me, too, and my excogitated contemplations of future marriage and family would soon transpire. But perhaps I was getting ahead of myself.

"David, that song is so beautiful. I love it," Lorna said.

"It's all for you, my dear."

From the tips of my toes, I mustered the courage to continue. The words hovered on my lips. An awkward pause. I took a deep breath.

When I was a boy, my father cautioned me: "Never tell a girl you love her unless you are ready to marry her." His words had stuck with me all these years. I thought of dad as I sat next to Lorna. *Yes*, I thought. *I'm ready. She's the one.*

"Lorna, I want to tell you something that I have never said to anyone else."

She was nervous of what I might say. I noticed the glistening perspiration on her palms, and she fidgeted.

"I want to tell you that..." I paused for effect. The thought lingered long enough for the romance to settle into the moment.

It was the perfect setting. The final hues of the Manila Bay sunset reflected in her pupils. The ripples of the South China Sea ebbed and flowed, creating a romantic synergy. The air stilled in subtle warmth. *This is going to take our relationship to a whole new level,* I thought.

"I want to tell you that I love you."

I had never said that to another girl, and Lorna had never heard a man tell her those three words.

I considered the profoundness of love, how it could be such a fearful phenomenon. To love and to be loved; nowhere does greater danger reside. John the Evangelist tells us that there is no fear in love, but that perfect love casts out all fear. Perhaps that fear was presently in flight, but lingering concerns about such transparency still gathered at the forefront of my mind.

"I love you," I said.

Lorna's reply came unrehearsed, unexpected, and abrupt.

"Um, thank you," she replied

The color drained from the sky, startling the South China Sea at the sudden injection of sunset. The ocean shuddered. The screeching of taxi tires on Roxas Boulevard set nearby sparrows to flight. My heart dipped into my belly, a sinking sensation.

"Thank you."

It was the most natural response for her. *But, wait, isn't there more?* I found that after nearly four years of pursuing this young woman, I could not choreograph to perfection an intricately detailed response. I could not make Lorna love me, or at least not coerce an articulated expression of her emotions.

My heart bobbed and waggled in my gut. I expected so much more. *Thank you? How about, "I love you, too!" Why not, "You're my hero, my man, the sweetest guy on the planet?" How about a kiss?*

"Uh, you're welcome." My reply sounded stupid.

This evening was meant to progress otherwise. I misjudged the power of harana, assuming an unequivocal romantic response. Had the music somehow bled from my lips and become nothing but noise?

But within the recesses of my being, I sensed her quintessential connotations. I knew her heart. The melodious intonations of love were not yet fluent on her tongue, but within her heart brimmed a deeper truth. Though her acknowledgment of my vulnerability had not yielded the response I sought, I found her reservation laudable.

Lorna's modesty and demure nature were delightful. She was shy, *pakipot*, not in its derogative, Filipino connotation of playing hard to get; but in the more complete definition of "chaste reservation".

The sun had set by now, so we set off, hand-in-hand, in search of public transportation back to her parents' home in Tondo.

Regardless of the length of our ongoing courtship, I still sang her sweet serenades. Hundreds of love letters were still to be penned and posted from China to the Philippines, to Tondo, Manila, to her mailbox, where her heart would gain clarity as to the depth of my love for her. Still, we would listen intently to the subtle tones of ethereal reverberations in the symphony God orchestrated in our midst. And come what may, we would dance to the musical whisper of the divine.

———————•———————

After ten days in the Philippines, I returned to my mission field in China. The motif of the music modulated to the momentum of Kunming; the strain and structure of the song shifted to a slower pace. I rocked along the ripples of love's wake, rising slightly with the melodic accents, then ebbing lower with the altered timbre.

Leaving Lorna again was not easy. Thankfully I was part of an active Christian community in China.

I was privileged to be one of the worship leaders at the Kunming International Fellowship, the home church to over thirty nationalities from every continent, mostly missionaries.

Service started at 10:30 am every Sunday morning in Jinkang Gardens. We met on the top floor of a five-story building at the northern district of the city. The office-space-now-turned-church-auditorium was deprived of the basic tech equipment of most Western churches: flashing LED lights, fog machines, modern sound system, an elevator. But it boasted the beauty of Ecclesia, a relational network of like-minded believers with a passion for the advancement of God's Kingdom.

Before the service began, a spirit of a united community could already be felt in the sanctuary as people conversed about each other's ministries over coffee and tea. This sense of kinship was paramount within our bodies. Everyone had a voice. Every Sunday, the stage was filled with testimonies from ministry leaders, with individual prayer requests, with prophetic words from God.

The value of Christian community remained integral since inception, brotherly love and acceptance at the nucleus of the fellowship.

Worship was also one of the essential valued aspects. There were little time restraints to snub the presence of the Holy Spirit, and a bulk of the service provided ample opportunity for corporate laying on of hands, jubilant dancing, the waving of banners, and free flowing merriment.

Our international church was to me the model church, with plenty of room for God to interrupt the agenda, surprising us with palpable habitation and manifestations of His presence.

I loved leading worship at the Kunming International Fellowship. Though not an expert musician, I had always carried within me a worshipper's passion: to lead people into the presence of God. With the reverb raised to five on the soundboard dial, my guitar became an eloquent guide into the sacred. As my clumsy fingers strummed six strings, celestial acoustic consonance coalesced.

The church began just before my arrival to China in 1998 in the apartment block of a missionary family, Chad and Mindy Layman, and their two boys, Jacob and Caleb. At that time, it was just a small home group of mixed nationalities, numbering no more than fifteen on any given Sunday.

Random police visits came with the territory. It was the nature of the beast as China's political scene underwent a massive overhaul.

There was the public proclamation of religious freedom, but the law of the People's Republic of China was left mostly to interpretation, dependent upon circumstance and evidence; or chiefly, whether or not a governmental higher up had felt the loss of face by an existing religious entity.

One Sunday morning in the year 2000, while the curtains drew shut, I led worship on my guitar when a commotion occurred. My eyes were closed in adulation, so I tuned out the distraction of shuffling feet and audible chatter. I kept singing, probably "Our God is an Awesome God," the chorus repeating in climactic repetition. Enjoined voices at the small Sunday service abated to a rustling silence, at which point I finally opened my eyes to observe what happened.

Standing there in the center of the worship circle were two Chinese police officers, wearing blue, wrinkle-free uniforms tucked into their black pants. The sight of these two authoritative figures may have been startling had I not already been interrogated on numerous occasions while traveling with Chad Layman to rural ethnic villages in Southwest China. The feeling at present was more one of sapping enervation as I contemplated how long this particular bout of questioning might last.

I had been blessed to be mentored by a man like Chad, who had little reservation—or fear, for that matter—in publicly proclaiming the name of Jesus where it had not yet gone. He showed me the ropes. I was his young padawan while we hiked up minority trails in thick brush, camped in impoverished regions of the 10/40 Window; inhaled the black soot of smoky fire pits in the homes of the Wa, the Dai, the Bulang, Yao, Miao, and Yi. We had been questioned and interrogated by police over five times, typically in the late evening hours, sometimes until dawn. Chad had modeled for me the innocence of doves, coupled with serpentine wisdom, an authoritative posture with brash boldness.

Never had I seen Chad waver in fear while being questioned by the police for countless hours. He already had been the main attraction at multiple rodeos. This, he shrugged, was just part of the territory.

Early 1990 Bible smugglers in Hong Kong referred to him in jest as a missionary Rambo: bold, persuasive, cocksure. The man was a formidable presence, three-hundred pounds of evangelistic fire and animated cheer. A Pennsylvanian by birth, he was now more Asian than he looked. His wife, Mindy, brought a balanced energy to their ministry with her Malaysian hospitality and Eastern charm.

As mentors of my early China memories, the Laymans were the quintessential image of a family on mission, heroically bringing their young missionary kids to regions that made even the most-seasoned veteran missionaries wince in wonderment.

Chad patted one of the rigid officers on the shoulder in typical jovial manner, offering him a cup of green tea and a slice of butter cake. He continued with pleasantries about the weather and how charming our host country was; how happy we were to enjoy living as expats in China.

One thing to be learned in restricted access countries where the Gospel of Jesus Christ is often seen in a negative light, or even as a menace, is that it's okay to be yourself. The Western craving for, shall we say, comfort and security are not Christian values. One of the sure promises of Jesus to His followers was that in pursuing His Kingdom, persecution was sure to occur. And in the midst of questioning authorities, thanksgiving and jubilation—not fear—was the proper response. Personal safety had never been the main issue. Propelling the message of God's glory and grace to nations beyond was central, for which courage and self-denial had to be mustered.

I learned that the missionary endeavor was a slow death to self. Jesus had not promised His disciples that bringing His message of grace and glory would be an easy task. He had promised that He would send His Holy Spirit as an ever-present help in time of need; that His footprints would line the path alongside ours.

These promises in the midst of persecution were the propelling force behind 1st century Church expansion. They evoked radical obedience at every challenging interval.

Paul and Silas sang.

Peter prayed.

John journaled.

Only then did prison doors open, redemption arrive, victory eventuate.

The cops were congenial, clarifying that they represented the foreign affairs office, and were only there to understand the nature and intent of our gathering. Both officers made it clear that no local nationals were to be included at our weekly meetings; that according to the laws of the People's Republic of China, proselytization would not be tolerated.

The conversation took place in Mandarin, and Chad fluently articulated that we, as a small group of foreign Christians, would uphold the laws of the land. No Chinese would be invited to our non-government sanctioned gathering.

"This fellowship is part of our Christian cultural heritage," Chad explained. "We respectfully request that you allow us to continue meeting weekly as foreign nationals, and as long as we meet, we pledge to honor your requirements."

We did not divulge the fact that we were missionaries. We defined ourselves only as Christians, never alluding to the ongoing ministry that took place outside the fellowship and throughout the week. After all, "missionary" was a four letter word in China.

Chad's candid tact was precisely what the police wanted to hear. After finishing their cups of green tea, he shook the hands of each police officer, and they departed.

Over the next number of months, the police would make random appearances at our growing home group to ensure that there were, in fact, no Chinese citizens present. At each occasion, they were relieved to see that we had stuck to our word. And during each visit, more green tea and butter cake was consumed, followed by fruit platters, coffee, and warm handshakes. This relationship between the authorities and our fellowship, namely Chad Layman as the pioneer, became the backbone of trust, which allowed our growth and longevity as an unregistered, international foreign fellowship in Southwest China.

Within a year of that first police visit, the missionary community grew in unity, and new harvesters arrived from their home countries. We needed a new location to handle the increase of Western Christian presence. Thankfully, our friendship with the police had been solidified, opening special doors no man could shut.

In 2000, we rented a large office space on the fourth floor of Jinkang Gardens. Over two hundred foreign Christians met there every week. An array of world flags hung overhead, perfectly depicting the rich diversity of the church. The fellowship that was enjoyed before and after church often lasted longer than the actual service itself.

This was, to me, the definition of true church, not simply a service to be attended. It was not a time slot diced up into predictable motions; but a living, breathing organism, sometimes seemingly unmanageable—a good problem, we decided.

The four walls of this unique church never felt like obstacles to be traversed. Week in and week out, Christians shared testimonies of powerful weekday ministries. These were met with enthusiastic applauses as each member delighted to see the other succeed in their God-given callings.

The Kunming International Fellowship was a free-flowing juncture of time where relationships and shared experiences formed so deeply that I have yet to discover another Christian gathering like it.

———— ◆ ————

Beyond the four walls of the church, I went, encouraged and inspired. Sunday morning services and weekday connections with the missionary community fed my soul. I felt as if I was surrounded by a great cloud of witnesses, and that propelled me further to serve the Chinese.

Nearly every weekend, I traveled twelve hours by bus to the ancient city of Dali. I put my weekday Mandarin lessons to the test, immersing myself in authentic cultural scenarios.

I sat on a cement bench along the cobblestoned walkway on Foreigner's Street, just west of Revival Road. I watched the Bai minority tourist guides adorned in baby-blue slacks and fold-over blouses lead large groups of visiting Chinese tourists through the small town.

This was the new tourism, a growing Chinese middle-class demographic, sightseeing adventures around their country. They ogled in wonderment at diverse ethnic culture, catching glimpses of destinations they had previously only had the opportunity to see in newspapers and television shows. These wide-eyed tourists fondled ethnic relics and knickknacks that lined the narrow alleys.

Middle-aged women stroked the blue, tie-dyed tablecloths, and handmade fabric tissue boxes, pondering where they might place them in their homes were they to bargain down the price and make the purchase.

The men flipped through the pages of Mao Zedong's miniature Little Red Book. They tested chrome Zippos as their cigarettes drooped on their lips, falling onto the ornaments spread on the table. Sellers scowled at these uncivilized gestures, dusting the ash onto the sidewalk.

Dali city was replete with the clinking of hammer on hard marble as artisans chiseled the characters of buyers' names on the tips of Chinese chops. The clickety-clack of mule hooves on uneven cobblestone passed by, pulling antiquated, rubbish wagons from bin to bin. The constant shuffle of tattered black dress shoes and the clopping of high heels rattled beside street-side vendors. There was the crowing of roosters and the crying of babies, hammocked in colorful slings suspended from the shoulders of local mothers. The guffaw of energetic haggling between buyer and seller. The guttural grunting of gruff throats being cleared and sputum discharged from the lips of smokers to the unlucky footpath.

Music was everywhere, not merely meaningless noise. But the ethereal symphony was difficult to recognize when veiled by the unusual sounds of China.

But there were other sounds, too, influenced at times by foreign presence, musical introductions to choruses from the Christian Church.

I sat on a cement bench under an ancient marble gate that arched over the entrance of Foreigner's Street. I sat there, singing, worshipping, ushering in the presence of God where it was not known. My guitar case laid open in front of me, the orange lining visible to passersby. I did not hesitate from receiving the occasional donation of crumpled Yuan and Renminbi coins.

This was not a get-rich-quick scheme. Admittedly, in my nearly twenty years in China, that plan never panned out for me. It was a street performer act, an attraction, baiting spectators. It was a sort of street evangelism through musical worship.

Local street vendors knew me by name. Tourist guides waved, followed by their stupefied, gawking tourists. For most Chinese visitors, it was the first time they had ever seen a foreigner. That fact alone made it easy to gather a crowd in Dali. An American round-eye with an instrument was a novelty.

Longfellow once mused that music is the universal language of mankind. I have no choice but to concur. Add to that the spiritual element of worship, and some might even sense the voice of God Himself. It was my joy to give witness of God's marvelous grace in my life through relationship and music.

As the sun waned, I packed my guitar and headed to Number Four Guesthouse, a dingy dive at which I often roomed.

Like a sheet of serenity, gently blanketing the sadness of the township's diurnal noises, twilight cloaked the city, enveloping Dali's four gates and towering Three Pagodas. Sleep came to each occupant, and with sleep came new sounds. As our eyelids closed and led us into the subconscious, a holy anthem swept through the valley. In the streets of the sky, night walked, scattering poems. It was as if God was singing, with gentle whispers at first, while His angelic hosts accompanied Him in rhythmic fashion.

It was a celestial symphony, kisses blown from a Heavenly Father, hallowed and immaculate.

It was God smiling as He sang over us a divine harana. A sweet nocturne, the intonations of which soothed the bruises of the heart and nightmarish battles of the mind. He made no distinction between believer and unbeliever. He simply recognized His beloved creation, and His fierce love was adamant that each might sense His presence.

"Quiet now," He came to me in my dreams. "Hush. Just listen to My lyric-less song and be at peace."

Anxiety fled then. Fear of failure in my missionary calling was quelled. The loneliness I felt in Lorna's absence departed in haste. Bewilderment of each day's mounting pressure vanished away. And suddenly, even in my subconscious state, I realized the astonishing power of a serenade.

Chapter 6

OVER MOUNTAINS AND VALLEYS

"In the vast plain to the north, I have sometimes seen, in the morning sun,
the smoke of a thousand villages where no missionary has ever been—
villages whose people are without Christ, without God,
and without hope in the world."
ROBERT MOFFAT

We stood on the raised tip of a precipice in Dehong Prefecture, panting heavily after many miles of trekking. The hilltop curved at a thirty-degree angle down into a valley of erect, leafy sugarcane. The sun waned, hovering precariously close to a jagged mountain range that towered in the distance to the west toward Myanmar. The air was still, the humidity stifling and sticky with a certain peculiarity to it. The atmosphere was both crackling-dry and oppressively humid. As far as the eye could see, there was not a single body of water for hundreds of miles. Yet, the troposphere filled with moisture, misting the greenery and dampening every visitor who dared make their way along these pathways.

We were slow-traveling dots on a colored map, moving reluctantly over a baked and dank landscape of never-ending mountains. Although fatigued, there was another force at work in us. We sensed the Divine and Providential there atop the mountain, a tugging urgently drawing our hearts into the unknown.

We could have easily never traveled there. We could have been sitting in our Kunming apartments, sipping coffee, absorbed in a good book. And who would have blamed us? Hadn't these mountains been so long overlooked by evangelistic efforts of the global Church that no one would have batted an eye at the lack of our presence?

But God's merciful prompting propelled us over mountain and valley, to regions where no missionary had gone before.

A hushed, ethereal music resounded with subtle baritone notes and elevating crescendos. Glenn must have heard it in between his panting breaths; he stood, hunched over, his hands resting on his knees. He removed his backpack and plopped it carelessly on the dusty trail. He squatted in the dust, cocked his head, and listened. Muffled echoes of worship danced overhead, suffocated slightly by the humid air.

"Good to be here with you guys," he said gruffly, still trying to catch his breath.

His words, less like transcendent reveling, were more of a suggestive celebration.

Glenn Robinson, a six-foot-four-inch tower of Irish masculinity, stood upright. The map of wrinkles on his forehead told of the most incredible journeys. His eye lines tinged with Celtic memories, of dewy heather, of vast open skies, and of rain. There was a warm deviousness about his trimmed, black beard. There always seemed to be a quirky smirk lurking on the corner of his lip, as if he was about to erupt in laughter in response to his own wit.

"But I'm telling you," he continued, "I really hate being in the bush!"

He wasn't joking. Glenn had been living in China for many years by that time and preferred the convenience of developing urban centers. By his own admission, he would much rather be in the capital city of Kunming than these backward rural regions.

I found it endearing, admirable even, that though he did not particularly favor laborious village treks among unreached people groups, yet here he was. And I sensed that God was pleased by this kind of obedience.

For God is always on the alert, constantly on the lookout for people who are totally committed to Him. His eyes move to and fro throughout the whole earth that He may strongly support those whose hearts are fully His. He is searching, not only for those with ability but availability; for those who would say, "God, I'd rather be elsewhere. Yet here I am, Lord. Send me. Use me." Over this kind of simple obedience, I have seen God's good pleasure.

"Now, let's get on with it," Glenn said. "No more of this meandering around. Let's go, you pansies!"

I laughed, lifted my backpack from the trail, and stood to my feet. Frederik, our Danish counterpart, and Tim from Holland sat up from the trail, exhausted. We lingered for one last look at the village across the sugarcane valley.

"That's where we're headed," Tim said. "I guess the only way across is through."

Frederik nodded reluctantly. He gazed over the precipice and down into the valley. He wasn't thrilled at the idea of leaving the trail for the rugged hinterland. But the sun quickly lowered, and our options were limited. The sky shifted from blue to pink, here and there lined with looming purples. The trail turned sharply to the left around the ridge of the mountain, off into the distance where it disappeared. We knew that the path would take us to the village opposite the mountain. But we did not have time to follow its long-drawn-out course.

"Well, what are you girls waiting for?" Glenn asked, a smirk curling on his lips. "Let's get on with it!"

Down the ridge, we walked, over thick brush toward the sugarcane field, our legs aching with every jolting step.

———— ◆ ————

Glenn, Frederik, Tim and I each joined the Kunming International Fellowship. We had been present at the forming of the apostolic missionary team, which focused on reaching the least reached peoples in Yunnan Province. Our shared passion for serving the Chinese drew us together as a band of brothers.

Nearly every month, a few of us scheduled a trip to the countryside. We boarded overnight sleeper buses to rural regions tucked deep in the backwoods of Yunnan Province. From the bus terminus, we rented minivans that ran between small counties and mountaintop villages. From the roadside village, we then trekked deeper into the bucolic settings where tribes untouched by the Christian message resided.

We traveled over mountain and valley, to the forgotten junctions where true worship was not. We journeyed to the distant boundaries where ethnic animism and historical Buddhism intersected; where ancestral cultures lived in constant fear and torment of the spirit world. There, we beheld the spine-chilling ceremonial rites of animistic communities. We watched as shamans and witchdoctors convoked the spirits of the dead. We witnessed imperious wizards summon hungry ghosts from the underworld. At their feet lay the bloody, feathered carcasses of sacrificed chickens, waiting to be lapped up and consumed by the demigods. In return for this blood-curdling ritual slaughter, the unseen spirits were believed to bestow a blessing upon the fields, livestock, and community.

We went where most Christians dared not. And in our going, our hearts enriched with felicity.

———— ◆ ————

As we hiked down the mountain, my backpack seemed unnaturally cumbersome. Glenn led the way, pushing aside the tall brush, making a path where there was none. Tim followed close behind, Frederik trailing his steps. I brought up the rear of the pack as we edged down toward the sugarcane valley.

At the bottom of the slope, we slowed to a halt.

Glenn wiped the perspiration from his brow. "Well, here goes nothing," he said and pushed his way into the thick plantation.

Inside the labyrinthine maze of eight-foot-tall sugarcane, our only visible guide were the stratus clouds streaming slowly overhead. The waning sun allowed for little clarity during our unpredictable parade.

We strode single file, shoving aside each thick reed far enough to pass. I paused to snap the base of a sweet stick, peeled its rigid bark down like a banana, and tore off a sugary chunk with my molars. It was at that point that I noticed my bleeding knuckles and forearms. The razor-sharp husks of the sugarcane field had been bruising and slicing us during our twenty-minute footslog, shredding our skin and confusing our directional senses. We began to question the validity of our decision to take the treacherous shortcut.

After what seemed like hours, Glenn, Frederik, Tim and I emerged from the fructose field, licking our wounds like wounded dogs after a ravenous fight.

Up the slope to our right, Penghei Village mounted atop the adjacent ridge. Prodding toward a steep precipice, we came to a clearing. The village was home to the Zaiwa people, a branch of the

Jingpo tribe. They erected their houses with cement and packed earth. Grassy shingles topped each structure, capping ancient secrets.

I set my backpack down at the edge of a concrete slab, pulled loose the straps, and flipped open the top. I removed from my bag what had become to me one of the greatest missionary ice-breakers. I might even go so far as to say the cultural key to passing through the barriers of mores and folkways. I grabbed a handful of long, multicolored balloons, filled them with air, then pinched and twisted them into nothing short of miracles: purple puppies, colorful kittens, swords, and sombreros. The nearby grannies were cautiously curious. The children froze, stunned and astonished, staring incessantly at my bag of goodies. Parents and middle-aged uncles and aunties stood awkwardly dubious and fascinated. Rarely, if ever, had a foreign presence been made in this Zaiwa community. The sight of travelers from afar brought a subdued exhilaration to the bucolic community.

Throughout our long trek, Glenn lugged around the weighty sound system battery in his backpack. No wonder he had an acute distaste for trekking through rural China. But his grunt work was about to pay off. We arranged our speakers in the center of the village, connected electrical cords, and slid a CD into our walkman. Glenn pushed play, the symphonic notes commenced, and the music coursed through the countryside.

It was a notable sight to behold, quirky and fantastical. There we stood—four Caucasian men in an agrarian milieu, set deep in the heart of rural China—flailing our arms to the beat of the music and cavorting about whimsically. It was dramatic presentation, albeit, puerile and fatuous. It was an amusing disport, a playful parade, an outlandish spectacle to create a scene.

We performed The Heart Skit. We belted out Father Abraham. We nailed Ragman. The entire performance imbued with sparkle and elan. And just as expected, the ludic commotion quickly lured a crowd.

When the congregation of Zaiwa people had reached over one hundred and fifty, I picked up the microphone, stood in the center of the throng, and began preaching the Gospel.

The last dying hues of the sunset passed beyond the mountain range to the west. The dim foreground of the village framed a shadowy atmosphere. Curling, grassy rooftops became silhouettes contrasted against the cobalt blue sky. Swaying light bulbs dangled from electrical wire, and the warm glow mingled with the dusky ambiance.

Shortly after I began speaking about the things of God, the spirits gathered. I could feel them. The little gods who governed the land began to appear, paralyzing its inhabitants with fear and servitude. I could sense that the netherworld vexed at our presence; as if we had infiltrated the chasmal caverns where a dragon lay, happening upon the golden treasure guarded by his vicious claws.

A battle for the souls of men was underway. Angelic swords clashed against demonic scimitars. The heavy warfare was palpable; the atmosphere was tense and rigid. But our limpid hearts remembered that we had arrived in the village for such a time as this. And so, a sudden, triumphant joy filled our hearts. Come demon, demigod, or netherworld deity, we were there to attest to the grandiose of the one true God.

"Oh, while you live, tell the truth, and shame the devil," Shakespeare once said. I opened my mouth, and the words gushed out like living water. "Today is the day of salvation!" Truth, so long obscured, had made its arrival, and the advent of God's presence began to shift the atmosphere.

After a ten-minute oration about the life, death, and resurrection of Jesus, we took the time to pray with people individually. We laid hands on the sick, claiming their healing. We prophesied life into the community. We prayed for salvation and spiritual transformation to occur in the lives of the precious Zaiwa.

Seeds were planted, the fruit of which we would never see. But by faith, we stood on the promises of God, that He desired that none should perish but that all would come to repentance. Perhaps some of the seeds sown have grown into robust plants by now. Perhaps, even now, they are blooming in the humid landscapes that stretch along occasional streams in Southwest China. Of this, I am unsure. But I am confident that God sees every hopeful harvest dream; that He gathers the healthy crops between His fingers, breathing life into the previously parched lands.

After our silly performances and our public prayer ended, a group of young men arrived, lugging six-foot drums into the center of the crowd. The instrument was popular in those parts; its drumhead made of stretched goat skin; its long base resembling the leg of an elephant.

A lively presentation commenced. The young men began beating the elephant foot drums, and the crowd joined in the rhythmical, toe-tapping performance. The assembly erupted in song, the tonal lyrics sung in local Zaiwa dialect. Old men clapped their hands. Young women undulated to the beat, their colorfully ornamented headdresses swaying in rhythmic fashion. We joined in as best we could, comprehending not a word of their traditional folk songs.

Penghei Village had never seen this kind of cross-cultural performance before. It was a rare occasion for this rural village to host guests from afar, let alone those from across the Seven Seas.

We spent hours together with the Zaiwa community, laughing, dancing, and sharing God's love. For most of them, it was their first time hearing anything about the Christian Gospel.

In the midst of the singing and dancing, I noticed a group of four middle-aged women on the outskirts of the crowd. There was a certain spark in their eyes; a hunger for the things of God dimly reflected in their pupils. So, I approached them and introduced myself in Chinese.

"Ni hao," I began. "My name is David."

"I'm Zhang Daonan," one of the women replied.

"Auntie Zhang, have you ever heard of Jesus before?" I asked.

Her eyes lit up at my inquiry.

"Women ye xiangxin Yesu!" Auntie Zhang replied in a hushed tone. "We believe in Jesus, too."

She cautiously glanced back and forth, obviously nervous about the content of our public conversation. She told me that there was a small gathering of Christians in the village, six women and two men. They were hungry for the things of God, but they did not own a Bible.

"Can you read Mandarin?" I asked her.

"No. But my husband can," she informed me.

I pulled a Bible and a VCD of *The Jesus Film* from my backpack and handed it to her.

"This is a gift for you," I said.

Auntie Zhang's eyes filled with moisture as I placed the book in her hands. It was the first time she had ever seen a Bible. She gently stroked the front cover with her fingertips, caressing the slight indentation of Chinese characters. Her lips formed the words for Holy Bible, *Sheng Jing*, in Mandarin, and a teardrop stained her olive cheek.

"Xiexie ni!" she said, bowing. Her voice cracked with emotion, and it seemed that the heavens lit up with the slightest luminescent glow at the bloom of holy joy. But the moment was cut short as she nervously glanced around at the crowd.

"We have to go," she said suddenly.

The women rushed through the crowd and disappeared between two hutted homes.

———— ♦ ————

Past ten o'clock, the crowd began to disperse, returning to their thatched homes for the evening. Glenn, Tim, Frederik and I continued to converse with a small group of people, sharing in-depth details of how to be saved.

Suddenly, a woman with a stern look on her brow approached us, interrupting our conversations. She was uninterested in formalities, and her commanding intonations were terse.

"Nimen guolai yixia," she requested in Chinese. "Please follow me."

Although abrupt, it did not extinguish the innate courtesy that typically marked Yunnan's ethnic peoples. We followed her to a small room in the center of the village where we were instructed to sit and rest. The woman served us green tea and boiled peanuts before continuing her undisguised inquiries.

"My husband is the village elder," she began. "He is not here right now, so I want to know why you are here."

Frederik explained that we were tourists interested in learning more about the ethnic people groups in the area. But the woman didn't seem to buy his story.

"Show me your passports," she retorted in Chinese.

Glenn leaned toward me. "This isn't looking good," he whispered.

We were in the middle of nowhere, more than fifty miles from the nearest county seat. The situation had become precarious, and should the police make a visit to the village, we were like sitting ducks.

The woman picked up her phone. But when she tried to dial out, the call would not go through.

"Gai si!" she said vehemently, cursing her phone, then setting it back on the table. Someone handed her another phone, but the second phone had the same issue.

"Looks like Someone is looking out for us," Glenn whispered to me again.

It was nearly midnight, so the village elder's wife had no choice but to allow us to stay in the area. She knew that it was illegal for foreigners to spend the night in a village, but we were too far off the beaten path to return to a nearby city.

"Tomorrow morning, you need to leave," she informed us.

"Don't worry," Frederik replied. "We will leave at first light."

Satisfied, she left the room and closed the door behind her.

From the middle of the ceiling, a single light bulb cast a dim glow upon the cement floor where four thin blankets laid. We flipped the switch and curled up side-by-side to keep warm.

"Thank God her phone was broken," Frederik said.

"Yea," Glenn replied. "A good way to end the evening."

Glenn, Tim, Frederik and I huddled on the bedbug-ridden blanket, trying not to think about the spiders and rats scurrying along the floor. Sleep came at intervals throughout the night, interrupted by the shuffle of feet and hushed whispers outside our door. Gusts of chilled air drifted through fissures between the windows, and the rustling of a tree branch against tiled roof created an eerie, sleepless mood.

Early the next morning, moments after the sun had risen, I awoke with a start. My legs were numb from sleeping on the hard floor, and I wiped the sleep from my eyes. Frederik was already dressed and ready to depart.

"We have to go, guys," he said. "We better not wait around for the police to arrive."

We packed our bags and opened the creaky door. Faint rays of early morning sunshine gathered along the cement slab outside, and the chilled air brushed against our cheeks. Before a single soul in Penghei Village had awakened, we began our trek down the narrow pathway.

After hiking along a dusty trail for ten minutes, we paused on the mountain ridge, overlooking the valley below. We stretched our hands back toward Penghei Village and prayed for the small group of Christians who resided there. We prayed that the Gospel message would take root in the community and that they might experience the presence of God.

"Lord, watch over Your people," I prayed. "Protect the seeds we have sown. May salvation come to these mountains."

———— ✦ ————

We hiked through the mountains for two hours until we finally came to a paved road. We flagged down a dump truck headed in the direction of Ruili; and for the next hour, we jolted along the road in the trembling bed of the truck. At noon, we arrived at the Myanmar border, our muscles taut and quivering from the brutal journey. We found a cheap hotel, cleaned up, and spent the night in the city.

The next morning, we slept in for the first time in days. It was the much-needed rejuvenation our worn bodies craved. But it was short-lived. At ten o'clock in the morning, we boarded a twelve-hour day bus south to Nansan County on the Myanmar border. We were on a mission, driven to the outermost edges of the landscape, passionate about reaching unreached peoples.

The long trip needs not descriptive articulation as the winding roads tended to intertwine with those of our recent experiences. The mountains bejeweled with bamboo; the valleys studded with sugarcane. The blurred landscape streaming past our bus window disposed with such similar scenery that a mild boredom overtook us, and we nodded off at moments along the journey.

Hours past sunset, we neared the small town of Nansan. To our right, along the unpaved road, we heard gunfire across the border. Ammunition discharged from AK-47 barrels launched skyward like the red glare of rockets. These were dangerous hinterlands controlled by notorious narco-traffickers. The mountains and valleys laced with ripe poppy, and closely trailing Afghanistan, Myanmar was ranked the world's second highest producer of methamphetamine. This was United Wa State Army territory, infamous for its juntas and dictators; well-known for its drugs, brothels, and crime.

As bullets laced the night sky, Glenn was struck by a sudden, sardonic epiphany.

"Can someone please remind me why we're here?" he asked facetiously.

I replied with nothing but a nervous smile, edgy about our momentary arrival at the precarious location.

At ten o'clock at night, our bus pulled into the county terminus. The town composed of a single unpaved road, and we quickly found the only hotel in the area. The staff at the front desk were surprised to see us so far off the beaten path.

"Bu hao yi si," a young lady greeted us with an apology. "Foreigners are not allowed to stay in this hotel."

"Well," Glenn began, "looks like we're screwed."

We slumped onto the lobby couch and considered our options.

Little did we realize that the hotel staff had already alerted the authorities, and within five minutes, four cops arrived. They escorted us to the police station, and for the next two hours, the suspicious police interrogated us. They seized our passports and questioned us about our purpose for coming to Nansan County. But we stuck to our story: that we were simply tourists, interested in learning more about the ethnic people groups in the area.

At midnight, they finally escorted us back to the hotel, and made an exception for our overnight stay, warning us to leave the next morning.

Again, we awoke early, unable to explore the nearby villages because of the watchful eyes of the police. Instead, we boarded an eight-hour bus southeast to Gengma County in the Wa Autonomous Region. We arrived late in the afternoon, exhausted from our long travels. The trip seemed a monotonous jaunt of long bus rides through China's untouched inland.

———— ✦ ————

Outside the bus station in Gengma County, we sat at a roadside stall and purchased four glasses of homemade lemonade. The shop owner prepared mango sticky rice for us, and we watched farmers and peasants stroll their goods leisurely down the road. We reclined on flimsy plastic chairs as the humidity infiltrated our pores, softening our aching muscles. What we really wanted was a soft bed and a good meal, perhaps a massage.

But there were places to go and people to see. There were unreached peoples waiting at the other end of our obedience. There was a heavenly calling beckoning us onward. It was for the joy of joining God at work that compelled us to such extreme geographical locations.

Our glimpses of extraordinary poverty, our run-ins with the police, and the physical fatigue we presently suffered paled in the presence of heavenly joy. We felt as if Jesus was there, sitting on a plastic chair beside us, jovial in the midst of trials. He had been here before. He had undergone much more. Poverty and human wreckage did not unnerve the Savior. He was here to bring the Kingdom of God, plain and simple. He was unwavering in purpose, and would see His Father's will be done on earth—among China's unreached communities—as was always the case in heaven.

So, we sat there for some time, quieted and reassured that God was pleased in our comings and goings to the ends of the earth.

We might have dozed off into a late afternoon nap had it not been for Glenn's sudden prompting.

"Well, you sissies, it's about that time."

We groaned but knew he was right.

"I thought you didn't like the backwoods," I reminded him.

"Hey! We're on a roll here," he smiled. "No point in stopping now."

"Where are we headed?" Tim asked.

Frederik unfolded his map. "It looks like there are more Wa villages to the east."

"To the east, boys!" Glenn shot up from his chair, stretched, then hoisted his bag around his back. "Move out, you pansies!"

That's all we needed to hear. Frederik grabbed Glenn around the neck and barked, "Get him, boys!"

"I'm too tired to jump him right now," I laughed.

"Fine. But soon enough." Frederik released his playful grip, sat down in his chair, and strapped on his backpack.

"I'm so relieved," Glenn retorted in long, drawn out sarcasm.

And with that, we were back on the road, slogging along the dirt lane toward the edge of the town. In our exhaustion, evangelistic exhilaration hovered on the forefront of our hearts. In our enervation, enjoyment came at junctures along the journey.

I was reminded of Oswald J. Smith's provocative words: "Why should anyone have the right to hear the Gospel twice, while there remains someone who has not heard it once?" And so on we went to peoples still unreached.

This was our steady sacrifice, our small road to Golgotha, a slow death to self. This was our denial of fleshly desires, our white flag waving in surrender to God's will and not our own. And in the yielding of ourselves came euphoria. "Delight yourself in the Lord," said David, the psalmist, "and He will give you the desires of your heart." In our docility, our desires were gradually aligning with the divine.

One mile beyond the outskirts of Gengma County, a seventeen-year-old Wa boy met us on the trail. Surprised at the sight of foreigners, but bold enough to strike up a conversation, he introduced himself as Tian Guangrong, whose name translated to English meant "Heavenly Light and Glory." The young man asked us where we were headed.

"We want to visit a Wa village," I said.

"Lai wo jia," Guangrong implored. "Come to my home. It's not far from here."

The sun quickly lowered over the distant mountains. We picked up our pace and followed our young guide to his village. As we walked, Tian Guangrong, Frederik, and I conversed about the meaning of life. We talked about purpose. We shared about life after death, about heaven, and about man's need for a Savior.

"Have you ever heard of Jesus Christ?" I asked him.

Guangrong scrunched his eyebrows, racking his brain in thought. "Is that some kind of herbal medicine?" he asked innocently.

"You're close!" I replied, laughing. "Jesus is like good medicine. He will not only heal your body but your heart as well."

The minority trails wound around the hilly ridges, past terraced rice fields, and sugarcane plantations. We trekked for over an hour until we finally arrived at Mangguo Village, home to the former headhunting Wa tribe.

A crowd quickly gathered at our arrival. It was the first time they had ever laid eyes on a foreigner. We blew balloons for the children, twisting them into the shape of dogs and giraffes. We passed out candy. The whole village filled with smiles, excited by the impossible occasion of foreign visitors.

"Gen wo lai," Tian Guangrong said. "My home is this way."

His house was made of packed mud, brick, and mortar. It was crumbling at the corners. There was a gaping hole in the clay shingled roof, which was overlaid by a blue tarpaulin.

"Please sit," he said, setting the table with porcelain tea cups. He scooped homegrown loose leaf tea into each cup and poured in boiling water. The earthy scent of steeping green tea filled the room. Glenn, Tim, Frederik, and I sat on small wooden stools, our muscles aching, our eyelids drooping in exhaustion.

Information traveled quickly in the rural villages. The locals heard that there were foreigners who had come to visit, and soon Tian Guangrong's home was filled with friends and family who were anxious to see us.

"It's no accident that we are here," I said. "The God of heaven and earth wants you to meet Him. He wants to bless your land and your family. He wants to give you abundant life. God's gift of salvation is for the Wa people."

As I spoke, it was evident that Guangrong's heart was open to the things of God. But he had never heard the Gospel message before.

"How can God save us?" he asked.

His question reminded me of biblical accounts from the Book of Acts. "What must I do to be saved?" The question revealed his hunger for truth. At the trembling of prison doors and loosening of iron shackles, a revelation of the Divine was unveiled to him. I felt that his soul hovered on the cusp of eternity, waiting for the gentle tug of the Holy Spirit to propel him over the edge into the deep waters of God's grace. An invisible earthquake shook the foundations of his being. A war for his soul was underway, the unseen realm of angels and demons writhing in fury for the souls of men.

"Believe in Jesus Christ," I urged him. "Confess in your heart that He alone can save you from hopelessness. God is here, now, waiting to reveal to you His power and glory!"

"Our people do not believe in the religion you speak about," Guangrong replied. "The elders in our village tell us that we must sacrifice chickens to appease the hungry ghosts. If we stop, they will torment our families and our homes."

A sudden word of wisdom befell me.

"What we are talking about is not as foreign as you think," I told him. "The only difference is that your people have never heard that the final sacrifice has already been made. You no longer need to appease the gods by your own merit and by the killing of animals. Jesus became the final sacrifice for our wrongdoing."

With my forefinger, I wrote the Chinese character for "righteousness" on the dusty table. Stroke after stroke, the deeper meaning of the character began to emerge. The pictographic elements of a "lamb," *yang*, combined with the character for "I" or "myself," *wo*, illustrated the word for "righteousness."

The group of Wa locals waited for an explanation.

"Yi," I said with falling Mandarin tone. "When I am hidden under the Lamb, I become righteous," I explained. "China's language and history are laced with tales of God on a mission to make man righteous through His Son, Jesus, who is called the Lamb of God. This truth has been hidden within your culture for thousands of years; but today, God wants you to know that He will make you a new creation when you give your life to Him."

I stretched out my hand and squeezed Guangrong's shoulder. "You see, Jesus, the Son of God, sacrificed Himself on a cross for you and your people. He is the final sacrifice. In God's Book, He is called the Lamb of God. Abundant life resides in Jesus alone. You can only become righteous in Him. When you place yourself under His Lordship—you under the Lamb, as your own language depicts—His blood will wash away your sin and return honor to you. Only then, the God of heaven will no longer see your shame. Instead, He will see His Son overshadowing you, covering you, making you new."

The group was silent, riveted by the spiritual conversation.

"We traveled long and far to tell you about God's love," I continued. "In the past, your people have not understood how to receive God's peace. You chopped off human heads to appease heaven. And you are still slaughtering animals to find that peace.

But Jesus Christ already sacrificed Himself so that you could have a relationship with God. He is the final sacrifice. And right now, He is here to save you from your wrongdoing."

There was a holy solemnity in Tian Guangrong's home. The men sat silently around the table, slowly puffing on their cigarettes, pondering the things of which I spoke.

We waited, soaking in the silence of the providential moment. The Holy Spirit was moving in the hearts of our Wa hosts, touching the hidden parts where no man had access. The crackling of the fire pit, the monotonous pulse of human hearts beating—these were the only audible sounds in the room. So, we waited even longer, allowing time for God Himself to reveal the depth of His heart for His people.

Glenn, Tim, Frederik, and I laid our hands on the men who sat around the table. We dedicated them to God, leading them in a prayer of salvation. It was a divine hour, one that every missionary prays for at the culmination of arduous travels.

Late that evening, Tian Guangrong's mother prepared our sleeping arrangements in two separate rooms of the little home. But I could not sleep without penning one last journal entry.

Journal entry, October 7, 2000: "It is past midnight, and I am finally in bed after a long day of travel over mountain and valley. Besides the chirping of crickets outside, all is quiet. A canopy of stars blanket the sky above Mangguo Village, and I sense God's pleasure in the atmosphere. Here I am in Southwest China, sharing life with unreached people groups. I was made for this. My heart is at rest."

———◆———

The following morning, we awoke to the sounds of the rural countryside: the crowing of roosters, the clanking of iron pots, and the bubbly percolating of boiling water. Guangrong's mother prepared a rustic meal of rice noodles and collard greens accompanied by steaming herbal tea.

When the light breakfast ended, we said our goodbyes and began our trek back to Gengma County. That afternoon, we boarded a final bus for what we thought would be the usual twenty-four-hour trip back to Kunming. Little did we know that our long travels would be extended by the unexpected.

Four hours into the trip, at around ten o'clock at night, we heard a commotion above us on the upper bunk of the sleeper bus. An intoxicated Chinese man had crawled into the bunk bed where a young woman laid. When he began touching her inappropriately, she yelled, trying to push him away. As was typically the case, none of the passengers came to the girl's aid.

Chinese culture had been permeated by the ancient idiom, "The nail that sticks up gets hammered down." It was generally unadvisable to meddle in the affairs of others, regardless of their plight. But Glenn, Tim, Frederik, and I did not share the same worldview on this matter. A chivalrous response was inevitable.

I stood to my feet in the aisle between the bus bunk beds and asked the girl if she needed help.

"Is he your boyfriend?" I questioned.

"No!" she replied, flustered. "Tell him to get away!"

I pulled the drunk man away from her and told him to leave the girl alone.

"Cao ni ma!" he cursed. "This has nothing to do with you."

"Don't touch her again," I warned. "Go back to your bed."

In a fit of rage, he began yelling at the top of his lungs. The man jumped down from the upper bunk, stumbled to the back of the bus, cursing in Chinese. He opened his bag, pulled out a machete, and made his way toward me.

"Wo hui sha nimen dajia!" he shouted. "I'm going to kill everyone on this bus!"

That was all we needed to hear. Glenn and Tim jumped on the man, grabbed the knife, and wrestled him to the ground. His machete fell to the floor, and Glenn kicked it underneath the lower bunk bed. Frederik and I rushed to the front of the bus to inform the driver what was happening.

"Stop the bus!" we shouted. "You need to kick this man off the vehicle!"

The bus driver glanced in the rearview mirror, smirked, and kept driving. Frederik and I could not believe it. Again, we shouted for him to pull to the side of the road, but he would not listen.

I returned to the back of the bus and made sure the knife was out of reach. Glenn and Tim had the man pinned face down on the floor as he shouted murderous threats. The passengers watched, alarmed but unwilling to get involved.

"The driver won't stop the bus," I told Glenn.

"Tell him he'd better," he replied. "He doesn't want an angry Irishman on his hands!"

For the next hour, Frederik and I implored the driver to pull over, but he would not. We were appalled, unsure why he was unwilling to kick the drunk man off the bus.

Finally, I grabbed hold of the steering wheel, and the driver slammed on the breaks. The sleeper bus skid to the side of the dirt road. I pulled the door lever, and Glenn dragged the man down onto the street. The bus driver stepped off the bus to calm the irate man.

Our heart rates pulsated at a frenetic pace. We could feel the adrenaline coursing through our veins.

"What is going on with these people?" Glenn quipped.

"Psychopaths," I agreed.

For the next thirty minutes, as the bus driver argued with the inebriated man, it became apparent to us that the two were acquaintances. That explained a lot. He did not want to leave the man on the side of the road in the middle of the night.

Frustrated, we waited inside the bus with the rest of the passengers. We listened to the bus driver and the drunk man argue for ten minutes more, when at last, the shouting subsided. Under the light of the moon, I watched the bus driver shake the man's hand and send him off into the night.

At midnight, the driver returned to the bus, nonchalantly strapped on his seatbelt, and started the engine. We breathed a sigh of relief as the bus slowly rolled down the mountainous road toward Kunming.

We danced on the precarious cusp of the missionary endeavor. Our week long trip through the rugged mountains of western Yunnan Province was the most grueling trip I had ever taken. We had close calls with the police along dangerous international borders. The ringing of AK-47 gunfire still rang in our ears. Images of extreme poverty had been imprinted upon our pupils and etched into our mind's eye. The degradation of humankind was real. The struggle for survival was palpable. But the long, twenty-four-hour sleeper bus ride back home to Kunming was far from over.

Hours past midnight, somewhere beyond Lingcang District, the bus jolted to a stop. I awoke with a start, startled by the sudden strong scent of bus emissions and dust. Outside, all was dark but for the faint gleam of headlights. I sat up in the sleeper bus bed and peered out the windshield. As far as the eye could see, rows of vehicles were stopped, each one hugging the ridge of the mountain road. Our bus driver cursed, unstrapped his seat belt, and laid down on a vacant bed.

"Must be a landslide up ahead," Frederik said, rubbing the sleep from his eyes. "Looks like the trip ain't over yet."

Glenn rolled his eyes, cracked the window, and sighed. "Well, it looks like I'm stuck with you ladies longer than I expected."

"You'll grow to love us soon enough," I said.

Sleep came over us as chilled air wafted around the vehicle, enveloping the passengers in a cold whisper. The grumble of bus engines were silenced, and headlights on the rural road ahead gradually switched off. All was dark and quiet but for the occasional sound of snoring.

At first light, I awoke to the sound of chatter in Chinese. I rolled over in bed and looked out the window. Below me, the sheer mountain bluff dropped five hundred feet into the valley where a slow-moving river coursed between rugged ranges.

"Who wants to go check out the situation?" I asked.

Glenn nodded in response, too tired for verbal utterance.

A row of dusty vehicles parked along the narrow mountain road. Glenn and I walked for nearly half a mile until the precipitous mountain obscured our bus from view. As we followed the curve of the road, the tragic explanation for our delayed trip emerged.

A colossal landslide had dragged half the mountain down the steep slope, taking with it a passenger bus. The bus hovered on its side on the soft embankment, threatening at any moment to plummet into the valley below.

There was no way across. It would take days for backhoes and bulldozers to clear the scene.

"Looks like we better go get our stuff and hike across the wreckage," Glenn said.

"Looks that way," I agreed.

We hiked back to our bus, and the four of us gathered our bags. We made our way back to the landslide, surveyed the wreckage, and rambled over the rubble. On the opposite side of the avalanche, we crammed inside a dilapidated minivan and continued the journey back to Kunming.

After many days of intensive travel through some of the most backward regions in Southwest China, we finally made it home to Kunming, exhausted and elated. Hidden facets of God's great love for the nations were revealed to us. It was a journey that would linger in our memories for years, inspiring future ministries among unreached people groups tucked within forgotten mountains and valleys.

———— ◆ ————

This was the missionary venture I had dreamt of. This was my China. It was not the China my friends had seen on the internet—the Beijings, the Shanghais, and the Hong Kongs. It was not the sweeping panoramas of towering skyscrapers and flashing fluorescent LED lights. It was not the expansive boulevards that stretched into the distance at the base of towering residential apartment blocks. Nor was it the incessant squabble of locals haggling over cheap gimcrack in an urban market that smelled of fish eyes, pig carcasses, and stinky tofu.

This was another memory of China altogether—a memory forgotten or never known.

Back home in Kunming, I sought to recollect my experiences. I thought of the quiet moments and noisy junctures in Jingpo villages. I recalled the half-clothed children and toothless grannies. I thought of the former headhunting Wa tribe and the desperate conditions in drug-ridden communities. I remembered the sound of AK-47 gunfire, the looming police presence, and the struggle for existence of those who had never heard the Gospel before.

My heartbeat began to murmur to the rhythm of God's heartbeat. I could still feel the sweat glistening on my neck and forearms as I drifted through the humid air of border regions. And somehow I knew that I was made for this.

I knew that many of my friends from Prescott, Arizona would never traverse geographical coordinates to this distance. And that was okay. I simply knew that this was the life to which I was called, the life I had chosen. I was created to stand at the edge of a village in rural China where no missionary had gone before. For a hundred miles in any direction, families—real people with real dreams and aspirations—still lay beyond the reach of the global Church. Hutted homes slowly slipped through the cracks of our evangelistic efforts. The plight of those unreached people groups saddened me. It confused me. It spurred me on to say, "Yes Lord, here am I. Send me. In all my inabilities, I am available."

THE SPACE BETWEEN

*"When I can no more stir my soul to move, and life is but the ashes of a
fire; when I can but remember that my heart once used to live and love,
long and aspire—Oh, be Thou then the first, the One Thou art;
be Thou the calling, before all answering love,
and in me wake hope, fear, boundless desire."*

GEORGE MACDONALD

There is a secret alcove in Confucius Temple hidden beneath mossy
fir trees and olive-green weeping willows. The scabrous, uneven
rock walls that surrounded the courtyard converged at the northwestern corner. A stone guardian lion loomed over the quoin, his
mouth open, his beady, petrified eyes stock-still, a cruel stare suspended upon his brow. A dragon and a phoenix slithered around
each temple column, bodies entwined around one another in the
shape of a ying yang. Splotchy orange and red koi glided just beneath
the surface of a placid pond where Chinese children dropped bread
crumbs from an arch bridge.

A bronze statue of Confucius stood erect in the center of the courtyard, green patina enveloping his forehead; verdigris bluing his long mustache. Old men gathered under the canopied patio, strumming pipas, bowing erhus, clicking clappers, making music. Old women sang doleful songs in high-pitched voices, their eyes closed, the intonations of song drawing them back down the pathways of memory. A melancholy nostalgia blanketed the temple grounds.

Potted plants lined the patchwork walls all the way back to the northwestern nook where there lay a single wooden bench. There, the noise of Kunming quelled. The blare of buses, the buzz of bicycle tires, the moan of mule carts on potholed boulevards—all these were forgotten in the secret corner at Confucius Temple.

I often found solace in that little corner, upon that bench, underneath the cloudy, gray skies. It was a perfectly absurd place for quiet times of Bible reading and of intercessory prayer. The shrill, alien accents of Chinese music seemed to reveal unique facets of God's character that I had never recognized before.

Often, in the most unexpected locations, the presence of God is made known. He is the Master of the mysterious, ever revealing Himself in the subtle space between the divine and the secular. I think He makes little distinction between the two.

Nearby the ringing of church bells and in the proximity of chanting Buddhist monks, God startled me with His omnipotence time and time again. Within the choruses of Christian worship and in Confucian courtyards, He showed me repeatedly that His presence could not be constrained. He did not live in a box, and could not be bothered to display Himself in ways I found most appropriate. I believe He finds a certain wit in this. I envision Him laughing with delight at the pounding of my heart when, lo and behold, there He is where I thought He could not possibly be. For He is the Father of Lights. There is no turning in Him, like the obscurity of the moon when the sun casts oblique shadows upon its outermost brink.

I have sensed Him both on the highest mountaintop and in the deepest valley. His footprints have always lined the sand alongside mine, while smuggling Bibles from Hong Kong to China, or hiding in a thicketed ditch near Myanmar, or swooning at first love's allure. Even during my midnight interrogations, He was there.

I have seen the edges of His garments fluttering in the blustering squall. Amidst the violent seismic undulation of an earthquake, I have caught glimpses of His majesty. Near the incandescent blaze of a wildfire, I have noticed the glow of His glory. But most often, I have heard Him in the gentle whispers after the feverish frenzy of life fades.

I call it the space between. It is an oasis in the desert, a sanctuary of solitude found in lulls between the busyness of missional lifestyle.

I am driven. I always have been. Status quo bores me. The commonplace is just so common. The mundane and mediocre make me fidgety. I am inspired by Ralph Waldo Emerson's encouragement: "Do not go where the path may lead. Go instead where there is no path and make a trail." But there is a quiet space between pioneering where I paused to catch my breath, close my eyes, and take in the moment. To rest.

In the northwestern corner of Confucius Temple, I felt the Good Shepherd's weathered staff curl around my neck, lovingly drawing me closer into His embrace. While the shadow of false gods fell at skewed angles along my chest, the King above all kings pulled me into His bosom and whispered of His affection for me. Tears streaked down my cheeks then.

In moments like these, I was not "David the missionary." My identity was not found in my work nor in my calling. The labels man had stuck on me curled at the edges and peeled from my skin.

There was no praise in purchasing a one-way ticket to the Orient, no acclaim to be solicited for simply following the beckoning of the Holy Spirit. I needed not the accolades of man. There was no applause in those moments. Man's recognition and approval—which, admittedly, I secretly craved—became a flimsy facade in the arms of my Savior.

A gentle breeze blew through the courtyard. The weeping willows swayed, brushed against the stony walls, and dangled on my bench. I shuttered at the gust of chilled air. The spell broke for a moment, and my mind wandered, as was my natural tendency.

I thought about friends and family back home. Remembering the churches in America who were financially supporting my mission filled my mind. I considered the vision partners who faithfully donated their hard-earned money for me to stay in China. I did not want to let them down. *Can I really make a difference in this country?* I questioned. *What if the money stops coming in?* I doubted. *What if I fail in my missionary endeavor?*

The Good Shepherd drew me closer. "I own the cattle on a thousand hills," He said. "Trust Me."

But I was spiritually dense and prone to doubt. My impulse was to gather all the tangled threads together, to organize the strands in my mind into a single, united ball. My habit was to control what could not be managed by man.

I thought of the Wa tribe. I wondered if Uncle Xiao was in his fields, breaking the earth, preparing to plant seeds for a new harvest. Perhaps he was in his hut, sipping mijiu, smoking his water bong, thinking of *The Jesus Film*. I wondered about his neighbors. Had their divine encounter with the Man on the cross begun to transform their hearts? Were they reading the Gospel tracts I gave them?

The Holy Spirit wrapped me in a warm embrace again, drawing my consciousness back to Himself. "I am in control," He seemed to remind me. "Stop worrying for a moment. Be with Me."

And for a fleeting moment, I remained there, reassured; my apprehensions abated. That was until I thought of Lorna and the precariousness of our long distance relationship. *What if, after all these years, she will not have me?* I worried. I reached into my backpack and pulled out a handmade paper card. I considered writing her another love letter. *If only I could convey to her my true love. If only we were together now.*

The voice of the Comforter rose ever so slightly from a gentle whisper to a droning murmur. A flurry of wind rustled the trees above me. A quiver on the surface of the pond sent ripples drifting to the water's edge as startled koi fish darted into the deep in search of safety. The gray clouds had thickened overhead by now, and the sky was heavy with moisture. Rain began to sprinkle the courtyard, slowly at first, until a heavy shower fell from the heavens, soaking the trees, and drizzling over the bronze statue of Confucius. Raindrops spiraled around the temple columns, streaking down the etchings of dragon and phoenix, pooling around my shoes.

I sat there, motionless, as stationary as the stone guardian lion on the cornerstone above me.

"David!" The voice of God echoed across the temple grounds like a susurrus amidst the condensation. "I know all things. The world is in My hands. The burdens you carry are not made for you alone. Take My yoke upon you and learn from Me. In My gentleness, you will find rest for your weary soul."

The rain mixed with the tears on my cheeks, and something in the recesses of my heart severed. Like the temple veil was torn from top to bottom at the death of Jesus, my own staunch will split in two; and the holy of holies found access into my being. Once again, I sensed the luminescent gleam of God's presence glimmer inside me. The space between the dense and the divine illuminated everything within.

And all turned silent.

The man-pleasing spirit absconded. The spirit of control escaped through the fissures left from the tear inside. Worry and doubt disappeared with the advent of the Divine.

The gentle voice of Jesus came to me again: "I desire your wholeness. Cease striving in the calling I have given you. You cannot save China. That's My job. You cannot control every juncture in time. Simply rest in Me, My son."

To my right sat a shrine ornamented with joss sticks. They had been burning since early morning, emitting the slight scent of jasmine and rose like ceremonious prayers to appease the gods. I watched the final smoldering wisps of incense spiral upward then vanish from their wetted tips. The rain had smothered their flaming apex and snuffed out their spiritual capacities.

I remained there on the bench for a while, soaked in the rain. It was cold and cleansing. I, too, like the joss sticks beside me, had nothing transcendent to offer; no way to appease Heaven through human piousness. All the services I had extended to God, all the sacrifices I had made in the missionary endeavor paled in comparison to His presence. These were but dead works, silly, wet ceremonial embers. I was left with nothing to do but respond, "Not my will, but Yours, be done."

When the rain stopped, I stood to my feet. My clothes were saturated with moisture, my shoes soggy and dank. I made my way to the courtyard exit at the edge of Renmin Road. Under the arched gate of Confucius Temple, I watched the commotion of the city: the incessant stream of bicycles, swerving buses, and foot traffic. In a few minutes, I would be absorbed by the momentum of Kunming. I took one last moment to pause, to reflect upon God's grace. I whispered a defiant declaration into the space between rest and restlessness.

"It is well with my soul," I exclaimed, and stepped out onto the sidewalk.

Chapter 7

UNENGAGED

"A man who becomes conscious of the responsibility he bears toward a human being who affectionately waits for him, or to an unfinished work, will never be able to throw away his life. He knows the 'why' for his existence, and will be able to bear almost any 'how.'"

VICTOR FRANKL

Southwest China is home to the highest percentage of unreached people groups in the country. Not once have they heard about Jesus. They have never met a Christian. There are no missionaries among them; zero churches, zero Christian bookstores, zero Gospel radio broadcasts, zero opportunities to understand Who God is.

I lived where the zeros resided, and I was uncomfortable elsewhere.

The People's Republic of China officially recognizes fifty-six ethnic people groups within its geographical borders. Yet, an enormous number of ethnolinguistic peoples have been grouped together with other tribes and generalized under a majority title.

Smaller populations of people have been merged into larger blocs and are now recognized as the same people group. Despite their distinct histories, unique ethnic heritages, diverse cultures, and languages, they are no longer officially recognized as independent tribes. But dissect China's fifty-six nationality minorities, and the picture becomes clearer: nearly five-hundred various people groups, each with their own cultural identities, ethnic significance, and transcendent value.

I traveled among the lesser known tribes with smaller populations. Even the Chinese themselves had never heard of the people groups I came to know and value.

In rural China, I came alive. In the homes of the Kongge, the Kemu, Ake, and Lawa—ethnic peoples you will not find on China's list of minority nationalities—my heart bloomed and my countenance brightened.

I was made for pioneer missions among the unreached people groups of the 10/40 Window.

But there is another, more-disturbing term that missiologists refer to. It is the word "unengaged." A people group is unengaged when there is no church planting strategy, consistent with Evangelical faith and practice, under implementation. There is no church, no missionary, no mission agency, no one who has yet taken responsibility to tell them about Jesus Christ.

When I hear the word "unengaged," my heart drops. I am equally sickened and saddened at its utterance. On the scale of Gospel presence, unengaged people groups are a step below the unreached. Among them, there is no unanimous Christian effort seeking to target these three-thousand ethnic tribes with the Gospel.

They are simply overlooked, forgotten, and despised.

But they are still precious to the heart of God. He cares for them. He numbers the hairs on their heads as He numbers ours. The unengaged communities in Southwest China matter.

I questioned why there were so many unengaged communities

still waiting for the truth of the Gospel. With all the technological resources we have at our disposal in the 21st century, how are there still so many without access to Christianity? With such a large missionary task force, why has the global Church overlooked these groups?

It seems clear to me that it is less an issue of ability than it is of priority. Harsh truth be told, we simply don't care about bringing the Gospel beyond the zip codes of Jerusalem, Judea, and Samaria. And meanwhile, the ends of the earth lie untouched—though not out of reach. The fruit of the harvest hangs heavy on low-lying branches, waiting for laborers in the field. But so few come, and the fruit drops to the ground, rots, and returns to the dust.

Do we really think that Jesus did not consider these precious peoples when He spoke of the Great Commission?

Despite our forgetfulness and neglect of unengaged peoples, I believe Jesus' passion for the lost still remains intact. I think that He would still leave the ninety-nine, safely tucked away and for a time, to search for that one lost sheep. And in this case, the one lost sheep equals over one billion people who have yet to hear the Christian message of salvation.

Linger there for a moment and notice a little more of the breadth and depth of God's heart.

———◆———

The seventeen-seater bus barreled down the dusty, curving roads on the borders of China and Laos. The blurred landscape would have been alluring—even romantic—had it not been for the potholes and loose gravel sending me bouncing eight inches from my seat toward the ceiling every few seconds.

We had been traveling for over an hour on the rugged roads, but the journey felt much longer. Bus rides always seemed unimaginably prolonged on country lanes like these, as if we were traversing an alternate universe, hovering outside the dimensions of time.

I shared a seat with an elderly Chinese woman, probably in her late sixties, who was returning home to her village after purchasing living necessities for her family. Thankfully, she was situated on the window side of the bus, which left more treasured legroom for me. I stretched my left leg into the aisle, trying to maintain my balance as the bus tore around sharp bends in the road.

Chad Layman sat across the aisle to my left, knuckles white, squeezing the headrest of the seat in front of him. Mindy was a human seat belt for Jacob and Caleb, cradling them in the seat behind her husband.

The dilapidated buses that crisscrossed the countryside from Xishuangbanna City to the surrounding villages transported everything from humans to furniture, market goods, and animal carcasses. And in our particular case, the roof filled with slaughtered pigs, bundled in tarpaulin, and tied to the top of the vehicle. It was only after an hour of trembling over bone-shaking roads that we realized the contents being transported overhead.

As we barreled around the bending lanes, the ropes began to slacken, and the tarpaulin above flapped in the wind. Pig blood began streaking down the bus windows, coating the vehicle in gory red.

"Mommy, look!" Six-year-old Jacob marveled at the vivid crimson dye smearing down the sides of the bus. His little brother, Caleb, laughed with delight.

"What in the world?" Mindy shrieked, and pulled her boys tighter into her lap.

We had been down endless miles of rural road before, but this was a first. We watched in disbelief as the window tinting gradually grew rusty red and the landscape outside seemed brushed in a rosy film.

But the local passengers must have seen this scenario before. Their occasional, nonchalant glances displayed little emotion, and the journey continued casually and uninterruptedly.

The roads wrapped between mountain ranges, here and there hovering precariously over ridges that descended into chasmal valleys. We passed through verdant terrain ripe with tea fields and juddered past pockets of modest villages. And the deeper inland we journeyed, the more scarlet our bus became.

After what seemed like an eternity, our bloody bus finally reached the end of the road and parked at the bus terminus.

We stepped off the vehicle and stretched our muscles. Our faces were covered with dust; our clothing infused with perspiration. Dried pig blood plastered the bus exterior. Bright red smeared the roof, crimson streaks spreading down to the wheel wells. It was like a scene straight out of a horror movie.

"That was the porky blood bath from hell!" Chad grinned at his description, and we burst into laughter, which made our muscles hurt even worse after the ride we had just alighted.

Outside the bus station was a row of street-side stalls and vendors. I bought a can of Spam and instant noodles—the perfect combination for a trip in the backwoods of China.

We were on our way to the Kongge tribe where our local missionaries had seen breakthrough after regularly traveling from the county seat to the village. These local heroes initiated ministry among poor communities; met new tribal people; sipped local tea in shoddy homes; shared the Gospel to families; and ushered people into the Kingdom of God. We were their backup. We were there to inspire and support local ministry efforts, as should be the goal of every Western missionary. Working ourselves out of a job never sounded like a bad idea to Chad Layman, and under his tutorage, that spirit transferred to me as well.

The Kongge were one of the lesser-known tribes of China, both unreached and unengaged. Not only did Western missionaries cock their heads and rack their brains to recall the people group, but most Chinese believers had never heard of them as well. They were the unknowns, the invisible ones. They were the precious despised. But we saw them. And standing from our vantage point on the borders of China and Laos, we were only a few kilometers from their residences.

Thick, cumulous clouds blanketed the overhead sky, threatening to burst at any moment. A subtle breeze blew steadily, shifting the firmament until fissures between the vaporous masses grew wider. A gentle drizzle began to fall. The raindrops pitter-pattered upon the tin roof of the bus station like a percussive symphony of liquid music.

"It's gonna be a wet walk to the village," Chad said.

"And muddy too," I agreed.

Jacob and Caleb had already found the attractive puddles forming on the pavement and were delightfully jumping one to another, splashing each other with bursts of hysterical laughter.

After consuming my Spam-instant-noodle delight, we bought cheap umbrellas for our hike into the bush. The looming clouds spread across the horizon, graying the already dismal landscape. The sky cracked with sudden forked lightning, and the drizzle transformed into a deluge of tropical rain.

Mindy called her boys to join us under the canopy cover on the corner of the bus station. There, we waited for the rain to subside.

Soon the downpour began to dwindle; and, as usual, Chad was ready to rock and roll.

"Let's head on out!" he said. Chad opened his umbrella and stepped onto the street. "Ain't no point in hanging around here."

We walked to the furthermost edge of the small town road where it intersected with a narrow minority trail leading to Kongge villages. Up muddy inclines we trudged, our shoes suctioning deep into the spongy earth with every step.

Tall, bending bamboo lined the tapered trails, between which we caught occasional glimpses of hutted homes perched along the terraced fields.

Chad held Mindy's hand, supporting her along our footslog. I followed close behind, watching Jacob and Caleb happily trudge uphill.

The Laymans were the epitome of a family on mission, making excursions together into China's backwoods. The boys were troopers—city kids who were perfectly at home in the countryside. They were world wise. At this young age, they had already journeyed with their parents to every corner of Yunnan Province.

By the time we reached the Kongge village, we were covered in mud from our knees down. Our cheap umbrellas were saturated with rain, and the dripping leaks had soaked our frames.

At the village entrance, the minority trail split into five alternate routes, so we followed the rising path up a swampy stairway to the elevated homes. At the top of the hill, we came to a clearing, wondering in which of the stilted homes the new Kongge believers resided.

A steady shower continued to fall, sprinkling residents who were returning home from their fields for a midday meal. We asked about the whereabouts of our local friends, and an elderly man motioned toward a home tucked at the end of the trail.

"It looks like our local brothers are well-known around here," Chad said.

"I hope that's a good thing," I replied, considering whether or not they were regarded with contempt for their newfound faith.

The Gospel took root in this unengaged village, but as was often the case, not without repercussions. To break from the norm of animistic rites for a new religion was frowned upon, and was sure to cause rifts between world views and relationships. We were anxious to see how these new Christians fared in their community.

At the heart of an animistic belief system was the notion that natural objects, natural phenomena, and the universe itself possess souls. This belief in spiritual beings or agencies naturally paralyzed local inhabitants with fear and servitude. Ancestral cultures who cling to such convictions live in constant fear and torment of the spirit world.

Animist villages shared many similarities, yet each revealing glimpses of cultural facets unique to the particular tribe. The features of Kongge homes may very well feel like those of the Bulang or Yao—rickety structures with leaking roofs, livestock living alongside families, and smoky fire pits ever billowing fumes from the central living space. There, an elderly woman often stood hunched over a blackened wok, the aroma of brothy vegetables permeating the fibers of cloth and skin. The Kongge huts shared similarities with the homes of the Wa, the Lahu and the Dai. Each were inhabited by farming communities struggling to make a day's wage. Their livelihood hinged upon the success of their crops of sugarcane and Pu'er tea, bananas, pineapples, and rice.

We hiked to the homes at the end of the trail. There, we were met with the warm smiles of the new Christian family. Our local missionaries informed them that we would be coming, and they were grateful for our arrival.

"Nimen hao," the family greeted us. "Welcome! Please come inside and drink tea with us."

We climbed the wooden stairway leading to their raised living quarters and shook hands with each member of the household. They served us hot tea and introduced themselves one-by-one.

"We hear that you have decided to follow Jesus," Chad queried.

"Shi de," the man of the household replied. "Every day, we learn more about God as we read the Bible together. But we still have many questions."

They had only recently given their lives to the Lord after local Chinese missionaries shared the Gospel with them. Their hunger for spiritual truth was evident, and so Chad began to explain more clearly how to hear the voice of God and serve Him wholeheartedly.

It was a prodigious meeting. The Holy Spirit had supernaturally revealed Himself to the family and allowed us to witness the initial stages of their faith journey.

We spent the entire afternoon encouraging these believers in their newfound faith. I wanted to tell my vision partners that the Kongge were no longer unengaged. We were engaging them! It took two thousand years for the Gospel to come to the tribe, and Christian light now glimmered in their midst. I considered what a blessing it would be to inform the global missions community that the Kongge were on someone's radar. But I knew that this small breakthrough was a drop in the bucket. The general population had little Christian witness. Statistically, the ethnic people group was still immensely unengaged.

Did these few lives matter to God? I was convinced that they did. Did not the angelic hosts dance with delight at the transformation taking place in this previously overlooked region? No doubt, there was jubilation that new names were penned into the Lamb's Book of Life. But thousands of Kongge homes dotted the landscape as far as the eye could see, and countless communities still waited for a light to shine in the darkness.

Chad continued fellowshipping with our new Christian brothers and sisters, and I stepped outside onto the flimsy balcony. The bamboo creaked beneath my feet. I watched the low-hanging clouds sweep across the sky. An impending storm brewed on the horizon.

There was hope for the Kongge. The seeds of revival were being watered at this very moment. There was a strand of expectancy that this ethnic people group would someday stand before the throne of God, clothed in white, and offer palm branches to their Creator.

They would join the anthem of the redeemed from every nation, tribe, people, and language with choruses of praise. They, too, would have the opportunity to cry out, "Salvation belongs to our God, who sits on the throne, and to the Lamb!"

I had met some of the first Kongge Christians that day. I shook their hands, conversing about life, death, spirituality, and hope. Thankful for this moment, I whispered under my breath and watched the warmth of my lungs vanish into the sunset.

"Thank You, Lord, for calling me here. Thank You for showing me that You are at work, restoring lives and bringing salvation."

I stared into the distance. The valley grew murky and overcast but for the flickering lights twinkling in distant Kongge villages. Still, there in the mountains and valleys beyond, forgotten communities remained untouched, waiting to be engaged by the arrival of Christian hope.

———— ◆ ————

The definition of engagement by Merriam-Webster looks like this:

To offer (as one's word) as security for a debt or cause;

To bind (as oneself) to do something;

To hold the attention of;

To deal with especially at length;

To pledge oneself.

As I gave myself to the ethnic tribes of China, God had pledged Himself to me. His dedication was not a formula of cause and effect. Mercy such as His was not dependent upon my obedience. The guarantee of His presence was without conditions. There were no strings attached. I was not a mute marionette, suspended from heavenly heights, dangling and frolicking this way and that by regional variations.

I was engaged to my Maker, His inexorable love pursuing me.

In a similar way, I gave myself to Lorna over the last six years. I never stopped pursuing her. Courting her was a form of engagement and devotion.

The length of time involved in our long distance relationship required a fair amount of tenacity. But it was perseverance without strain. For in the giving of my love to Lorna, I felt fulfillment. She was the object of my adoration, and I sought to serve and encourage her. There were no conditions to my love; there were no marionette strings. But oh how I prayed that she would someday become my wife!

Khalil Gibran articulated beautifully a love without conditions by saying, "If you love somebody, let them go, for if they return, they were always yours. And if they don't, they never were."

Since that providential day in 1997 when our lives intersected in Hong Kong, Lorna became a part of me. She was mine. We were partners in crime, stealthily smuggling Bibles into the borders of China. We were best friends, exchanging intimate dreams and journal entries. And we were now becoming lovers as we flung open the veils that guarded unknown hurts and pleasures. The alcoves that retained secrets from the world—the deep chasms where pain and felicity resided—we shared with each other.

In recent months, we conversed about her visit to Kunming. She wanted to experience what life in China was like. Giving herself to me meant leaving her country, her church, her friends, and her family. It was a life-altering decision, and she needed time to decide when she would dive head first into the enigmatic ocean of overseas missions and cross-cultural marriage.

But there had been confirmations from the past. From a young age, God drew Lorna toward the missionary endeavor, imploring her to reach forgotten peoples.

———— ◆ ————

At eleven years of age, Lorna sat in a row of plastic chairs in the sanctuary at Christ, the Living Stone Fellowship in Mandaluyong, Manila. Standing at the podium, Pastor Dan Balais spoke about the plight of the unreached; about the heart of God that beats for every tribe; about the missionary call to which Filipinos should respond.

In typical mellow-mannered gentleness, the pastor spoke with tender tones and amiable fervor. The appeal to his congregation carried no manipulative undertones, only a supplicated exhortation toward obedience.

After providing scriptural context for the massive harvest, the lack of workers, and the need for Great Commission fulfillment, Pastor Dan requested the congregation to stand to their feet.

"Close your eyes for a moment."

Piano keys rang bell-like, and a hush like autumn cool after a light rain shower fell over the church. The voice of the Holy Spirit was given free reign, not only to whisper but to be heard.

"Ask God to what country, land, or people will He use you, either by sending or in going."

Lorna's eyes closed. She was just a new Christian at the time: impressionable, sensitive to the voice of God, and innocent. Angelic wings stirred the air. Thick, celestial presence permeated the atmosphere, and Jesus leaned near to her ear with a secret.

"China," He whispered, and the flower of missionary passion began to bloom within her.

Lorna opened her eyes, startled and in awe. Her heartbeat quickened at the presence of the Divine. The young Filipina girl began to weep with a mixture of joy and trepidation.

"Yes, Lord," she whispered in reply. "Where You send me, I will go."

———◆———

On the first month of 2003, Lorna and her parents boarded a China-bound plane from the capital of the Philippines. I flew from Southwest China to Hong Kong to ease them during their international travels.

I waited in the arrival area at Hong Kong airport, blending into the crowd of Cantonese businessmen and families. I gently cradled the bouquet of flowers I purchased for Lorna. The arrangement of red roses, Oriental Lilium stargazers and baby's breath blended into a beautiful medley. I unfastened a single, fulvous rose for Lorna's mother. Her father would have to settle for a pat on the back and a bear hug.

Journal entry, January 17, 2003: "My whole body feels alive. It's hard to articulate. There's a tingling sensation in my stomach, and I am aflame with anticipation. Lorna will arrive at the Hong Kong airport in thirty minutes. The moment has nearly arrived, and I am a nervous wreck!"

Time passed in slow motion. I watched the digital arrival board flick from Chinese to English. Finally, Lorna's plane landed. I shuffled my feet back and forth, then stood still again. I raised the bouquet of flowers to my face and breathed in the fragrant aroma. The floral scent calmed my nervous elation.

Although I met Lorna nearly six years earlier, we had only spent half a year in each other's physical presence. The thought of being together again carried an ecstatic anticipation.

From around the corner of the arrival hall, Lorna glided along the tiles, suitcase in tow, followed by her mother and father. Her smile was as wide as the ocean, brimming with euphoric charm. For a moment, I forgot about the flowery bouquet, and I flung my arms around her. The romantic embrace made our hearts flutter with emotion. Lorna buried her face into my shoulder. We cried for joy, happy to be together once more.

"This is for you, my dear!" I said, handing her the bouquet of flowers.

"Thank you!"

I greeted her mother with a single red rose and a warm hug followed by a strong embrace for her father.

I took Lorna's hand, slid her fingers between mine, and started toward the train turnstiles at the airport exit.

"We'd better get going," I told her mother and father. "Our flight from Shenzhen to Kunming departs in a few hours, and we still need to cross the border."

We would take the same routes where I led short-term Bible smuggling teams in 1997. The MTR train snaked along underground tunnels, intersecting with the KCR line toward the China border. At Lowu international customs, we stood in the same staggered queues where Lorna and I had carried Christian literature across the border six years earlier.

The moment infused with sentimental nostalgia. Memories of the Shenzhen we once experienced together were recalled from the recesses of our minds and now felt distant and fabricated.

"It's so different," Lorna exclaimed. "Where are all the banyan trees?"

I shared the same sorrow at the loss of our mutual memories. What was once the meeting spot for Bible smugglers under the shade of ancient banyans was now a gaping chasm of earth and metal. The digging was underway, as it seemed it always was in China's urban developmental boom. The clanking and roar of drills and backhoes tore through the stony earth. Soon, a state-of-the-art subway system would carry commuters to the city center in record time. But for those of us with an acute aptitude toward nostalgia, it evoked the sinking sensation of loss.

"I know. I can't believe they're all gone," I said. But some memories were still within reach. "Remember when Kyle and I took you to that hole-in-the-wall restaurant? The Cantonese one with black and white checkered tiles?"

"Yes," Lorna recalled. "That place was delicious!"

"I wonder if it's still there."

But we didn't have time to explore. Our flight from Shenzhen to Kunming was scheduled to depart on time, and we still had to taxi over an hour to the airport.

That afternoon, our plane departed from the southeastern province toward China's rural western mountains. For Lorna, it was an exploratory trip. She knew that her life would be dramatically altered if she were to give herself to me in marriage. She wanted to experience Kunming for herself; and in typical Filipino custom, she wanted her parents to be on board with her decision.

It was a frigid evening in mid-January when we landed at the Kunming airport. The icy climate was a shock to Lorna and her parents. They had never experienced such cold weather in the Philippines.

After taxiing to Kunming's northern district, we dropped off their luggage, bundled up in borrowed coats, and headed outside for a meal. We ordered Over the Bridge Rice Noodles at Brother's Jiang, a popular chain specializing in Yunnan Province cuisine. Lorna's father cupped his hands around his hot bowl of rice noodles and watched the steam wisp around the lip. Lorna's mother shivered, her breath hovering in the chilled air.

"Are you enjoying the weather?" I quipped.

"It's freezing!" her mother replied. "But we are happy to be here with you."

Lorna's mother and father had always been supportive of our relationship. I was blessed to have such loving future in-laws.

"I am so happy that you are here with me, too," I said. "I'm excited for you to see the China I have come to know and love."

Truth be told, I wanted to quell the concerns that were perhaps lingering in their minds. I wanted to assure them that I would take care of their daughter were she to join me in China.

Midway through our meal, I excused myself. I selected this location because I had to run an errand at a nearby jewelry shop.

"Can you wait right here?" I asked. "I'll be back in ten minutes."

As I stopped outside, a gust of glacial wind buffeted my cheeks. I jogged across the street to the adjacent jewelry shop. The week before, after careful deliberation, I selected an elegant, thin band of white gold set with a single diamond. But because I had yet to confirm the size of Lorna's ring finger, I had not yet made the purchase. So today, one day before I planned to propose to my girl, I bought her engagement ring. I tucked it safely into my coat pocket, then hurried back to the restaurant.

Nonchalantly, I rejoined them at the table and continued my bowl of rice noodles.

"If you don't mind, I'm going to take Lorna to Lijiang," I announced to her parents. "You'll be okay here in Kunming, right?"

"We'll have a chance to explore the city!" her mother said.

I did not disclose the fact that the destination was over three-hundred miles away, and we would take a plane to get to Lijiang City.

"Have fun," Lorna's mother said. "And be careful."

———— ◆ ————

We booked two rooms, separated by an open Chinese courtyard at a charming inn hidden by the curving labyrinthine cobblestone walkways. Rows of ethnic Naxi tribal architecture lined the narrow alleys; there, shingled corners of curling, grassy rooftops nearly collided as each structure was set mere inches apart. Along the ancient Dongba paths, the sound of trickling water passed from its source on northern glaciers, the current moving we knew not where.

Sprawling in a half moon panorama, clockwise from north to south, around the towering hills of Lion Rock Mountain, the sleepy town of Lijiang was a romantic glimpse of China's disappearing ancient beauty. To the north, fifteen miles past the mist of Black Dragon Pool, where statues of imperial guardian lions peered quietly into the waters, the snowcapped Jade Dragon Snow Mountain loomed ominously in the wintery mist.

This was the perfect setting for proposals, for romance, and for love.

Lorna was not feeling well after the tumultuous flight from Kunming to Lijiang. She decided to rest in her room, and I took the opportunity to put the elaborate plan of my proposal into motion.

I gathered the articles required to create an amorous ambiance: a kettle of hot water, a plastic basin, two chairs, a small table and tablecloth, a vase of flowers, two glasses, and a bottle of red wine. I volunteered two employees from the quaint inn, and the three of us jogged up the zigzagging stairway toward Lion Rock Mountain. We carried the equipment to a serene slope under swaying fir trees.

I arranged the site to my liking. I draped the white tablecloth over the table, set the red wine and glasses side-by-side, and placed the basin of hot water between the chairs. I instructed one of the young men to keep a watchful eye on the location. To the other, I gave the responsibility of recording my proposal with my camcorder.

Brimming with euphoria, I ran down the mountain. Moments before I arrived at the inn, I stopped to catch my breath, compose myself, and brush my hair back into place. I walked through the arching threshold into the small garden where Lorna sat, reclining on a bench under the open-air courtyard.

"Want to go for a walk?" I asked as if nothing out of the ordinary was about to occur. Still, I thought her heartbeat quickened at the possibilities.

"Sure. Where are we going?"

"I want to take you to Lion Rock Mountain." I pointed up toward the five-story wooden Dougong tower set on the nearby hilltop. "There's a beautiful view of the city from there."

After a fifteen-minute stroll, we reached the final step; and from the heights of the acclivity, we surveyed the plain over which we had passed. Ten thousand antiquated rooftops spread before us like a sea of halcyon gray shingles.

We turned toward Wangulou Tower, and suddenly Lorna noticed an unusual scene set between the forested hilltop.

"What's that?" she questioned.

"I'm not sure," I played dumb. "Let's go check it out."

As we neared the quaint setup, I asked Lorna to take a seat in one of the chairs. She blushed, and the ecstasy on her cheeks was evident. I kneeled down in front of her and washed her feet in the warm basin of water. After toweling them dry, I sat down at the table. I poured two glasses of red wine, held mine up, and toasted.

"To the most beautiful girl in the world," I began. "I am so happy to share this moment with you, Lorna."

"Thank you," she replied.

"Thank you?" I joked. "You mean you're happy to share this moment with me, too, or 'Thank you' as in the day you thanked me for telling you 'I love you'?"

We burst into laughter at the thought of that moment on Manila Bay nearly two years earlier.

"You know what I mean!" she giggled.

"I know, I know," I admitted. "But seriously, I have loved every minute of this joyous journey with you. To be here on this mountaintop with you now is, well, I'm speechless. But I pray that many more sweet memories will be made between us. Cheers!"

"Cheers."

We clinked our glasses together. The echoing resonation of a gong rang from Wangulou Tower, startling a flock of birds to our right. The trees rustled as a chilled breeze passed through the forested hilltop. From the lower end of the slope, I thought I heard the shrill tones of an erhu being played and the hushed timbre of a Chinese ballad.

I lowered my left knee to the earth, bowing in front of Lorna. A burst of courageous masculinity and chivalrous gallantry surged within me. I looked up into Lorna's eyes. I meant to make her my bride, to protect her, and to cherish her.

From my coat pocket, I presented a red velvet box. I held it in front of her.

"Lorna, my dear, I want to ask you to be my wife."

I flipped open the jewelry box. The reflection of a rainbow danced upon the multifaceted, diamond engagement ring. Time stopped for a moment. I swallowed a lump in my throat.

"Lorna, will you marry me?"

Her eyes welled up with moisture, and a single tear slid down her blushing cheek. She squeezed my hand with feminine delight.

"Yes!" she exclaimed, "Yes, I will!"

A joyous delight brimmed within me, expanding deeper and wider until it burst, and laughter escaped my lips. I was given to joyful tears, but they would not come. Instead, a kiss. Her lips pressed against mine, and we embraced there atop the hillside. The bloom of affection grew ever higher, transforming into agape love.

For the longest time, we stood silently atop the mountain, embracing one another, taking in the moment. We looked out over the city, staring in the same direction, our hearts intertwined. We had always stood this way, side-by-side, our horizons aligned and the path before us.

On January 22, 2003, Lorna and I were engaged in Southwest China, far from the countries of our birth, yet more at home in each other's arms than we had ever been before.

Not far from here, our lives would soon merge in marriage. Our hearts would finally be united with holy purpose to engage those who were yet unengaged by the love of God.

Chapter 8
THE BIG DAY

"That sanguine expectation of happiness which is happiness itself."
JANE AUSTEN

The tailored blades of grass in Puerto Real garden edged against quaint pathways and under dim palm tree shadows, sprawling up an incline to impenetrable Intramuros walls. Glimpses of a bygone era echoed through the stone corridors and arching gateways. Centuries earlier, Spanish conquistadors arrived on these very grounds, colonizing the Philippines for 333 years.

Dungeons and torture chambers inset into dormant colonial walls, revealing the once-laid bones of anti-Spanish Katipunan revolutionaries. Mere minutes from this spot was the execution site of the Philippines national hero, Jose Rizal.

Stories of tragedy, struggle, and victory now lay silenced where soldiers feet once tread, bruising the green lawn. In the not so distant past, Spaniards and Americans, Chinese, Japanese, and Filipinos carried loaded rifles over these historical grounds.

Intramuros was the seat of the Philippines' government for nearly four hundred years; but whispers of harsh colonial occupancy could only be recalled by the surrounding flora and in the pages of history books.

The greenery of Puerto Real gardens was now tranquil and mute, swaying gently in the humid tropical breeze.

The previous week, I proposed to Lorna, and we were engaged atop a romantic hilltop setting. Then, after a one-week guided tour around Southwest China, I traveled to Manila with Lorna and her parents.

We began arranging the detailed preparations for our upcoming wedding on the last month of 2003. We selected the popular Puerto Real garden, reserving the venue nearly one year in advance. We organized invitation cards and caterers, and secured bubble machines, butterflies, and doves.

The countdown to the big day had begun. Lorna and I were ecstatic. Traversing the vast Metro Manila landscape in the balmy tropical heat to arrange wedding preparations was exhausting, but we were simply happy to be together.

The time flew by. We grasped at the moments, like granules of sand slipping through the narrow neck of an hourglass. And after one joyous week in the Philippines, we found ourselves melancholy and teary-eyed at NAIA International Airport in Manila.

I have mixed emotions about airports. They sit in a no man's land, like territories of another dimension, lonely and silently somber. Yet, all human life can be found in an airport. Luggage that had traversed the globe strolled past us. Travelers of every hue and skin tone sidestepped around us, darting through sliding doors to catch their flights.

Amidst the frenetic pace of shuffling shoes skirting around each other with aspirations of punctuality, airports are otherworldly, an oasis of imagination and daydreams. Young people look at the planes; the older ones look at the passengers with a watchful incredulity.

An array of polarizing emotions occupies airports. Tiled floors stretch beneath rising elevators and looping escalators, espying intimate parting kisses, warm hugs, and teary farewells.

Saying goodbye to my fiancée was not easy. I felt Lorna's tears staining my shirt as we embraced outside NAIA terminal one. I longed to remain with her in Manila, and I was vexed at my necessary return to the mission field. Visiting short-term American missions teams were scheduled to arrive in Kunming, and they counted on me to guide them through uncharted territories in Yunnan Province.

I was angry with China, at my missionary calling, even agitated with God. The missionary endeavor required a certain amount of self-denial and dedication to the purposes of God's heart. It required fervent devotion and commitment. Still, I hesitated to leave the one I loved so dearly to fulfill that calling. *Could not God watch over those without access to the Gospel for a few months in my absence?* I questioned. He was more than capable, I knew. But He wanted all of me. He was calling me toward unwavering obedience to the task.

This kind of self-sacrifice was ever an inner battle of the mind. I was immersed in inherent self-preservation and want for my own comfort. Though on paper and in my missionary updates, I gave the illusion of my utter abandonment to the will of God, the reality of my self-centered narcissism and undue fascination with personal comfort often sought to highjack God's perfect plans for me.

Yet, He was ever faithful, ever patient, relentlessly beckoning me toward His heart and purposes.

"My flight is departing soon, my dear," I whispered into Lorna's ear as her face nestled beneath my chin.

"I wish you didn't have to go," she cried.

"I wish so, too."

We shared one last kiss—a lingering repose—and I departed, leaving my beautiful Filipino fiancée in the sweltering embrace of Manila's humidity.

————•————

I returned to China on February 6, 2003. The months progressed in slow motion, lapsing at a snail's pace without Lorna by my side. Visiting short-term missions teams from America kept me busy. I led them to rural villages and on bicycle rides in urban metropolises. I escorted them to the Great Wall, Tiananmen Square, and Beijing's Forbidden City.

When the teams departed, I kept myself busy, leading worship at the Kunming International Fellowship, journaling under dim lamplight at Salvador's Coffee House, and conversing with Chinese college students in English corners at Green Lake Park. Once a month, I traveled outside Kunming City to unreached villages with my missionary counterparts.

> Journal entry, May 7, 2003: "This morning I woke up in a village miles from modern civilization. I want to worship and pray, but a million little things distract me from this moment. Lorna is always one of the sweetest distractions. I am tempted to pen her a letter instead of digging into God's word. But I sense His voice now, 'Am I less important than your woman?' I have ample opportunity to touch the hem of His garment, but I reach out slower than He reaches to me. Still, in His mercy, we make contact. I need a continual touch from God today."

Trips to unreached villages entailed scrutiny over the stack of government maps from 1980 that I had found in a Kunming bookshop. I purchased the set, including Yunnan's 129 counties, a detailed topography of the province, and nearly every single village in the region.

But even with an intricate mapping system, each trip required continual pauses on mountainous roads, querying local minorities about the specific trails and narrow pathways we should take.

On one particular trip to the countryside, Chad drove Betsy, his faithful, army-green Beijing Jeep. He steered precariously around the precipice of a winding road, overlooking chasmal cliffs and valleys below. I rode shotgun, navigating from a paper map. Mindy sat in the back seat with her boys, rattling over the rugged terrain.

Plateaus of endless terraced rice fields stepped down the hilly slopes into the valley. We were in central Guizhou Province, passing the street-side day-market in Bajie where Miao minority women adorned in beautiful multicolored fabrics. They gathered in groups on the roadside, buying and selling their local products. We scouted out ethnic Bouyei communities, searching for open hearts among the unreached people group. So, we drove on, down the dusty road, inquiring random pedestrians as to the whereabouts of Bouyei homes.

After a search that lasted more than seven hours, we parked at the entrance of a dilapidated shelter in Nakong Valley. A farmer meandered along the road, leading his donkey past our vehicle. His wife sat atop the animal, gawking at us from the saddle, her long, jet-black hair tangling in the breeze.

"Is this a Bouyei village?" Chad inquired.

The man nodded, and continued on his trek. That answer was all Chad needed.

"Alright guys, this is it," he announced. "We're camping here tonight. I ain't driving another second!"

Mindy unloaded plastic bags of instant noodles and packaged snacks. Jacob and Caleb were already blowing up balloons for a group of children. Chad reclined in his camping chair, exhausted from the long drive. I set up our tents outside the tilting, wooden structures of the village.

There was a hubbub of commotion about us. Curious kids thronged around our makeshift campsite, their wind-burned cheeks gathering around giddy smiles. Bouyei women peered dubiously from the threshold of their homes. Chickens pecked at the earth near the doorways.

"Looks like the whole village is coming out to see us!" Chad said.

He was tickled at the thought. He had not driven hours over rugged mountain terrain for nothing. Our evangelistic journeys were all about people. We sought the crowds, the dirtier the better.

Jacob and Caleb twisted long balloons into colorful swords and handed them to the children. Rowdy boys dueled with the flimsy sword balloons, flitting about like young kungfu masters. Jacob and Caleb joined in the sword fight, and a raucous chase ensued.

I was proud of the two missionary kids. Without effort, they naturally blended into unique environments, whether in the polished shopping malls of urban megacities or the rustic backwoods of ethnic villages. Their upbringing as third culture kids offered them glimpses of diversity; and everywhere they went, they settled in comfortably.

The sun set beyond the adjacent mountain range, shading our lowland campground. Chad set up our film projector, and I draped a white sheet over a protruding tree branch. When dusk turned to darkness, we planned to play *The Jesus Film* in Mandarin Chinese, accompanied by other evangelistic movies.

At eight o'clock in the evening, after an unsophisticated meal of instant noodles, we estimated that there were over three-hundred locals present for the airing of *The Jesus Film*. It was the first time they had ever witnessed a Gospel presentation.

After the film had ended, a group of young men lingered, and we spent time sharing that God wanted to bless their families with salvation. We passed out Bibles and Gospel tracts, encouraging them to learn about God's love for them.

In moments like these, we always looked for young people who were hungry for spiritual things. We invited them to return to the city with us where they could be introduced into underground house churches and integrated into our discipleship process. Over the years, this strategy had proven successful. After receiving salvation and discipleship, many young men and women returned to their hometowns, leading their communities to an understanding of God's heart.

It was past ten o'clock at night when I noticed a middle-aged man in army attire retreat to his doorway. He thumbed through one of our Bibles while discreetly making a phone call. There was just enough duplicity about him to recognize that he was a village cadre. Instantly, I knew that he was alerting the authorities about our arrival.

"Chad, it looks like we have ourselves another Judas," I announced.

That afternoon, we passed a local township on our way to the village, so we knew that the police station was roughly four hours away.

"It'll take them a while to get here," Chad said. "Let's leave at five o'clock in the morning."

It was already too late to depart by that time. Our tents were arranged and our sleeping bags laid inside. The village was pitch black but for the shimmering stars that punctured the inky sky. We would leave early the next morning so as to avoid conflict with the authorities.

But at two o'clock in the morning, we were surprised by an unexpected visit. We awoke to the zipping hum of an opening tent, followed by an inquiry in English, "Where is your translator?" The village cadre who made a phone call to the police station alluded that Chad's wife, Mindy, the only Asian in our company, was our interpreter.

"We don't have a translator," Chad yawned. "That's my wife, and she's not coming out of the tent!"

For the next two hours, Chad and I were interrogated by three police officers in a sugarcane factory not far from our campsite. Only one of the officers was able to communicate in a second language, so the dialogue continued in English. We felt it unnecessary to disclose the fact that we were both proficient in Chinese.

"Did you show a movie last night?" the cops questioned us.

"What do you think?" Chad was exhausted, but still a facetious smile formed on his face.

"Did you show a movie last night?"

Again, Chad answered with rhetoric. The looping conversation lasted over an hour until at length, the police officers grew weary of repetition.

Our answers carried a certain serpentine wisdom accompanied by the innocence of a dove. It reminded me of Jesus' trial before Pilate. For hours on end, Pilate questioned Jesus, accusing Him of the charges brought before Him.

"Are You the King of the Jews?" Pilate questioned.

But Jesus remained silent.

"Are you or are you not the King of the Jews?" Pilate asked again, flustered and agitated.

Again Jesus spoke not a word.

"They say You are the King of the Jews!" The fury of Pilate's accusation percolated through the palatial chamber.

"You have said it," Jesus finally responded.

But we often overlook the wit and facetiousness of Jesus' reply in the scriptures. Perhaps His response to Pilate's vexed questioning sounded more jocose than we realize.

"You're saying that I'm the King of the Jews?" Jesus quipped. "Why thank you very much. I appreciate the compliment!"

His response during interrogation bore the sagaciousness of a serpent and the virtue of a dove. Jesus modeled guiltless morality in His reply, aggrandizing the fear of God higher than His admiration for man's approval.

After one hour of seeking to pry a confession from us, the police shifted course. One of the officers removed a Bible from his bag, revealing that they had evidence from our affair in the village.

"Did you pass out books last night?" the officer questioned, shaking a Bible in front of our faces.

"Yes, we passed out that book," Chad happily replied. He snatched the Bible from the officer's hand, opened the book to the first page, and revealed a red stamp with underlying Chinese characters on the inside cover.

"Can you read this? Or do you want me to read it for you?" he challenged them. Chad continued in English, "This Bible was printed by the Three Self Patriotic Movement, the official Christian Church of the People's Republic of China. Do you understand what that means?"

The police officers were speechless, unsure how to reply.

"It means that we gave away legal copies of a book that is permitted by law within this country. So, now, what's your next question?"

If there was one thing to be praised about Chad Layman, it was his boldness in the face of persecution. Never once did I notice a tinge of fear or willingness to back down in his replies. Never would he divulge unnecessary information that would incriminate our Chinese counterparts. He was a missionary. But before that, he was a family man who would stand for his loved ones at all costs. And that included the spiritual children whom he had raised up in the Christian faith over his many years of missionary service.

For years to come, this was an aspect of Chad's mentorship that I would be required to emulate during numerous police interrogations and in dangerous situations. I am forever grateful for the strength of this man for sowing godly boldness into my life in more ways than he perhaps comprehends.

The officers were left without incriminating evidence. But knowing that their higher-ups at the police station required a confession, they cordially requested a written report about our activities.

We obliged, playfully constructing our confession in English. The condensed version went something like this:

"We enjoyed movie time together with the local community. We made many friends. We offered gifts to the locals, books printed by the People's Republic of China. We had interesting conversations about life and culture. We apologize if we caused a commotion, and agree not to create any more unnecessary disturbances in this village. Sincerely, Chad and David."

The police transcribed information from our passports, and apologetically accepted our report.

"Thank you for your time," they said graciously. "Please be on your way early tomorrow morning."

We agreed, shook hands with the officers, and waved as they drove away down the rural country road.

"Well, that wasn't too bad, now was it?" Chad slapped me on the back. "Another one in the books!"

I smiled, and we returned to our tents to catch the few remaining hours of sleep before sunlight.

The next morning, after packing our belongings, we stretched our hands out toward the unreached Bouyei homes. The valley shrouded in a misty haze, pierced here and there by the early rays of sunlight. We prayed that God would watch over the lives of those who expressed interest in the Gospel; that He would cause the seeds that were sown to grow into a mighty harvest of souls. We prayed that there would be a spiritual awakening among this tribe, and that many of their names might be written in the Book of Life.

The proceeding day was monumental for the Bouyei. It was

the big day of Gospel advent in a region untouched by Christian presence.

Carl F. H. Henry once stated, "The Gospel is only good news if it gets there in time." In the midst of persecution and interrogation, we were honored to be the ones to take the message of life to the Bouyei.

———— • ————

I had been in China for a total of five years by then, and ministry began to click. I knew it was not of my own doing, but because of God's grace upon my life and through the relationships He had brought along the journey. Connections with pastors and Christian leaders in the underground Chinese Church grew into friendships. A mutual trust flourished. They knew that I desired to stand behind indigenous missionaries, providing ministry platforms for them to succeed in their own unique callings.

I built a team of like-minded Chinese young people, raising them up in their faith, and discipling them as Great Commission Christians. I traveled to unreached villages with them. We sat side-by-side in some of Southwest China's most remote areas. And as they matured in their cross-cultural abilities, I sent them to the homes of ethnic-minority nationalities.

These relational partnerships with local ministers were inter-connected vertically and horizontally by an individual relationship with our Heavenly Father and through the unified brotherly love in the community. The fruit of these relationships led to thriving church plants among unreached people groups.

Through my studies of "Perspectives on the World Christian Movement" and by personal experience in the missionary endeavor, I came to the conclusion that my role should be one of empowerment of local ministry efforts. I knew the power of indigenous missionaries. They spoke the same language, shared a similar history, consumed the same delicacies, and understood the cultural nuances and intricacies of the target people group. They lived, breathed, and would die an intrinsic part of the society, not as an outsider looking into the culture through a foreign lens, but as an integral part of the whole.

The Gospel always enters an unreached area from the outside. That was one of the many unique roles of the foreign missionary: to create breakthrough and make headway. But during the course of a thriving church plant, permeation of culture could only have longevity when local missionaries spearheaded the movement.

God's gifts and callings for each Christian—whether foreign or local—are both unique and irrevocable. But serving in the capacity where we could be best utilized was paramount. For me, that meant standing behind the underground Chinese Church and seeing their ministry efforts thrive.

I vowed to assume this attitude of servant leadership far into the future, regardless of how my roles expanded in apostolic nature.

———— ◆ ————

One month before our wedding day, I returned to Manila, Philippines to help arrange final details. During this time, the relationship between Lorna's family and I grew closer. Lorna's mother had already begun referring to me as her son-in-law. I was blessed to be marrying into a family who loved and accepted me. Their care served to quell the nervous considerations of entering into a cross-cultural marriage.

As for Lorna, she had yet to meet my parents face-to-face. She heard their voices over the phone and spoke with them on Skype. She was assured of their love for her, but not until the final days before our wedding would she meet them in person.

Some of my missionary friends from Kunming flew to Manila to attend our wedding as well. Their presence was of utmost value to me.

The big day finally came. It was the culmination of the long-distance relationship Lorna and I had been waiting for nearly seven years.

December in Manila was usually a dry month. But today was atypical. I stood in Puerto Real where our wedding took place, nervous about the thunder clouds looming over the open garden. The gray sky hovered uncomfortably low over Manila Bay. I glanced toward the South China Sea, praying God would withhold the rain. We had not rented tents or canopies, and were not prepared for a wet day.

Lorna was in Diamond Hotel with her parents and bridesmaids. Makeup artists applied the final strokes of foundation and blush to her cheeks as she sat gazing out the window. She sent me a text message.

"I'm so nervous!" her text read. "I hope it doesn't rain. That would be terrible."

"I hope it doesn't, either," I replied by text message. "But whatever happens, today is going to be a memorable day!"

My mother stood beside me in the garden, wound tight with excitement and maternal pride.

"You're getting married today!" she reminded me.

"I know," I said. "I can't believe it!"

A cameraman signaled for our attention. My father stepped into the frame, and our euphoric smiles were captured in time with a single click.

The wedding party busied itself by arranging last minute details: tilting to perfection the silk lilac bows on the backs of white chairs; setting dinner tables symmetrically by number. They laid silverware beside each plate, folded pink napkins diagonally, and slid them between fork tines. The caterers added final dashes of salt to each dish as the musicians practiced their romantic melodies. Friends and family greeted me with warm hugs and excited handshakes.

"Oh no! It's starting to rain!" Lorna texted me again from Diamond Hotel. I imagined her standing in the reflection of a tall window, surveying the storm.

"It'll be okay, my dear," I replied by text. "Don't worry!"

But as soon as my text was sent, clouds shifted course from the sea toward the colonial Intramural walls, and the sky above was cracked with forks of lightning. I watched with horror as a torrential downpour soaked everything in sight. The finely trimmed lawn turned to a spongy, wilted bog as guests trampled the grassy life in search for cover from the storm. I stood under a stone arch, paralyzed with distress as one year of wedding preparations transformed into soggy shambles.

I thought of Lorna's efforts over the past year. I imagined her heart sinking at the thought of her special day being dowsed by the torrential storm. But come violent monsoon or typhoon, we were getting married today. The show must go on. I had not chased her seven years for nothing!

Then suddenly, as quickly as the deluge had begun, the waters ceased, and a single ray of sunlight burst between a crack in the clouds. To my left, on the far end of the corridor, at the Puerto Real gate, a vehicle pulled to a halt at the entrance of the garden. On the side of the car shown the logo of Diamond Hotel. The door opened slowly. Lorna stepped out of the vehicle, and plunged her silver high heels into a deep puddle. Her mother fumbled with her long wedding veil, trying desperately to keep the mud from staining her elegant, semi-translucent organza.

My heart leaped at the sight of her stunning beauty. She looked across the drenched lawn, and our eyes met. I noticed a single tear streak down her cheek as she waved at me. I blew her a kiss.

"David, you're not supposed to see the bride before the wedding!" My mom flung me around by my shoulders and blocked my view with her arms. I appreciated her traditionalism, laughed, but turned to catch one last glance of my bride before she ducked back inside the vehicle.

For over an hour, we waited in the marshy greens as the wedding party scurried over the grass, tidying up the décor. Our officiating pastor was stuck in one of Manila's infamous traffic jams, moving toward our venue at a snail's pace.

At five o'clock in the afternoon, on December 13, 2003, after everyone in the wedding party arrived, our ceremony began nearly two hours past schedule. But at that moment, when the symphony sounded, time was irrelevant. I walked down the white veiled isle, soaked in a memory that we would one day tell our children. I stood to the left of our minister and Lorna's pastor, Dan Balais.

White lanterns hung from twisted banyan tree vines, flickering with warm luminescence. The final hues of sunset departed beyond the expanse of the South China Sea.

I recall few of the formalities that took place until the bridal chorus commenced. Everyone stood to their feet, wide smiles stretched across their face, their shoes sinking into the mushy earth. The crowd erupted with applause as Lorna strode ever so slowly down the aisle. She carefully tried to maintain her balance while her high heels submerged into the grassy turf with each step.

Our wedding day was filled with magic and applause; with two golden rings, a promise, and a lingering kiss. White doves and butterflies were released, flapping their wings and fluttering in the amorous breeze. Bubbles wafted skyward as confetti floated to the earth. Two individuals merged into one that evening, never to be torn apart or separated again.

Our parting teardrops over the past seven years evaporated in the folds of a memory. Sadness faded away as the flower of hope bloomed within our hearts.

"I love you, Lorna."

"I love you forever, David."

Later that night, we returned to Diamond Hotel, embraced one another, and gazed down at the silent commotion of the city. We lingered there—side-by-side, like we always stood—and looked out into the distance. Come what may, we were no longer alone. Perhaps we had never been alone after all, cradled in a holy embrace over the last seven years.

The rain fell only once that month, on the thirteenth day of December, a romantic tale that would permeate our imaginations for a lifetime.

Chapter 9

BARREN

"The Lord will comfort Israel again and have pity on her ruins.
Her desert will blossom like Eden, her barren wilderness like the garden
of the Lord. Joy and gladness will be found there.
Songs of thanksgiving will fill the air."
ISAIAH 51:3

Five weeks after our wedding, Lorna and I boarded a flight from Manila to Kunming. She peeked out the plane window with watery eyes, watching a blur of tropical greenery stream past her view. A megacity of skyscrapers and scattered homes nestled between verdant green, which disappeared beyond view as we soared over the South China Sea. The islands of the Philippines perched stalwart upon the surface of the ocean.

Warm tears trickled down Lorna's cheek. Her parents were somewhere below, perhaps pointing at our plane, waving their last goodbyes. Her sisters were no doubt crying like my young bride beside me. Lorna wept, lamenting the loss of family, friends, and all that she held dear in her home behind us to the west.

The sting of separation was new to her. I sought to comfort her with an embrace; I knew all too well the sensation of loss that accompanied obedience to the missionary call.

On February 3, 2004, Lorna and I moved to China. We embarked upon the adventure of cross-cultural ministry, no longer alone, finally together, seeking to advance the Kingdom of God to regions that knew it not.

In presenting cultural intricacies to my helpmate, China became fresh again. What had become commonplace—even boring—now bounded with newness. Lorna's China adventure had begun, and in her eyes sparkled the childlike wonder that was once mine.

She moved into my apartment at Jinshi District in northern Kunming. In the morning, as early sunlight fell in skewed angles through the window, we sipped coffee and read the Bible together. In the evening, the aroma of Filipino dishes permeated the dining room. The space between was filled with romantic gestures and sweet whispers as our honeymoon lingered far longer than planned.

Lorna hung flowers around the edges of family portraits, and we painted our apartment walls in a colorful faux finish. She set decorations on corner tables, scrupulous about every detail. A home began to emerge within the walls of our little apartment.

We lived between cultures, appreciating the American and Filipino values we shared, absorbing the varying aspects of China's ethnological mores.

Lorna began to study Mandarin Chinese. Her tutor came twice a week, and I sat in the living room, listening to my wife repeat her teacher's tonal sentences. It was Lorna's third language, and I was proud to see her thriving in her missional calling. I was blessed to be on this adventure with her.

Our missionary life as newlyweds on the field brimmed with the dazzling mosaic of exotic colors, sights, and sounds.

We lived in the midst of millions of college students and ethnic peoples. That excited us. Our callings were merging in unison, and we found constant joy in the journey.

We teamed with vision, watching the purposes of God unfold before our eyes, and anticipating greatness. We did not yet comprehend the impact our ministry would one day mature into. But every day in China seemed like a big day to us, one that might tip the scale of souls rushing headlong into Heaven.

———— ◆ ————

Every Thursday night at eight o'clock, week after week, Lorna and I bused downtown to Green Lake Park where Chinese university students gathered to practice their foreign language skills. It was the most popular English corner in the city. University students had been assembling on the sidewalk for over a decade. Lorna and I routinely joined the cross-cultural exchange, and gradually became well-known foreign guests.

The regulars were there, friends and acquaintances, eager to strike up a conversation regarding US/Sino relations or American perception of Bill Clinton's presidency. The students queried our stance on the renegade province of Taiwan, on the validity of the communist party, and whether or not we could introduce them to a foreign boyfriend or girlfriend.

Personalities of every type huddled together, encircling visiting foreign guests. There were handshakes and pleasantries, shy introductions, blushing cheeks, and broad smiles. Particularly extroverted pupils shamelessly requested our contact information, volunteering to tour us around the city and show us the sites. The introverts generally remained silent, tucked at the fringes of the crowd, trying to make sense of the conversation. Their English skills were not up to par with the outspoken types, and they struggled with the basics.

"What is your name?"

"Where are you from?"

"Do you like Chinese food?"

At English corner, no one was a stranger. It was easy to make new friends, to catch glimpses of China's cultural values and survey the landscape in search for hungry hearts. Lorna and I found it the perfect setting to share the Gospel with college students and young professionals who showed interest in spiritual matters.

There were two geographical settings of our early ministry together: the rural and the urban. Village work required intentional mapping, long hours of travel, strategic missional efforts among culturally distinct tribes, and deliberate styles of evangelism, discipleship, and church planting. Christian ministry in rural regions of the province was not easy, hence the shortage of missionary presence outside the populated cities.

But there was a new social landscape forming in China as pockets of society made their way to burgeoning urban centers in search for jobs, college degrees, and a brighter future.

China was historically known as an agrarian country. Eighty percent of the massive population resided in the countryside, and only twenty percent made their home in the cities. But that was changing. China's great uprooting had commenced. A new urban migration plan prompted millions of residents to leave their rural homes for the city life.

The migration demanded new ministry methods to reach transient communities. We called it reaching unreached people groups in urban settings. We gravitated toward the college student population. This spiritually-hungry demographic broke kinship ties, lived in a pluralistic environment, and were open to new ideas. It was not difficult to make disciples of them.

Fruit fell from the trees in modern China. It was ripe and ready for the picking. A great cloud of witnesses had gone before us—

missionary heroes of the past—many of whose blood stained the soil, causing scattered seeds to germinate for generations.

There was British missionary James Hudson Taylor, who arrived in Shanghai in 1854 after a five-month voyage from England. He spent fifty-one years ministering in China, spearheaded pioneer missionary work and founded China Inland Mission. His mission society was responsible for bringing over eight-hundred missionaries to the country, resulting in tens of thousands of salvations. His faithful obedience paved the way for countless others to impact China.

Samuel Pollard was posted to Yunnan Province in 1888 and remained in China as a missionary until his death from typhoid. During his mission, he traveled extensively, founding churches and training other missionaries. His greatest achievement was the invention of a written language for the Miao people. He used the script to translate the New Testament, and countless thousands of Miao came to Christ.

James O. Fraser first arrived in Yunnan Province in 1910 and spent nearly thirty years working among the Lisu tribe. He created an alphabet for the Lisu, which was used to translate the New Testament. After six arduous years of ministering among the Lisu people, he and fellow missionaries saw scores of families convert to Christianity, enthusiastically pursuing a new life without the fear of the spirits that had previously characterized them. Less than one-hundred years later, the Chinese government acknowledged that over ninety percent of the Lisu in China were Christian.

Born in China to his missionary parents, Eric Liddell was enrolled in a boarding school in London at six years of age. He later won an Olympic medal in the 400-meter sprint, and in 1925 he returned to China to serve as a missionary teacher. He died in China twenty years later due to overwork, malnourishment, and an inoperable brain tumor.

Harold and Josephine Baker began a rescue mission for street children in Yunnan Province, and in the 1930's the children in the home began to have spiritual experiences, claiming to have seen heaven through a series of visions.

In 1934, John and Betty Stam were new missionaries to China, with their three-month-old daughter, Helen. Shortly before his beheading and the murder of his wife, John Stam concluded a letter to his mission agency with Philippians 1:20: "May Christ be glorified whether by life or death."

Gladys Aylward took in abandoned orphans, intervened in volatile prison riots, and risked her life many times to help those in need. In 1938, the region was invaded by Japanese forces, and Aylward led over one-hundred orphans to safety over the mountains, despite being wounded herself.

These little-known heroes brought the Gospel to China's inland and ushered in the Kingdom of God to regions that knew it not.

But despite the expulsion of all foreign missionaries in 1949, the Spirit of God was alive and at work in the country. The dark days of China's Cultural Revolution ended, and echoes of revival reverberated over the expanse of time.

Lorna and I were now in China for such a time as this. We were small parts of the missionary task force, and our glorious calling was to be end-time harvesters.

We began by gathering a small handful of college students. We invited them to our apartment for home-cooked meals and walked them through a discipleship process. We started our own English corner; and gradually, the gathering of young people grew.

Our strategy was simple and organic. It was built upon relationships. We cooked together, ate together, laughed together, and wept together with students as they disclosed family struggles they faced.

It was life-on-life ministry, a transference of spiritual DNA, a welcoming of the Holy Spirit's presence. Our task felt effortless because God was always at work. We simply joined Him where He was, and He supernaturally weaved us into the tapestry of the local fabric.

It seemed like the stars were aligning. The ministry was thriving. Things were on the up and up. After my years of toil in Southwest China, my wife and I began to see fruit. It was a gift of grace to us. Mere months after we were married, we enjoyed the harvest together with little exertion. Though there were occasional setbacks and struggles, we continued on with more merriment than plodding.

Our relationship with local Chinese Christians deepened. We partnered with an underground Bible school on the outskirts of the city, imparting into them a mission's passion and challenge for purity in their relationships. Lorna was an excellent speaker on the topic of love, courtship, and marriage. After seven years in a long distance relationship, she had much to share from her personal experience.

Young Chinese believers asked if they could join us on our travels to the rural countryside. Many of the Bible students themselves grew up in village settings and represented a number of China's ethnic people groups. We were honored to have them join us, and the beginnings of a small local missionary team was birthed.

While in the city, they helped us disciple college students who were coming to Christ. The harvest was ripe, but the willing hands were few. Our new Chinese team brought a fresh approach to ministry through an indigenous style of outreach.

Nearly every month, we spent long hours on the road, traveling to unreached and unengaged villages. The experience was different than it had previously been. Our local missionaries were steeped in the culture, able to penetrate invisible ethnologic boundaries with more ease than foreigners. A whole new horizon opened to us. The possibilities were endless. Partnering with local Christians would become paramount in reaching the least reached peoples of Southwest China.

———————— ◆ ————————

In May 2004, during my morning quiet time, the Holy Spirit spoke to me from the book of Isaiah: *"Every valley shall be raised up, every mountain and hill made low; the rough ground shall become level, the rugged places a plain."*

Immediately, I recalled my previous travels to Hekou City, which bordered Vietnam on the Southeast corner of Yunnan Province. Years earlier, Frederik and I traveled extensively throughout the area, trekking from village to village, sharing the Gospel. I was reminded of the Yao tribe, an unreached people group who resided high in the mountains.

At times like these, when the Lord spoke to me about a particular geographic location, I rarely deliberated whether or not God was calling me to the area. His purpose seemed clear in Psalm 37:4, that when my delight was in the Him, my desires naturally aligned with His desires. I gave little consideration to the validity of His voice. I knew that He was calling Lorna and me to go to the mountainous region.

"Honey, I feel like God is telling us to go to Hekou," I told Lorna.

"Sounds good!" she replied, ever eager to follow the leading of the Holy Spirit.

That was all it took for us to head south to the border town the following week.

On May 27, 2004, Lorna and I borrowed a friend's truck and drove seventeen hours from Kunming to Hekou. We departed at five o'clock in the morning and arrived past ten o'clock at night. I was exhausted after a long day of driving. We grabbed a late dinner, checked into a cheap hotel, and crashed for the night.

The following morning, we set out to find Yao villages. Traveling these country roads with my wife was an altogether new experience. My journeys with missionary counterparts over the years were full of adventure, but Lorna became my favorite traveling buddy.

We traversed the hillsides together, passing slowly along precipitous inclines that overlooked banana and pineapple plantations. Yao Mountain was rich with tropical fruit that supplied many cities throughout China.

For five hours, we edged along the mountain roads in search of the tribe, but to no effect. We were perplexed that there atop Yao Mountain we were unable to find Yao communities.

The arduous drive brought fatigue. I became increasingly agitated. Exhaustion set in and my mood turned cross. But still, I drove over the dusty lanes, exploring narrow trails that forked along the roadside.

At long length, we came to a makeshift shack where two young men perched in the shade, severing banana clusters from their thick trunks.

I leaned out the window and called for their attention.

"Are you Yao?" I asked in enervated tone.

"Shi de," one of the young men replied. "We are."

I turned off the engine and stepped down from the vehicle. Lorna and I joined the young men in the shaded space beneath the roadside shanty. We slumped upon the small stool they offered us and reclined against the lean-to.

We rested there for ten minutes, chatting with the young Yao men. But they seemed indifferent to our conversation.

Suddenly, a middle-aged man emerged from the mountain slope behind the shack. At the edge of the trail, he stopped in his tracks and stared at me. An incredulous look washed over his face. He squinted, seeking to recollect a memory buried in his mind. A broad smile gradually stretched across his face.

"Wo gen ni jian guo mian!" he announced enthusiastically. "I have seen you before!"

"Zhen de ma?" I responded. "Where did we meet?"

I considered my journeys with Frederik many years earlier. We had crossed these mountains before, but I had no recollection of the Yao man.

"Five years ago, I was working at a restaurant in Xishuangbanna City," he told me. "You arrived with a group of foreigners, and I waited on your table."

I was surprised by his memory. I remembered the short-term missions team I led to the southern city many years ago. And now here we were, hundreds of miles across the province, sharing a providential moment with the Yao man. But his story did not end there.

"I remember after I brought food to your table, you and your friends bowed your heads and prayed. At the time, I did not know what you were doing. All I remember from your prayer was the word 'Amen.'"

The man paused, caught in the nostalgic folds of memory. The moment from a time long ago began to open, like the bloom of a flower awakening after a long winter.

"I asked my coworkers what 'Amen' meant," the man continued. "One of them had seen an American movie, and he guessed that it was how a prayer should end."

He told us that after that experience, his interest in spiritual matters piqued. He began to search for answers about God, but he did not know any Christians. He knew of no churches in Xishuangbanna City, and so his fascination waned with time.

The years shifted into forgetfulness, and he returned home to Yao Mountain to manage his banana plantation. Now, Lorna and I were here, on one of our first rural trips to the countryside together, unaware that we stood on the cusp of revival.

"Ni jiao shenme mingzi?" I asked the man.

"My name is Deng Chunfu," he replied.

"I'm David," I introduced myself. "This is my wife, Lorna. It's nice to meet you officially!"

I stretched out my hand, and the moment our palms clasped in a handshake, something supernatural happened. There was a sudden spark of divine revelation, a quickening of spiritual understanding at the human touch. I sensed the Holy Spirit reveal Deng Chunfu's situation to me, and so I boldly began to speak into his life.

"You left your wife and children at home," I said. "You have not been faithful to love and provide for them. It's time you returned to your family."

I was surprised by my own words. It was unlike me to be so direct, calling to the floor personal issues with a stranger. But I felt the truth being spoken through me was relevant and applicable. So, I continued.

"God wants to tell you that He sees your heart. He recognizes your desire to be a godly covering for your family. Today, He is giving you another chance to meet Him. He is ready to help you become the man you were created to be."

This was not your typical cultural greeting. The atmosphere was thick with angelic presence. Still, I was unsure how the man might respond to such direct words of knowledge.

Deng Chunfu lowered his head, struck with the overwhelming shame of a secret exposed. The truth was out, the discovery had been made, and immediately he began to weep. He embarrassingly struggled to wipe the tears from his cheeks.

I pulled my small stool closer and embraced him with a brotherly hug. I felt his shoulders convulse as he wept in the shade of the roadside hovel.

His tears subsided and clarity formed in his mind. "What should

I do now?" he asked, mentally sifting through the realm of possibilities in his precarious position.

Lorna sat beside me, praying for wisdom and truth to be revealed to the Yao man.

"It's time for you to meet God's Son, Jesus Christ," I responded. "He alone can help you become the man of God that your family needs."

Lorna and I stood to our feet. There was an urgency about the moment that called for an immediate response. We were reminded of A Song of Ascents in the book of Psalm: *"Those who go out weeping, carrying seed to sow, will return with songs of joy, carrying sheaves with them."* The hour of reaping was upon us, and we filled with a holy delight.

Deng Chunfu stood to his feet and followed us in prayer. He gave his life to the Lord there on the hillside beneath his highland home.

It was a divine encounter that I had not anticipated. Humanly speaking, it was impossible to arrange a meeting like this. But over the last five years, God was at work, orchestrating our steps until we would meet atop this mountain.

When our prayer ended, Lorna and I challenged Deng Chunfu with a bold proposition.

"Do you want to come to Kunming with us?" I asked. "There are many Christians there who will teach you how to follow Jesus."

It did not take long for Deng Chunfu to respond. Though he had nothing prepared for a seventeen-hour journey to the capital city, straightaway he joined us in the back seat of our vehicle. We began down the rural road, excited about what may come from the first fruits of the Yao tribe.

For the next two months, Lorna and I discipled Deng Chunfu in his new faith. Local Chinese Christians modeled to him the grace of God, and he poured over the scriptures enthusiastically.

We sent him back home to Yao Mountain, instructing him to

share his Christian faith with family and friends. Within one month, he reported that his younger brother and cousin gave their lives to the Lord as well.

Deng Chunfu returned to Kunming with two new young men, eager to understand the things of God. And for the next month, they were also introduced to the underground Christian Church. They grew in their newfound faith, memorized scripture, and underwent our discipleship process. We baptized them in a public swimming pool before sending them back to their village.

Not long after they returned home, Deng Chunfu called us with good news. "I have twelve more young people who want to become Christians!" he said. "Can I take them to Kunming?"

Lorna and I were astonished at the quick work God was doing among the Yao tribe. A breakthrough like this had never been seen among the unreached people group. It was a prolific season of Spirit-led revival, and we were humbled to be a part of the initial breakthrough.

———— ◆ ————

It is a rare sight to behold a seed break the surface of the soil; to witness a fragile stem rise from the earth's crust. Rarer still is it to see the antrorse stalk bend upward, and its leaf begin the early formation. The sprouting of bud into flower is often overlooked, for such observations demand faithful patience.

I waited for years, restless and expectant. I hoped that my ministry flower might bloom. I prayed that the seeds sown into Asian soil would produce a substantial harvest. I heard the whispers of slow growth amidst the shacks and shanties, along stony paths that disappeared into distant wildernesses. But I had yet to observe the springtime crops sprouting bountifully across expansive landscapes.

Life transformation does not happen all at once. It is a slow growth, and often a painstaking thing to anticipate.

New souls came into the Kingdom, and the seeds of revival budded. But frontier missionary efforts never ensue without a struggle. We were reminded of that reality in July 2004.

Lorna and I returned to Yao Mountain to follow up with the many young people who had given their lives to the Lord. There was an excitement in the air and a stirring in our spirits. We spent days traveling from village to village in search of hungry hearts.

But little did we realize that everything was about to change. The demonic hordes who held Yao communities in their clutches for millennium were unwilling to surrender these young lives without a fight. They took to the mountains and valleys, piqued and positioned for battle.

It was yet another long drive from the Vietnam border back home to Kunming. I was particularly exhausted after traversing the rural countryside, so we decided to spend the night in Gejiu City, a midway point along the journey. In the back of our vehicle were two more young men whom we invited to join our discipleship course.

The day happened to be my twenty-sixth birthday. Lorna secretly packed a bottle of merlot and two wine glasses, and she planned a small celebration for me in the hotel that evening. At eleven o'clock at night, we checked into the hotel, travel-weary, but joy-filled at what God performed in our midst.

"Happy birthday, David!" Lorna clinked her glass of wine against mine and kissed me. "I am so proud to be your wife."

"Thank you, honey!" I was surprised by her romantic gesture. "I'm happy we get to experience this journey together."

But our celebration was interrupted by a sudden knock on the hotel door. I set my glass of wine on the table and peered through the peephole. Four police officers stood in the hallway outside. My heart dropped.

"I can't believe this," I whispered to Lorna. "The cops are here on my birthday!"

Before opening the door, Lorna hurriedly removed the Bibles and Christian materials from our bag, stashing them under the bed.

These were precarious geographic locations. Our ministry intersected with areas where the social and political struggle was palpable. We ministered along routes where young Vietnamese girls were trafficked into China as sex slaves. Numerous divisive, state-opposed cults infiltrated the region, causing chaos among uneducated residents. Government authorities struggled to maintain stability amidst civil disobedience and were unable to distinguish between upright Christian endeavors and anti-government upheaval.

I cracked the door and peeked outside.

"Can I help you?" I asked.

"Please come with us," the police ordered.

"Is there a problem?" I played dumb.

"We'll find out soon enough," came their unnerving reply.

Hotel staff alerted the police that foreign visitors were traveling with locals, so they wanted to question me about our intentions.

For the next four hours, I was interrogated in a dimly lit hotel room. They raised their voices in a show of force, seeking to pry information about the young men who accompanied us. They informed me that they would be taking our Yao friends into custody. I was adamant that I would not allow that to happen. I was dubious of their intentions, unsure how the young men would be treated. A paternal boldness overtook me. I, too, raised my voice, and the room rang vociferously. I stood up for the young lives in my care, infused with righteous fervor.

But I was outnumbered, and at three o'clock in the morning, after a prolonged shouting match, the police led me back to my hotel room. They departed with our innocent local friends.

I was overwhelmed by a sense of failure. Lorna and I wept in our hotel room, filled with deep grief and regret. We were unable to protect our young disciples. We did not know what the police planned to do with them. We tried to rest, but sleep was elusive. In the wee hours of the morning, we finally dozed off, flitting in and out of fitful dreams.

A few hours later, Lorna and I awoke, shaken and dismayed. Our new friends were gone. We had no idea where they were taken or how they fared. We were left with no choice but to continue our journey back to Kunming.

———— • ————

The recalcitrant event startled new Yao Christians and the revival we expected ebbed. A rampant harvest withered at the stem, ripe branches drooped to the earth, and fruit shriveled.

As time went by, Lorna and I were left disillusioned and downcast. It seemed victory had come to the enemy, and we felt the sting of defeat. We grew fatigued at the lack of fruit in our ministry, and we were on the verge of burnout.

We experienced persecution first hand, the outcome of which slowed the growth of our missional efforts.

Months passed, and the struggle ensued. It seemed that ministry among the Yao tribe had come to an end. The outreach appeared useless and dormant.

We gathered our local missionary team, questioning whether or not we should discontinue our efforts among the unreached people group.

I will never forget their enthusiastic response.

"We won't stop trying to reach the Yao people," one of our local missionaries said. "The ministry might seem barren. But remember, the harvest is in the seed."

His encouraging words propelled us to continue seeking to save the lost. Who knew if there was still an oak tree germinating within the acorn? It might take years to witness the harvest, but still, the seed must be sown.

Confucius once said, "If you are planning for a year, sow rice; if you are planning for a decade, plant trees; if you are planning for a lifetime, educate people."

We would continue to bring the message of salvation to the Yao. We would not throw in the towel just yet. We were set on educating them with God's truth: that He loved them, and that His heart burned for them.

But the months turned into years, and privation in ministry was only one side of our story.

———— ✦ ————

We desired to start a family; but month after month, the situation seemed impossible. We were unable to conceive, and so we sought the advice of doctors in China. We underwent a series of health check-ups to understand the source of our infertility. The results were disheartening. Every doctor we saw informed us that we would never be able to conceive.

It was a season of heartbreak that would last for years.

We traveled to the Philippines, Thailand, and America in search for an alternate medical opinion. But the results were the same. Doctors in four different countries told us that we would never be able to have children of our own.

The hypothesis of infertility plagued Lorna. "Barren" became a four-letter word to her. Still, she clung to the promises of God. She meditated on covenants in scripture from Psalm 113:9: *"He gives the childless woman a family, making her a happy mother."* She memorized the encouraging words from Psalm 127:3-5: *"Children are a gift from the Lord, they are a reward from Him. Children born to a young man are like arrows in a warrior's hands. How joyful is the man whose quiver is full of them!"*

But every month, we were reminded of the reality of our situation. Discarded failed pregnancy tests laced our rubbish bins; and we sat together, dismayed, praying God would open Lorna's womb.

Joy in the journey became difficult to find. We were mystified by our state of affairs, wondering if our home would ever be filled with the sound of a child's laughter.

We plodded on, of course, discipling Chinese college students who joined our English corners. We continued raising up young people in their faith, partnering with underground churches and Bible schools. And nearly every month, we found ourselves atop rural villages, sharing the Gospel among unreached tribes.

But the lingering cognizance of our family situation reflected in ministry efforts as well. A tinge of doubt and dismay percolated just beneath the surface of our activities. In the midst of it all, we knew that God drew us toward unswerving trust in His providential design.

Throughout my many years of life and ministry in Asia, I've found that God is ever the Master Artist, penning a marvelous narrative, painting a dramatic masterpiece, orchestrating a symphonic musical. His imagination was wild and creative with turns and twists in each artistic stroke genius.

His narration was explicit, though I would have rather the story take an alternate direction. Colorful paint splattered upon white canvas in seemingly careless fashion. But who dares doubt the inspiration of the Artist? Operatic accents filled my senses. The Conductor's hands gesticulated in an excited manner; He, Himself, lured into the ecstatic delight of the music.

And where God makes masterpieces, it is only natural that spontaneous joy emanates.

But at the natural state of things, uncertainty loomed at the forefront of our minds. "Hope deferred makes the heart sick," King Solomon once said. A chronic malady pervaded our hearts. We lifted our eyes to the hills, asking from where our help came from. But the Heavens seemed like brass.

Lorna began copying every promise from the word of God into her diary. She even started writing a special journal of notes to our unborn child. Within the pages of the little book, she penned ardent words. She shared the struggles of her present journey, and how she could not wait to meet her baby face-to-face. It was an emotional narrative, one that evoked faint hope in the midst of apprehension.

Journal to our Future Child, April 29, 2008: "My child, today I was inspired to write you a journal. I have been longing to see you, to hug you, to wrap my arms around you. I imagine your tiny body, your cute smile, and your faint whimpers. I am waiting expectantly for you to arrive!"

———◆———

Our tale of infertility lasted for nearly a decade. It took us over arid, sandy plains and scorched by the sun. It felt that we traversed the sloping desert banks, espying an occasional oasis in a low-lying basin. But as we stumbled in the direction of the aquifer, we found again that it was just a mirage.

The hot air played tricks on our senses, distorting distant images, an optical illusion of turbulence and vibration. And all the while, our lips chapped with an insatiable thirst in the barren landscape.

Hope deferred far too long. Over the years, Lorna underwent four intrauterine inseminations, but our every attempt to conceive culminated in failure.

The medical procedures took a toll on my wife's body, and her hormonal balance was interrupted. Her body began to decline, and insomnia set in. It was painful to watch Lorna struggle both physically and emotionally.

I, too, was emotionally drained. My prayers became peppered with expletives as I questioned the purposes of God. His ways were higher than my own. So lofty, in fact, that confusion clotted my senses. Still, He somehow managed to comprehend the deep longings of my heart; and in His mercy, He revealed Himself at intervals along the journey.

For eight years, Lorna and I lived through the highest of highs and the lowest of lows. We reveled in the mountaintop experiences. We rejoiced as many young people came to Christ. And in the valley of the shadow of death, we clutched each other, creeping forward in our dim surroundings, praying the next steps would lead us to distant, unseen light.

Barrenness. We would not allow the word to define our marriage. We would resist the fictitious guile that sought to cripple our ministry. Though month after month, we grappled with the knowledge of infertility, we would not accept the notion as actuality.

We clasped each others' hands, impregnated with a sudden burst of hope. Lorna looked deep into my eyes, and declared with conviction, "This too shall pass."

Rememories

THE BEGGAR

"What each man is in Your eyes, thus he is, and no more."
FRANCIS OF ASSISI

Wintery air flurried through Jinri Park, encircling bony, ginkgo trees, brushing against bare human skin. The last of stubborn autumn leaves gripped wooden limbs and jittered in the breeze like decrepit, quivering fingers. Careless passersby trod upon fallen leaves, crushing the veined blades beneath high heels and pointy-toed dress shoes.

I sat on the sidewalk outside Parkson Mall, releasing the week's journey into the blank leaves of my journal. My view from the raised stairway was the perfect vantage point. I surveyed the mismatched crowd of wealthy residents and street beggars, and both mingled inadvertently.

I passed the time people-watching, penning thoughtful prose. It was a therapeutic pastime, a sort of meditative means of releasing pent up missionary emotion.

Across the tiled plaza, a young beggar sat in the flow of foot traffic, imploring pedestrians for charity. She must have been seven or eight years old, far too young for a life of survival like this.

She wore tattered, dark-blue pants, soiled at the knees from long hours of bowing to strangers. Her pink shirt was torn at the hem; the neckline laced with embroidered red roses. Her cheeks smeared with dirt and streaked with dried tears. Her oily hair cinched in a ponytail, her bangs cutting across her forehead in particularly oriental fashion. Her eyes were black as the night sky, deep and hollow with occasional glints of starry reflections.

The little beggar girl was barefoot and had a stub where her left arm once grew. I found myself imagining her as a child, girlish and innocent. I imagined her cradling a rag doll while running along hilly plains in her countryside village. She ran across the sloping landscapes and pretended she could fly. The horizon was wide, and her imagination brought her as far as her eyes could see. She did not yet comprehend the earthbound grip of gravity.

But now those dreams vanished, faded memories in the back of her mind. Instead, she sat on the cemented grounds of Jinri Park, a stub for her left arm, her rag doll replaced with a tin can in her right hand.

I closed the pages of my journal and weaved through the crowded plaza toward the little girl. I stopped a few feet from her. When she noticed me, she bowed to the sidewalk then lifted her head again. Her deep, forlorn eyes locked in silent hopelessness, seemingly ready to burst into tears at any moment.

"Uncle, gei wo qian," she pleaded quietly. "Give me money."

Empathy took hold of me, and I dropped a few coins into her tin can. The clanking din rang in my ears. It was a dreadfully hollow resonation; a tinny sound I have never forgotten.

"Xiexie, shushu," she murmured without smiling. "Thank you, uncle."

My memory of that moment is drained of color. White high heels and black, pointy-toed dress shoes shuffled around the little girl in slow-motion. I stared at the wide seams between gray cement tiles that stretched across the park, and felt helpless.

Though I often extended small generosities to street-side beggars, it never made me feel like a saint. My deeds were heartfelt, but the offerings unreasonably meager. The scanty sums could not alleviate poverty or mitigate such terrible misery. For as Mother Teresa aptly stated, "Loneliness and the feeling of being unwanted is the most terrible poverty."

Poverty is deceiving. We have the lamentable tendency to see the exterior privation without recognizing the internal heart cry. We gather human value into inaccurate categories, classifying people merely by outward appearance. But tattered clothing and empty pockets don't tell the whole story of a beggar's life.

———————◆———————

I regularly traveled twenty-four hours from Kunming city to Dadong Village, home to the former headhunting Wa tribe on the Myanmar border. For years, I sowed the Gospel message into this people group and began to see breakthrough in the impoverished region.

On one particular journey, after many days of hiking through rugged, uncharted territory, my L5S1 disc shifted, and my back went out. Late in the evening, I fell to the ground in excruciating pain. I was unable to stand on my own. Two young Wa men lifted me into the back of a handheld tractor, and we began the eight-mile descent toward the hospital in Cangyuan city.

I laid in the rear wagon of the handheld tractor, wincing in agony. A tiny Wa granny cradled me in her lap, and lovingly brushed my forehead as we jerked and trembled over the rugged dirt trail.

The pale moon hung low over precipitous mountain ranges. Silhouettes of alpine bamboo swayed in the muggy breeze. And all the while, the affectionate eyes of the Wa granny gazed down at me with compassion.

In the midst of severe pain, I was suddenly struck by a divine revelation. The former headhunting Wa tribe—one of the sweetest people groups I traveled to—were lost without remedy. Their affliction was staggering, their poverty crushing. Though the fields were white for harvest among this tribe, their voices were muted, and the Christian world did not realize their plight.

In my weakness, it dawned on me. I was a voice for the voiceless. I was the pioneer missionary, the church planter, the fundraiser, and the connector. I was called to stand in the gap for the unreached, to pray for them and to solicit others to do the same.

Two days later, I woke up in a tumbledown hospital in Cangyuan city, still groggy from the heavy drugs that trickled into my veins through an intravenous drip. But something had shifted in my thought process. The tender care of a tribal grandmother taught me a lesson in genuine human concern. It freed me to ditch the missionary beggar mentality to pursue a path of righteous advocacy.

Flashbacks of every beggar I had come across flooded my mind. At the forefront of these reflections was the little girl with a stub for her left arm. I resonated with her sense of shame and embarrassment because I had so often felt humiliation by my apologetic appeals for missionary support. And I was not alone in this cogitation.

The missionary often struggles with a beggar's mentality. I knew the work of the Lord was not dependent upon the alms of sympathetic donors or gleanings from wealthy Christians looking for tax exemptions. But when I appealed to the affluent for financial assistance, I often felt like a scrounger.

Like many other missionaries, I had been paralyzed by this erroneous beggar's mindset. But God recalibrated my mentality and revealed my true identity in Him. I was His son, a prince in the Kingdom of God. And riches were being laid up for me in a world beyond my eyes.

Why such a simple act of service from that Wa granny so transformed me, I am still unsure. Her small gesture changed my way of thinking about mission. From that moment on, I never felt like a beggar when asking for prayer and financial support for the ministry. I could see clearly now. I was a conduit of blessing, assured of my part to play in global missions.

The pious platitudes had been swept away. My pride melted, and with it went the beggarly shame of soliciting funds for the Great Commission. I realized that I needed more than monthly financial support from donors. I needed friendship, prayer, and a team of like-minded vision partners who would bring the Gospel to the unreached with me.

I am not a beggar, I told myself. *I am an advocate.*

———— • ————

Jesus' interaction with the poor was subversive. He would rather reveal secrets of His Father's heart for the penniless than merely offer them coins. The currency of Jesus' Kingdom is different than ours. His economy is based on self-sacrifice, and His currency is love.

"A generous person will prosper," King Solomon said. "Whoever refreshes others will be refreshed." The generosity of Jesus was a holistic altruism that bequeathed the whole Self. This was to Him true religion. Anything less was a pious shadow.

God was asking more from me than mere charity. He wanted me to demonstrate His Kingdom by bringing good news to the hopeless. He envisioned what the world could look like, and was calling me to join Him in the process of making that vision a reality. I felt His hand outstretch to me, requesting that I exchange the currencies of the world for His currency of love.

I began to look at poverty through a new lens. The real tragedy of the poor was the poverty of their aspirations. I wondered if I might lift the indigent up from their ashes to a higher plain of honor. I felt this might just be the way of the Savior.

I wondered how Jesus would have responded to the one-armed beggar girl. Perhaps He would have lifted her up, cradled her in His arms, and told her that she was a princess. He would have told her that she mattered, that she was of utmost value to Him. Maybe He would have caressed her rag doll and reminded her that she would fly someday.

———— ◆ ————

I caught myself staring at the seams between the cement tiles where the little beggar girl sat. Wealthy businessmen in pinstriped suits sauntered by with gaudy-outfitted women on their arms. But the girl sat silent and forlorn in a blurry contrast of shifting gray hues, her dirty, wind-burnt cheeks streaked with dry tears.

I could still hear the faint din of my coins reverberate in her tin can, a meager charity at best. She looked up at me with her hollow eyes, and my heart broke with love for her.

Shushu, zenme ban? she thought silently. *Uncle, what can you do for me?*

A chilled breeze suddenly passed through the branches of a bony tree in Jinri Park. No one noticed a single browned leaf fall quietly to the ground. No one was aware of the crackling sound it made as it was crushed beneath careless, unintentional shoes.

The little beggar girl and the Wa grandmother represented Asia's poorest of the poor. Yet they presented to me a rich revelation of God's Kingdom. They were the oppressed and marginalized. Yet they showed me how to love the broken and needy. They inspired me to act justly, to love mercy, and to walk humbly with God.

What could I do to bring the Kingdom of Heaven and see positive social change? I could open my mouth and continue to speak on behalf of the underprivileged, for I was no longer a beggar. I became an advocate.

Chapter 10

CUT ME OPEN

"In my deepest wound I saw Your glory, and it astounded me."
SAINT AUGUSTINE

Day after day, nothing seemed to change. But when we turned to look back, we realized that everything was different.

The only constancy in our lives was change. We should not have been surprised by this, for there is certainty in the cycle of seasons. There is a time to plant and a time to uproot; a time to scatter stones and a time to gather them; a time to tear and a time to mend. Over and over, it occurs: growth then decay then transformation.

Season by season, this alteration takes place at the discerning hand of the Gardener. He understands the times, trusting that seed sown into the fertile soil will produce a bountiful harvest. He does not worry when spring turns to summer, and the scorching sun beats on the earth, threatening to destroy future yield. Time of reaping will come, He knows. So, He wipes the perspiration from His brow and enjoys the varied climates. As slow death befalls the summer green, causing orange and brown to appear on leaf and stem, He watches the steady descent of autumn colors crumple to the earth. The crisp chill of wintery wind stifles the final hints of life, and all is silent once again. A broad smile forms on His face as He waits, expectant of a new spring.

And all the while He cuts and prunes, fostering fresh growth from scarred branches and knobby knots.

A monumental transition was soon to occur in our lives. Something loomed upon the horizon. We sensed the whispers of its imminent arrival, and Lorna and I sought the Lord for direction.

Our partner churches grew in number. They sent short-term missions teams to join our college student outreach and village ministry in China. With the help of these teams, our reach extended far beyond what we were able to accomplish alone. These churches and individuals helped us cast the big net of evangelism into university campuses and rural landscapes. And the catch was substantial. Many young people heard the Gospel message for the very first time.

Our friends around the world recognized the impact being made through our ministry, so they joined our vision for unreached peoples. These vision partners were dear to us, not only because they sowed prayerfully and financially into our efforts, but because the compassion of Jesus united our hearts.

But the expectations were raised. Financial stewardship became paramount to Lorna and me. A sacred responsibility was placed on our shoulders, and we sought to oversee faithfully the ministry God bestowed upon us.

It was evident that our mom-and-pop's shop ministry was expanding. No longer was this the lonely ambition of my single years. It became larger than a family on mission. A legitimate platform would now be required.

In October 2008, Lorna and I established a 501c3 non-profit

organization. We called it "Within Reach Global." Unreached people groups at the fringe of global evangelization were finally within reach.

Our vision was clear: "Honor God and reach the unreached." Our methods remained intact: to evangelize, disciple, and plant churches. Compassion for the poor continued at the nucleus of the ministry. But now the platform expanded, and our missionary team was about to see breakthrough like never before.

Lorna and I were already blessed with a dedicated group of local missionaries. Among them, they represented six distinct minority nationalities. We traveled together extensively throughout Yunnan Province during our many outreach efforts.

Our local missionaries were nameless, faceless heroes. They were the forgettable ones of the world. You would never see their names in lights or their faces gracing the covers of best-selling Christian books. At first glance, you might not think much of them. They were the unassuming type: misfits and ragamuffins, a few bubbles off plumb. They were jars of clay, cracked and brittle, leaking. But they were filled with the all-surpassing power of God, and it flowed from their beings like a sweet oasis in desert plains.

Zhang Rong had been with us the longest. He was a fourth generation Christian from the Hani tribe. The gravestones of early 20th century Danish missionaries lay on a sloping flatland at the perimeter of his rural village, inspiring revival among his tribe for decades. Zhang Rong's shoulder length, jet-black hair curled at the edges, tangled and matted. His square jaw felt anomalous; his puffy lips and crooked smile awkwardly wonky and aslant. But his heart glinted gemlike. Grace and generosity mounted on his brow, and gentleness became the essential quality of his person. He was a gifted evangelist, a tenacious church planter with a pioneer spirit.

Liu Zhenmei brought a giddy, girlish jubilance to our missionary team. She was sassy and assertive, fearless in the face of adversity and unswerving under persecution. Stick-straight hair cut across her forehead in the most oriental fashion, fluttering back and forth with her eccentric gesticulations. She did not know how to suppress a smile, and so her crooked front teeth were invariably visible. She challenged the status quo, and compassion compelled her to the most impoverished regions.

Zhou Guangming joined our ministry team in an outlandish manner. We found him writhing on the ground, demon-possessed and foaming at the mouth. After the exorcism and deliverance, clarity returned, and he immediately committed himself to the purposes of God. After he had fallen from a tree at age six, the tragic childhood accident left his right leg shriveled and atrophied. But although Guangming could not walk without crutches, he grew so accustomed to his condition that he overlooked his handicap. We did not view him as a cripple but as a stalwart evangelist and powerful prophetic voice.

Then there was Deng Gaolin and Zhang Lifei, Li Fengwei, Li Tianliang, and Wang Jianming. These young men and women made up our indigenous team, and our foreign missionaries joined hearts and hands with them.

Hailing from the Philippines, John and Hannah Dela Cruz were the first of our international missionaries. John was a stocky Filipino man with trimmed goatee and mustache. There was a lightheartedness about him, a warmth within his taciturn manner. During his initial visit to China, he recognized grave hopelessness in the eyes of Chinese young people and compassion filled his heart. The fire of evangelism blazed, and a holy vision birthed within him. His wife, Hannah, joined her husband's passion for souls. She was a lovely, sweet-natured Filipina woman, a prayer warrior, and a peacemaker. Amity and fellowship were of utmost importance to her. Hers was a servant-heart, and her gift of hospitality blessed everyone around her.

This modest group of local and foreign trailblazers made up our missionary team. Some were focused on children's ministry on the border of Myanmar. Others impacted ethnic communities near Laos. Buddhist monks and witch doctors were led to Jesus. Young people were saved and set free at our English corners. Churches were planted and disciples were raised in China's most remote regions.

Everything we did was through relationship. We traveled together, dined on bizarre delicacies together, wept together, and shared each other's burdens.

This personal touch was paramount at Within Reach Global. Intimacy grew through proximity, shared experience, and trust. And though Lorna and I looked at our missionaries as co-workers and friends, they honored us as spiritual leaders and mentors. They playfully referred to us as "Papa David" and "Mommy Lorna." Yet, there was esteem in their terminology and the underlying tinge of veneration was heartfelt.

Our goal had always been to develop a ministry that operated by indigenous methods. We sought to empower local Chinese to reach their own country and beyond. We knew we would not be in China forever, and we prepared our local missionaries for this reality.

In July 2009, our ministry team gathered at Fuxian Lake on the outskirts of Kunming for our bi-annual missionary convention. We sat at the water's edge, listening to the monotonous ripples ebb and flow over the sandy lakefront.

Our eyes closed and the cadence of nature and praise played upon our senses. Zhou Guangming strummed his guitar, leading us in Mandarin worship: *Wode Shen wo yao jingbai Ni.* A chorus of bilingual voices blended in song: *Oh Lord, I want to worship You.*

Within Reach Global missionary conventions were a time of refreshing and refocusing. We shared prayer requests and praise reports from each of our outreach centers. Stories of persecution interweaved between testimonies of revival. The Kingdom of Heaven advanced in our midst. God was at work, and we reveled at each mission's report.

When worship ended, we closed in corporate prayer, thanking God for His presence and faithful leading. Our next order of service was future planning and strategizing. We sat in a circle on the sand, sensing a new season on the horizon.

"Where do you see yourselves in one year from now?" I asked the team. "What do you foresee in two years? In five years? What countries would you like to see God lead us to in the future? Take a moment to write down your thoughts, and we'll re-converge in fifteen minutes."

Our missionaries found private spots along the lakeside and sought God regarding the future of the ministry. It was a moment of stillness, of quieting our hearts, of recollecting our memories.

When we gathered again, each one shared specific direction from the Holy Spirit. Our list filled with multiple unreached tribes that we desired to impact. There were new ministry aspects to be considered, from drug rehabilitation to orphan care, ministry among trafficked women and serving the poor.

Five locations emerged as countries where we wanted to see breakthrough: China, Myanmar, Vietnam, Cambodia, and Laos.

After each team member had a chance to share, Lorna and I concluded the vision mapping with our personal plans.

"Though our hearts are in China, we will not live here forever," Lorna announced. "Someday soon, we believe God will call us to another nation."

Our co-workers gasped with surprise. Their love for us was unmistakable, and they were grieved at the thought of our departure.

"Don't worry," I encouraged them. "We're not leaving yet!"

But Lorna and I felt it necessary to prepare them for the day God would lead us elsewhere.

Within Reach Global continued to expand, but not without strain. New Chinese ministers joined our team. Individuals from America, Ireland, and the Philippines moved to China to volunteer at the ministry.

We saw new missionaries come, and others leave. It was a humbling process of learning to navigate the tides of Christian leadership while recognizing that we did not own anyone in ministry. We stewarded those who came to us until God moved them on. He was in control. He would watch over our efforts among the unreached. And it was amazing to see what could be accomplished when no one but God received the glory.

New outreach among the poor commenced. We partnered with like-minded ministries, sowing into the lives of underprivileged children and orphans. We began to make headway among drug-addicted communities in Myanmar. Over three-hundred kids came to Christ in the mountainous border region. They began prophesying and preaching the Gospel to their families. They prayed for the sick in their city. But the small revival would undergo severe persecution and the expulsion of our missionaries from the region.

As I reflected on the impact Within Reach Global saw in Southwest China, I was reminded of Pastor Samuel Lamb's words: "More persecution, more growth."

During the Cultural Revolution, the Chinese pastor underwent twenty-one years in forced labor camps simply for sharing the love of God. When he was finally released from prison, his church grew exponentially, and many more souls were added to the Kingdom.

During my early China years, I carried smuggled Bibles to Pastor Lamb's church in Shenzhen. I recalled Pastor Lamb's toothy smile as he reminded foreign missionaries of the truth he lived through.

"More persecution, more growth," he repeated the words like clockwork. "That is the history of the Church."

———— ◆ ————

Spring to summer, autumn to winter, Lorna and I experienced the shifting seasons cycle in a repetitive fashion. God's watchful eye was not only on our ministry but also on our hearts. We were like branches in His great vineyard, and in the quietness between each season, the Gardener came to tend His estate. He pulled back our thorny boughs, trimmed off our dry limbs, and severed our dead roots. God's knife was upon us. In His grace, He sought to grow within us eternal fruit. Few noticed these unpleasant moments of pruning. They watched from a distance and would only see the future fruit.

From a distance, a sprawling vineyard sloping over hilly plains is a beautiful sight to behold. But standing from within the verdant landscape, a closer look reveals more accurate details. The sweeping panorama is actually a series of broken branches, torn brush and bruised vine. Gashes where a hatchet once struck reveal age-old scars from which new offshoots sprout.

I pictured Jesus strolling along hilly landscapes like these with His disciples, perhaps through an orchard of pomegranates. Between the rows of plantation, Jesus ambled, His fingers brushing against the glossy, narrow-oblong leaves. The gentle caress of His skin upon the verdure elicited meditations of a Heavenly Kingdom, and He pondered eternal harvest.

"I am the True Vine and My Father is the Gardener," Jesus said to His disciples abruptly. "He cuts off every branch in Me that bears no fruit, while every branch that does bear fruit He prunes so that it will be even more fruitful."

His disciples were caught off guard. They followed behind the leisurely steps of the Messiah, pondering this harsh reality: Whether one bears fruit or not, cutting is inevitable.

Jesus sauntered quietly along the orchard, allowing this truth to sink in. After a few moments, as if His disciples required constant reminding, Jesus reiterated His thought with additional depictions.

"I am the Vine; you are the branches. If you remain in Me and I in you, you will bear much fruit." He did not beat around the bush. His parabolic narrative shifted from figurative to plain speech. "This is to My Father's glory, that you bear much fruit. For apart from Me, you can do nothing."

I was in the same boat as those early disciples. A glorious harvest was sure to come, but only as I remained in Jesus. So, I prayed a dangerous prayer. I asked God to search my heart, to remove from me everything that was not of Him. *Investigate my life, Oh God,* I whispered under my breath. *Find out everything about me; cross-examine and test me; get a clear picture of what I'm about; see for Yourself whether I've done anything wrong—then guide me on the road to eternal life.*

He answered my prayer with a swift strike to my tender branches, cutting from me recalcitrant tendencies; severing from me presupposed expectations of the future.

Lorna and I ached to start a family, but our busy ministry schedule would not allow her body to conceive. China's stressful spiritual climate mixed with our audacious diet left us continually ill. My stomach was always in a knot. I regularly struggled with bouts of "Mao's Revenge," and not even the strongest deworming medicine could cure my upset stomach.

As for Lorna, her hormones were totally out of balance and insomnia also plagued her. Every month for three days, she was bedridden in acute pain. We did not yet realize the severity of her medical condition. We were desperate for a professional to help assess what was happening in her body.

In January 2011, far beyond midnight during a sleepless night, she wrote me a note:

> *"Dearest David, my hormonal imbalance is interrupting my sleeping patterns, and once again I find myself unable to rest. But I sense the Lord's*

comfort right now. The heart of a mother is growing in me, and I see a father's heart in you. I am praying for you right now. Please do not worry about me. Please know that I love you and am committed to following you wherever you feel God leading us. I trust that the Holy Spirit will lead and guide you as we make big decisions together. Perhaps He is leading us to a new direction."

The next day, Lorna collapsed from pain. I rushed her to the nearest hospital where nurses administered an intravenous drip. Within thirty minutes, the doctor reported her shocking analysis.

"You have severe appendicitis," she said with a panicked voice. "You need to undergo surgery immediately!"

I had grown accustomed to this sort of silly guesswork in China's medical field, so I shrugged off the diagnosis. Lorna and I both agreed that another professional opinion would be required, but we were unable to find qualified medical practitioners in Kunming City.

We left the hospital and returned home, a take-out intravenous drip still attached to my wife's wrist. I babied her while she rested on the couch, propped pillows under her head, prepared soup before bedtime, and helped her remove the IV. She slept, weakened by the futile medical evaluation.

I laid awake that night, stared at the darkened ceiling and asked God for direction. I vacillated between two options: leave China for an undetermined amount of time or stay in the place where we had made a home for many years. But health considerations finally took precedence over the grief of leaving the community we loved, the friends we made, and the life we knew.

The next morning, I hastily purchased plane tickets to America. We scheduled to depart in one week, barely enough time to pack our belongings. I loaded our furniture into a rented storage unit. We would travel with only the necessities packed into two suitcases and two carry-ons.

Urgency and relief intermingled in our sudden departure. The new direction felt both refreshing and infused with uncertainty.

One week later, we boarded a flight from China to America, unsure the length of time we would remain in my country of birth. The plane taxied along the tarmac, and we stared out the window. Kunming City had transformed right before our eyes. Our memories of a podunk town lay buried below layers of pavement and cement. The city was no longer an underdeveloped agrarian landscape. Its burgeoning skyline now bejeweled with glass and metal high-rises; its thoroughfares jammed with Audis and BMWs. China's aggressive dream of modernization streamed past us, and as the airplane took off, we dizzied in its turbulent wake.

Our hurried departure made the loss of relationships feel particularly poignant. The Christian community at Kunming International Fellowship was a family with whom we shared similar passions and experiences. But there was little time to say our goodbyes, and that painful reality pricked our hearts.

A rush of juxtaposed emotions washed over Lorna and me. This foreign land had become a second home to us. Now, after many years of pioneer missionary work in Southwest China, we left behind all that was familiar.

Attempting to quell her uncertainties, I squeezed Lorna's hand as we looked out the plane window.

"America, here we come!" I blurted out. But there was a muted hesitation in my avidness.

"Here we go," Lorna repeated, unsure whether she should laugh or cry.

———◆———

I spent nearly my entire adult life in Asia, so settling into American culture was a difficult adjustment. Everything was strange; and I, ever-foreign, peered into my culture from an outside perspective.

It was cold in the forested, mile-high city of Prescott, Arizona. We found a small, semi-furnished studio-type home not far from the downtown courthouse square. One week after we moved in, the snow fell and blanketed the city with a six-inch layer of white solitude. Lorna and I sat inside the small home, warming ourselves under a thick quilt.

"What are we doing here?" I asked rhetorically.

"Let's just seek God about the next steps," Lorna replied.

My wife had always been the trusting type, hopeful for the future, expectant for the promises of God to be actualized. She contained as few answers as did I, but still she lifted her eyes to the hills, fully conscious from whence came her help.

The moments crept along at a snail's pace. Our schedule was empty. We felt out of touch and useless. In Kunming, we grew accustomed to a city with a staggering population. Now, here we were in my birth city, home to little more than 100,000 people.

Our Within Reach Global missionaries were halfway across the globe. We tried to push away plaguing internal thoughts that we abandoned them. *This is a new season, full of hope*, we told ourselves. But as we stepped away from China to pause and reflect, to wait on God, we were unsure if the ministry would thrive in our absence or crash and burn at our departure.

We stayed busy with medical exams and doctors appointments. We were determined to understand the cause of our infertility. After meeting with numerous medical practitioners, we became increasingly frustrated that Lorna's health remained the same. She was in acute pain, and no one had an answer for us.

But there was another problem. We did not have medical insurance and our short stay in America did not allow us to qualify for financial aid. Our numerous medical appointments began to add up, and the financial burden gradually became impossible to handle.

One doctor spoke to us candidly about getting the care we needed. Instead of staying in Prescott, she encouraged us to return to Asia where the financial burden was not as exorbitant.

The winds of change shifted and again we began to readjust our sails with the current.

"Does this mean we're leaving America?" Lorna asked.

"Whatever it takes for you to be well," I replied.

And so our stay in the United States was cut short by the necessity of medical care. Our five months in Prescott, Arizona was a difficult period of trying to decipher times and seasons. The moments filled with questioning tears and hopeful whispers, and God's reply came to us in subtle junctures.

We would now travel back across the Pacific to the Orient, unsure about the details ahead.

———— ♦ ————

The stimulating atmosphere of Manila was a welcome change from the measured downtempo of Prescott. With a population of twenty million strong, the vivid cultural landscape of the Philippines was the bustling metropolis we were accustomed to. We were home again and in our element on Asian soil.

Shortly after arriving in Manila, Lorna experienced one of the most painful months of her life. Her stabbing cramps were especially torturous, and she thought she might faint from the pain. We rushed to the hospital, desperate for help.

Doctor Delfin Tan was a gentle-mannered Chinese-Filipino doctor. He was well-known in the Philippines as "the grandfather of OB/GYN" and his grandfatherly aura brought a certain calm to our emotional and painful narrative.

But this was not our first exchange with the doctor. He was part of our infertility journey over the last five years. He performed our four intrauterine insemination procedures, each one resulting in failed pregnancy. Again he assessed Lorna's symptoms and gave his confident diagnosis: endometriosis.

"Women who suffer from endometriosis often encounter this sort of acute pain," he said. "It is also one of the leading causes of infertility. You will need major surgery to remove all the scar tissue."

Lorna and I were both alarmed and relieved. Her medical condition was much more severe than we realized. But in the doctor's diagnosis, we sensed light at the end of the tunnel. We could finally put a name to our distress. We could now begin to move forward with a sense of purpose.

Now we braced ourselves for the invasive laparoscopy and hysteroscopy surgeries that Lorna required. The prospect of having a child brought the buzz of anticipation, but I was still uneasy about my wife's safety. The only thing I could do was trust that God would watch over her.

I will never forget the day of Lorna's surgery. The date was January 9, 2012. The location: United Doctors Medical Association. At eight o'clock in the morning, just before Lorna was wheeled to the operating room, I stroked her cheek and kissed her forehead. *Oh God, please be with my beloved wife,* I prayed.

I was told the procedure would take two hours. So I waited, praying for Doctor Tan's hands, hopeful that everything would go well. He used small laparoscopic instruments inserted into Lorna's belly that resembled tiny scissors, knife, and cauterizer. A laparoscope camera inserted through her belly button projected images of her internal organs onto a monitor screen.

Doctor Tan began the painstaking task of removing every trace of scar tissue from Lorna's body. He clipped, cut, and cauterized, removing the unwanted lesions.

Ten o'clock came and passed, but Lorna was nowhere to be found. I waited impatiently, growing more nervous by the moment.

Hour after hour, trepidation gripped my heart. I inquired about the progress of Lorna's surgery, but no one could tell me how she was.

For thirteen hours I waited without a word of my wife's whereabouts. My heart sunk. *There must be some terrible complication*, I thought to myself. I prayed that I would not lose my wife. *Please, God, bring her back to me healthy and whole*, I cried. *Please don't take her from me.*

At nine o'clock at night, a nurse informed me that Lorna began to wake up, and was asking about me. I ran to the recovery room where she lay strapped to a hospital bed. I wept with joy and relief, thankful that she was still alive.

"Where is my husband?" Lorna cried.

The effects of anesthesia had not fully lifted.

"Where are you, David?" she whimpered in pain. "I can't see anything."

"My darling, I'm here!" I threw my arms around her and kissed her cheek. "Don't worry. I won't leave you."

It was as if she returned from death to life. The eight-hour surgery lasted much longer than expected, and she was still groggy after five hours recovering from the anesthetic.

Doctor Tan asked me to join him in the surgery room. He informed me that Lorna's was the worst case of endometriosis he had seen in twenty-five years of practice. He was exhausted but in high spirits.

"The surgery was a success," Doctor Tan informed me. "I did not realize how severe her case was until I operated, but I removed ninety-nine percent of the scar tissue."

He showed me the monitor screen where images broadcast from a laparoscope inserted in Lorna's belly button. There he watched his own ergonomic movements and rotations. His bloodied instruments still laid on a nearby table, and he wiped perspiration from his brow.

"You must be worn out," I said.

"Not really," he replied jovially. "It's kind of like playing a video game!"

"Well, Doctor Tan, you just beat the game." I threw my arms around the man, filled with a sudden surge of gratitude. "Thank you for saving my princess!"

———◆———

For the next three days, Lorna lay bedridden in the hospital. Her long road to recovery was slow and painful. The taxing surgery took a toll not only on her body but her memory as well. The lingering effects of anesthesia sunk deep into the corridors of her cranium, scattering her thoughts.

She struggled with this reality. So, three weeks after the surgery, I took her to a beautiful garden getaway south of Manila.

Sonya's Garden in Tagaytay was like heaven on earth for Lorna. The charming environment whisked her away with inspired rumination. The grounds were lush green and perfectly manicured. Dozens of distinct flower species laced the gardens, each blooming with particular beauty. Vibrant violet bougainvillea interspersed the lawn, and the scent of mint and tarragon wafted through the yard. Lorna breathed in the sweet, floral aromas and felt healing take place within her body.

Sonya's Garden was a prophetic atmosphere. It spoke life into our storyline of barrenness. The Gardener guided us through the valley of the shadow of death, then brought us out into spacious places where glory lit the dim pathways.

Lorna reclined on a sofa in the middle of the garden, penning her thoughts into the pages of her diary.

Journal to our Future Child, January 30, 2012: "Dear little one, exactly three weeks ago I underwent a major surgery for stage four endometriosis.

It was the hardest thing I've ever gone through. I felt like I was in the middle of the valley of the shadow of death. Just before the doctors administered my anesthesia, all I could think about was your daddy, the harvest we expect to see in China, and my hopes to see you and your siblings. My body is prepared for you, and I believe that you will come soon.

"There is something I want you to remember: God is always faithful. He is leading your daddy and me now. I sense His hand upon us at every step of our journey. You will experience His faithfulness, too. When you walk through dark valleys, you will never be alone. Waiting for the fulfillment of God's promises can be one of the hardest things to undergo. But trust in Him always. His promises are worth waiting for, especially when His promise is a beautiful child like you."

The pain that persisted for years was now removed from Lorna's body. All that remained were four small scars on her belly, reminders of the cutting she underwent. But the scars were more than that. They were reminders of God's omnipotence, of His ongoing presence and His trustworthy promises.

Every scar we carry is a quintessential mnemonic of God's grace and love. They remind us of the cuts and incisions we undergo in the garden of life. They are memories of shattered hopes and broken dreams from whence grow new limbs and leaves, flowers and fruit. So why would anyone covet a life without tragedy? The struggles we face—instances of pain, moments of loss, ache, agony, and discomfort—these are the things that press us deeper into the heart of God. For it is only after the swift strike of the Gardener's blade severs from us our impurities that new bloom appears.

But Lorna waited in vain to conceive for nearly a decade. The slow growth of the seed was indiscernible. Not even the slightest sprouting of life made its way through the crust of the earth. All that Lorna had to show for her years of hope deferred were four small scars on her flesh.

But she clung ever-tightly to the promises of God for our future children. She prayed again, "Lord, give me children lest I die!" Her ardent words ascended to Heaven, and God heard the yearning of her heart. He had been happily at work all along, pruning and preparing her garden for harvest.

Three months after Lorna's surgery, we moved into a new apartment in Quezon City, Manila. It was the beginning of another new season for our lives and ministry.

After the first night in our new apartment, Lorna woke up early. She sensed something strange happening in her body. At first, she thought it was the residual effect of anesthesia or the slow return of endometriosis. She slipped out of bed quietly so as not to wake me. I slept in, oblivious to the subtle divine movements within our small apartment. While I rested, Lorna basked in the presence of the Holy Spirit.

The sun rose slowly and crept over the balmy Manila horizon. Scintillant light rays leaked through the window blinds, spilled over the sill, and made my eyes twitch. From the bathroom, I heard Lorna gasp. She ran into the room and shook me giddily.

"David, wake up!" she said.

"What's wrong?" I asked dazedly.

"You're not going to believe this!" Lorna's face lit with effulgent delight. I noticed a youthful exuberance I had not seen for a long time. There was a childlike quality about her euphoria. In her eyes sparkled the charm and enchantment of her childhood; upon her lips hovered the blissful felicity of a little girl. But there was something more. I recognized in her a faint but unequivocally maternal countenance.

"I'm pregnant!" she announced, tears streaking down her olive cheeks.

"What?!" I could barely believe what I heard.

"I took another pregnancy test this morning, and the results are positive!" A sudden burst of emotion filled Lorna's heart and her voice cracked with delight. "We're finally going to have a baby!"

I bolted out of bed and embraced my wife. We spun around our little apartment, reveling in merriment. We cried for joy together, danced around the room, steeped in the hilarity of the moment. The barren valley we traversed for so long began to bubble with fresh spring water. For years, it percolated beneath the surface of the soil, watering the seed of faith. Now, the germination began, and new life would soon spring up in our midst.

Chapter 11

EVERYTHING IS NEW

"Come, and make all things new; build up this ruined earth; restore our faded paradise, creation's second birth."
HORATIUS BONAR

Far into the uttermost fringe of an impossible fantasy, hope carried us for years and finally placed us in the lap of the unknown. This was the stuff that faith was made of—not blindly following after vain hope, but an earnest trust in the faithfulness of God's plans and purposes.

In the darkest moments, we nearly gave up. When the road was hard and the path became treacherous, we threatened to return to the specious safety of skepticism. But God's tender hand led us through the dismal nightfall into a place where His glory illuminated the landscape.

On May 5, 2012, Lorna and I first heard our child's heartbeat flutter at 147 beats per minute. A new life skipped inside my wife's belly with rhythmic jubilance, and the world rejoiced with us. Family and friends joined our amazement at God's goodness. Our inbox filled with encouraging messages and heartfelt congratulations.

Journal to our Future Child, May 5, 2012: "Welcome, little baby! We prayed for you for so long, and now here you are. We are overjoyed. Every night I kiss your mommy's belly. Do you sense my love for you? You truly are a miracle.

"Only a few months ago, Lorna had stage four endometriosis. Do you know what that means? It means that it was impossible for you to join our family. But here's the thing: God is the God of the impossible. After four failed intrauterine insemination procedures, we were utterly hopeless. But on the other side of our sorrows lied joy unspeakable.

"Our situation was impossible, but you defied all that was against you. And as the power of God's hand steadily formed your infinitesimal beginnings, you grew and grew until two of the most beautiful red lines on a pregnancy test showed us you were coming soon. Now a father's heart is growing in me and a mother's heart in Lorna. We are preparing for your grand entrance, my child! No more shame. No more barrenness. The world around us is bright with brilliant, joyful hues.

"We love you, little one. We have had you in our hearts for years and soon we will have you in our hands. We dedicate you to God and welcome all that He has planned for you."

I found myself pausing at instances throughout each day, quieting my heart at the presence of the supernatural. I reflected on God's heart as a Father. He was faithful and trustworthy. Upon His promises could we rely. I heard His voice say "yes" and "amen" at every interval along the journey. "Come, My son," He called. "You were created for nothing more than to enjoy Me forever."

Though Lorna was glowing with maternal radiance, her pregnancy was not easy. Her low-lying placenta threatened miscarriage, so Doctor Delfin Tan requested she remain at home for the duration of the gestation period.

On August 8, 2012, an ultrasound revealed the sex of our child. "It's a girl!" the doctor told us, and happy tears streaked down my cheeks.

We returned to our apartment with pink paint, and I prepared a corner of the small room for our daughter's arrival.

Journal to our Future Child, September 22, 2012: "Dearest daughter, the tragedy of our past infertility is slowly fading. No, it's more than just a steady fade; it's a breaking forth into rapturous joy! The painful sting of barrenness is not as sharp as it once felt. New life glimmers from the shadowy recesses of our memories. You are the answer to our fervent, most heartfelt prayers."

———◆———

Lorna's pregnancy made it difficult to recall what the memory of barrenness felt like. Healing took place in her body, and new life grew beneath her scars. We saw the past through a new lens and questioned the validity of distant somber seasons.

Our memories jumbled and reconstructed. They were surprisingly malleable, and we could not fully trust our recollections.

The hippocampus is thought to be the center of emotion, memory, and the autonomic nervous system. This information-processing unit of the brain houses a multitude of tiny modifiable connections between neuronal cells. These cells, with their wispy, tree-like protrusions, hang like stars in miniature galaxies and pulse with electrical charge. The memories within are patterns inscribed in the connections between the millions of neurons in the brain. Each memory has its unique pattern of activity, logged in the vast cellular network every time a new memory is formed.

But my memories were not static entities; over time they shifted and migrated between different territories of my brain. They were less like books on library shelves or collections of self-contained recordings, pictures, or video clips; they may be better thought of as a kind of collage or a jigsaw puzzle.

The brain doesn't just create, store, and retrieve memories; it restructures them. Our memories mix with an awareness of the current situation. They work something like a pen and notebook. For a brief time before the ink dries, it is possible to smudge what's written. In the retelling of a story, memories become plastic, and whatever is present around you in the environment can interfere with its original content.

Memories are not frozen in time. New information and suggestions may become incorporated into old memories over time. Thus, remembering can be thought of as an act of creative re-imagination. My recollection of years past felt like memories that I had fabricated.

I looked back down the corridor of time. God's omnipotent glory cast a misty haze over my hippocampus. All that I experienced was called to attention. Meals of cat soup, grub worms, and pig brains—had I really dined on those delicacies? The bloody bus ride to a Kongge countryside and the midnight interrogation in a sugarcane field—had these things indeed occurred? Candid conversations with Wa headhunters; governmental persecution of our local missionaries; a one-armed Chinese girl begging on a bustling city sidewalk; years of bitter barrenness and infertility; stage four endometriosis—was it possible that these flashbacks were accurate? The memories were present, but the sting no longer acute.

I concurred with Mark Twain's witty retrospection: "I have been through some terrible things in my life, some of which actually happened."

But then the glorious mist lifted from my brain, and I saw

clearly. The restructured memories brought a peaceful calm, and the presence of God was indisputable. A single set of footprints in the sand spoke of His relentless love. I suddenly recognized a once-brass Heaven as God's veracious withholding that He might bestow upon me the greater things He has in store.

I stood on a precipice between my chasmal past and the vast expanse of my future. Multifarious instances led me to the present, and light broke forth over the horizon like the dawning of a new day. I closed my eyes and inhaled a deep breath of fresh air. I placed my hand on Lorna's belly. Beneath my palm, I felt my daughter's faint kick inside the womb and my heart fluttered with excitement.

———◦◦———

Two days before Christmas 2012, Lorna and I received the greatest gift of our lives. After twenty-three hours of labor and a forceps delivery, Cara Liana finally made her entrance into the world.

Time stopped, angels danced, and a broad smile formed on God's face. *They said you were barren,* I sensed Him chuckle with delight. *Doctors around the world said you would never have a child. Now look what I have done in your midst!*

I lifted up my daughter and cradled her tiny body. She fit snugly in my forearm. I pressed my lips to her forehead, staring at the little miracle. Her eyes were closed, and I felt the murmur of her heartbeat against my chest. "I love you," I whispered.

Forty-eight hours later—on Christmas Day—Lorna and I returned home to our small apartment, overjoyed at the arrival of our miracle baby.

But to our dismay, Cara's temperature spiked, and signs of infection after prolonged labor began to show. In the afternoon on Christmas Day, we returned to the hospital with our baby daughter. Cara was immediately admitted to the neonatal intensive care unit and placed in an incubator under blue bililights. An intravenous drip was inserted into her tiny wrist, bandaged with a splint and gauze to minimize her mobility. The fragility of her little life was evident. Lorna and I were exhausted and unsure of what to think. Again, our faith was tested.

For one week, she remained under blue lights. All I could do was watch her through the glass, wishing I could take her home.

Days passed, and Cara's temperature gradually returned to normal. The infection that gripped her little body and threatened to steal our abiding faith in God's promise waned. At the turn of a new year, we returned home once again with our miracle baby, this time for good.

A new year commenced with our newest family member, and life altered dramatically. My protective father heart was birthed; my plans and purposes shifted. Sleeping patterns changed, and I pondered new ways of providing for my growing family.

Months passed, each infused with new joy. We watched our daughter's eyes take in the wonderment of the world.

After nearly ten years of marriage, Lorna and I were finally parents. We were a family on mission, excited to introduce our daughter to our cross-cultural lifestyle. We planned to raise her on the mission field, sowing into her love for God and compassion for people—especially the poor and marginalized, and those who were unreached by the Gospel message.

But the Philippines was a predominantly Catholic nation with a flourishing evangelical Christian population. There were few unreached people groups in the country. Nearly every citizen had some context about Jesus Christ, the Christian Church, and an understanding of the One True God.

Lorna and I began once again to pine for the frontier mission field. We were made for pioneer missions among the unreached people groups of the 10/40 Window, but the Philippines was already blessed with a vibrant Christian presence. So, we began exploring new opportunities to move back to a predominantly unreached region.

Our missionary team was busy and in full swing, discipling Chinese college students in Kunming, reaching unreached peoples near Laos and Vietnam, and ministering to drug-addicted communities and orphaned children near Myanmar. We were proud of them. Part of us wished we could rejoin them in China, but we knew that for us medically, that option was impossible. We needed to find another location where our family could be based.

After much prayer and consideration, we zeroed in on Chiang Mai, Thailand. The city was relatively modern and well-developed. It was also known as a hotspot for medical vacations. We knew that should we make a big move back to the 10/40 Window, we required this kind of efficient medical care system.

Nearly ninety-five percent of Thailand's population adhered to Theravada Buddhism, a conservative school of Buddhism that drew its scriptural inspiration from the oldest record of Buddha's teachings. We had visited the city of Chiang Mai multiple times during our many years in China. The cultural mindset that "To be Thai is to be Buddhist" pervaded nearly every aspect of Thai society.

But while the vast majority of Thai people practiced Buddhism, religious tolerance was both customary in Thailand and protected by the constitution. So, the city of Chiang Mai filled with a considerable international Christian missionary population whose missional efforts focused both on Thailand and its neighboring countries. The total Christian population in Thailand remained at less than one percent, and we felt the country was the perfect spot from which to base our ministry.

Our church in Manila sent us off with their prayers and blessings. Pastor Dan Balais encouraged the church to stand with us, realizing that the Philippines was poised to play its part in global missions to the unreached world. We were blessed to be surrounded by friends and family, prayer warriors, and the bigger body of Christ.

Less than five months after the birth of our miracle child, we packed our belongings and set out on a new missional venture. Lorna's family sent us off from NAIA International Airport. Our departure was again filled with bitter tears and affectionate embraces. Lorna's mother cradled Cara securely in her arms and kissed her on the cheek one last time. Grandmother and granddaughter cried together. It was painful to watch. Lorna and I were again reminded of the sacrifice we made as cross-cultural missionaries.

———— ✦ ————

On May 6, 2013, we flew from the Philippines to China. A short-term missions team was scheduled to arrive for a two-week exposure trip, and we joined the Within Reach Global ministry activities.

It was a joyful time of reconnecting with our local and foreign missionaries. It was also a sort of "show and tell" as we introduced Cara to our team. But our local missionaries had been busy in recent months as well. Their families grew, and we rejoiced together at God's faithfulness. Zhang Rong and Zhou Guangming's wives had recently given birth to their children. Liu Zhenmei and her husband cradled their new infant, and Li Fuliang's wife showed off their new baby. We filled with delight to see these precious little ones.

Our time in China filled with underground leadership seminars and English corners. The short-term team joined our annual college student camp where for three days, over one hundred Chinese students were introduced to the Gospel. We traveled to unreached villages near Myanmar and saw new salvations among unengaged tribes. And at our missionary convention, we heard powerful updates and new ministry breakthroughs.

We watched with amazement and pride as our missionaries oversaw the many facets of ministry. In Lorna's and my absence, God solidified their callings and strengthened their giftings. Our faithful missionaries took the ministry of Within Reach Global to new heights and possibilities.

After two weeks in Kunming, we departed China for our new home in Chiang Mai, Thailand. The streets lined with ornate, golden Buddhist temples and tuk-tuks; alleys filled with bald-headed Buddhist monks in saffron robes. Orange cloth wrapped around their bodies, draped and folded in pious fashion.

We moved into a small home in a Thai neighborhood. Our landlords and next door neighbors were in their seventies. They were staunch Buddhists, but welcomed us warmly, thrilled that our daughter, Cara, joined their lives.

"I am happier now than I have ever been," our landlady said. "I already love Cara so much!"

Cara loved our landlady, too. We referred to her affectionately as "khunyay," which in Thai meant "grandma." Nearly every day, khunyay arrived at our door, bearing gifts of papaya and mango sticky rice. She sat in our dining room and fed Cara like she was her own granddaughter. After midday snacks had been finished, she wiped Cara's chin and sat on the living room floor, and the two played with play dough together.

Khunyay's hospitable sentiments touched us deeply. As a cross-cultural missionary family, such a welcome was exceptionally moving. We had never been accepted into a foreign culture with such amity.

I began part-time work as the social media and marketing director at ActsCo Printing, a company that provided Bibles and Christian literature for ministries throughout Southeast Asia. Kendall Cobb, the managing director of ActsCo Printing, moved to Thailand from Bibleway Ministries in Hong Kong where I smuggled Bibles into China in 1997. It felt like I had come full circle, reunited with old missionary friends who shared my passion for the unreached.

We joined an international church and connected to the Christian community in Chiang Mai. Though our new church shared similarities with the Kunming International Fellowship, still everything was new. Relationships took time, and we slowly began to make new friends.

Returning to square one was a humbling experience. We were missionary veterans in China, respected in our close-knit community. We spoke fluent Mandarin and could communicate at ease in China. We pioneered a Christian ministry and oversaw the outreach for years. We crisscrossed the rural country sides, planting churches in remote regions.

But in Thailand, we were the newbies. We were green again, starting fresh and learning to navigate our shifting roles of husband, father and minister, wife, mother and homemaker.

We began Thai language studies, grew accustomed to driving on the left-hand side of the road, and sought to find our place in the new cultural environment.

Every few months, we traveled back to Kunming, a mere hour-long flight to the epicenter of Within Reach Global outreach. Cara's passport filled with stamps from multiple countries; and by the time she was one-year-old, additional pages had to be added to her travel document.

Lorna and I had a tendency toward nostalgia and often reminisced about our early missionary experiences. Our "glory days" of traveling throughout China's forgotten landscapes were beautiful recollections. We recalled the rapture of pioneering new outreach centers together as newlyweds. We remembered the good and the bad, but the overall remembrance saturated with splendor.

Despite intermittent uncertainties in our new mission venture, the season imbued with hope and excitement. Our move to Chiang Mai, Thailand would reveal fresh new designs for our family and ministry. We would never experience the old glories like before. God had greater things in store for us. He would bring us from glory to glory, His spectacular purposes revealed along our journey in even greater measure.

———— ◆ ————

There were over 500 Buddhist temples in Chiang Mai, each with its own ornate grandeur. Serpentine forms capped the curved, undulating roofs, and at the sweeping apex rose blade-like projections. These ornaments suggested the fins and feathers of a giant humanoid bird-like creature called Garuda.

During the 10th century, Thai Theravada Buddhism and Hindu cultures merged, and Hindu elements were introduced into Thai iconography. Temples included popular Buddhist figures like the four-armed Vishnu, the eight-armed Shiva, and elephant-headed Ganesh. The naga, which appears as a snake, dragon, or cobra, could be seen twisting around temple spires and painted upon colorful interiors. The ghost-banishing giant, Yaksha, was usually present at ornamented temple grounds, palms pressed together in prayer-like fashion.

These sacred religious structures opened to the public, and laity came to hear sermons and say afternoon prayers. The chanting murmur of monks droned repetitiously through open halls, their prayers dissipating skyward alongside wisps of smoking incense.

On Loi Krathong, known as Lantern Festival, Lorna, Cara and I joined our Thai friends at Faham Temple. They invited us to join them as they bestowed gifts to orange-clad monks and sought holiday blessing. It was a Sunday morning, but we decided to skip church for a day of missional living outside the four walls.

We removed our shoes and entered the temple hall. Dozens of monks sat cross-legged on the floor, eyes closed and hands clasped in prayer. Sun rays fell diagonally through finely carved teak lattice window shutters, illuminating elaborate painted murals that depicted scenes from the life of Buddha.

Lorna and I sat in the back while Cara ran carefree along the red-carpeted floor. Our friends made their way to an enormous, golden Buddhist statue at the front. They bowed face down in front of an overweight monk, and he blessed them with a sprinkle of holy water. One of our friends raised her head surreptitiously from her bowed position, and with a spirited smile, motioned for me to take a photo of her. I found her desire to capture the in-action moment less duplicitous than whimsical. After all, the modern Buddhist needs a picture to post on Facebook like the rest of us.

I snapped a photo of our friends doing merit in the temple, and when the blessing finished, she returned to us in the back.

"Thank you for joining us," our friend said. "I'm happy you're here."

It was endearing to hear her appreciation. She was honored to share her culture with us, and we welcomed new awareness of the Thai way of life.

Cara still toddled around the temple, perfectly happy in her inability to distinguish the sacred from the secular. I picked her up; and as we prepared to exit the hall, I whispered into her ear.

"I'm happy that you're here with us," I said. "Lots of Christians might tell you that you shouldn't go inside a Buddhist temple. But that's just nonsense. It's good to bring light into the darkness."

My young daughter did not yet understand the gravity of my words. She smiled and wrapped her arms around my neck. All she knew was that her daddy loved her and she was comfortable wherever we went together.

If only every Christian were so childlike, realizing that their

Heavenly Father paid little attention to man-made religious vestiges. He was not perturbed to find us in Faham Temple on Sunday morning. He did not cringe at the monotonous chanting of devout monks. He would rather His children joyful wherever they went, running carefree around a Buddhist temple or between Christian church pews. For He knew that wherever His children went, the advent of His Kingdom was at hand.

Later that day, we returned home and joined our Thai neighbors for the evening Lantern Festival celebration. I held Cara, and Lorna and I stood beside our landlady, staring up at the night sky. Above us launched thousands of rice-paper lanterns, lit underneath by flickering orange flames. The Lanna-style lanterns resembled the large shoals of giant fluorescent jellyfish gracefully floating through the air. A warm glow fell over the city, and the black Asian sky was punctured by a myriad of prayerful afterthoughts.

The lanterns symbolized the release of one's defilement and of hopeful prayers. But to our family, it was simply festive entertainment.

Our landlady prepared two rice-paper lanterns, one for her and one for our family. I unfolded the delicate paper and wrapped it around the thin bamboo frame. I lit the fuel cell attached to the bottom and waited for the hot air to fill the interior. After a minute or two, the hot air trapped inside began to create enough lift for the lantern to rise. It wafted up, swaying in the gentle breeze. Cara's eyes sparkled with fascination. I wrapped my arm around Lorna, and we stood beside our landlady, admiring our little addition to the bejeweled azure.

At that moment, we felt connected to our host culture. Our hearts entwined with the locals and our lives mingled amidst Thailand's folkways. We were the newbies. We were the outsiders. We were the foreigners peering into a strange new culture. But at times like these, we felt at home in a foreign land.

We stood outside our home, watching the lanterns disappear into the distance until at long last we thanked khunyay for the experience and wished her goodnight.

After putting Cara to bed, I stepped outside to catch one last view of the remaining lanterns flickering along the horizon. The warm glow was gone, the flames consumed by the darkness of night.

Loi Krathong, like many other holidays around the world, was the perfect mix of joy and sadness. It reminded me of a poem by E. E. Cummings:

The city sleeps / with death upon her mouth having a song in her eyes / the hours descend, putting on stars / in the street of the sky night walks scattering poems.

I stood at the edge of the road outside our little home, contemplative and nostalgic. I thought of the quondam years filled with my whispered prayers. I launched them skyward; they floated across the horizon, and I waited expectantly for answers. Some answers arrived while many drifted into the expanse, seemingly overlooked and unnoticed.

My rumination was interrupted by an unlit lantern slowly descending back to the earth. Like a hollow, gray carcass, it collapsed on the roadside, crumpled and lifeless. Mere hours earlier, it was sent off as a hopeful prayer; now it was a hope deferred. Mystical otherworld deities were mute and powerless to reply to the supplication of the sender, and so the request went unanswered.

I thought of a nation gathered with eyes lifted toward the night sky. Some were expectant and hopeful; others exhaled a final auspicious breath in 10/40 Window wind.

I, too, raised my eyes to Heaven. Memories of the past, uncertainties in the present, and ambiguity for the future filled my mind. Everything about this new season was unfamiliar, and I pined for divine solace.

David, listen to Me, I sensed the Holy Spirit's gentle nudging. *I am not like the gods of the earth. I am the light of the world, shining ever brightly, scattering poems of life and redemption. Trust in Me to guide you. Even in the midst of bewilderment, be the light of the world with Me.*

In the mystifying mix of thought and body, there is a coalescing of God's handiwork. He reminds us of the value of each—the thinking life and the physical life—and reveals how to draw the best of these two.

The past had passed into the annals of time. There were countless instances when I misremembered moments of God's nearness during difficulty. There were whole portions of the story I unintentionally left out of my lifelong narrative. But He showed me how to remember what He wanted me to remember.

You're building memories, the Holy Spirit reminded me. *Make sure they're good ones.*

A vast amount of Christian scripture calls the world to the act of remembering. God beckons us to forget not the story we are a part of, the moments He has acted mightily, the things we have learned through difficulty and distress. God bottles our tears and understands our struggle. But more than that, He cares. He is concerned about the details. He desires that we find our joy in Him.

The journey of faith is one that requires memory. In every season of life, God has accomplished His purposes; and He is moving even now. Of this, we ought not to forget.

Chapter 12

THE CHASE CONTINUES

"There are far, far better things ahead."
C. S. LEWIS

Twenty-some-odd years later and I am still learning.

Along this winding path, the only destination in sight is an eternal kingdom. As long as I am clothed in this earth suit, there is no arriving; there are simply more roads to be traveled.

Some may presume that I have lived a risky life on the frontier mission field. Admittedly, there has been much risk involved with traveling to remote regions to reach unreached people groups. Conversations with headhunters under the dim glow of candlelight and bellicose police interrogations. These precarious episodes were par for the course. For where darkness pervades the atmosphere, light is generally not welcomed.

Hudson Taylor said, "Unless there is an element of risk in our exploits for God, there is no need for faith." Nearly every step along this journey has required active trust that God would continue to guide where shadows filled the pathway. Yes, there were risks involved, but great exploits were had because of them.

But the space between my memories is permeated with other more fundamental realizations. I would like to think that going from glory to glory only brings better days, but the truth is that the path is long and often leads to undesirable moments. I still grow weary of the arduous journey and forget to revel along the way. If the joy of the Lord is my strength, I need His constant joy to propel me onward.

The once alluring charm of the mission field has all but worn off. There are times I can barely see the forest for the trees. Asia's unique qualities have become obscured, and the mystique has dissipated. What was once so curious and peculiar to me has become second hand. I have learned to navigate anomalous cultural mores without flinching. I blend into my environment much better than I used to. But I am still ever foreign at every interval.

I have spent many a lonely season amidst a sea of strangers, and I will be lonely once again. I wish it were not so, but such is life. I have grown accustomed to this cross-cultural lifestyle, but I am still misunderstood. I forsook the temporal comforts of America for the sake of the Gospel, and some of my family and friends are still confused. They wonder what it is that I actually do at these distant geographical coordinates.

On numerous occasions, I have been tempted to give up my calling for an easier road. But in moments like these, I recall David Livingstone's daring declaration: "I never made a sacrifice," he said. "Of this, we ought not to talk when we remember the great sacrifice which He made Who left His Father's throne on high to give Himself for us."

God is still teaching me about the simple things in life; that He is at the center of everything; that He is still in control. And when at last these sudden epiphanies befall me, the temptation to think myself higher than but a bondservant of Christ is quelled.

There is another way to regard the last two decades of my life. Perhaps I never made a sacrifice; I simply bought a one-way ticket to China.

Years pass, and I am still susceptible to the ongoing struggle of frontier missionary work. After undergoing more interrogations than can be counted, I realize that risk is an integral aspect of the missionary endeavor. After seeing our local missionaries beaten by the police and observing governmental crackdown on Within Reach Global outreach centers, the sacrifice still feels poignant. But persecution is a promise from Jesus. "If they persecuted Me," He reminds us, "they will persecute you also."

What I am really learning is that a servant is not greater than his Master.

———— • ————

In May 2015, I traveled south from Kunming to Hekou City on the Vietnam border. I was accompanied by a short-term team and a group of Within Reach Global vision partners.

I planned to take the team to the same Yao minority villages where Frederik and I first traveled in 1999. I would introduce them to ethnic families to whom Lorna and I went eleven years earlier.

The team and I were joined by ten of our indigenous missionaries. Among them were Zhang Rong and Zhou Guangming, two of our most faithful local missionaries who made the long journey from our outreach centers on the opposite end of Yunnan Province. We were also joined by local Yao believers, Christian leaders we raised over the years to reach their own people.

Before departing Hekou City for Yao Mountain, our local missionaries treated the visiting team to a steaming bowl of dog soup and rice noodles. I amusingly observed the entertaining interaction between our Chinese missionaries and American foreign guests. For years, I was the instigator. I loved to introduce short-term teams to bizarre local delicacies. Our local missionaries must have been paying attention all along. I sat back and watched them giggle with delight as our visiting guests slurped their noodles, tentatively avoiding chunks of mutt meat.

As breakfast finished, we loaded into a minivan and began our northern ascent from the small city to the mountainous countryside. We bumped over narrow, winding dirt lanes, passing occasional roadside shanties that reminded me of my initial interaction with Deng Chunfu. We passed pockets of rural villages hidden among the precipitous ranges where we witnessed small breakthroughs among the Yao tribe.

I was in a particularly nostalgic mood. My mind filled with precious memories of missionary travels and God's faithful leading. I felt retrospective and emotional as I sat back and watched our local missionaries take the lead on this particular trip. I was filled with gratefulness and pride to see all that God had done in them. They were dedicated servants in the Kingdom of God, capable leaders in His missionary mandate.

Yao Mountain had not changed much over the years. Rustic lean-tos tucked within the banana and pineapple plantations, and the bucolic landscape bejeweled with a ripe harvest. The serene setting would have been romantic had I not known that a dragon resided in these mountains for millennium. The animistic Yao tribe was still largely untouched by a Christian presence, and the lurking spiritual darkness pervaded. I was unprepared for the surprising discovery awaiting me.

After an hour-long drive, we arrived at the foot of an expansive village. Ramshackle homes sprawled upward, gradually ascending the towering mountain peaks. We followed a winding trail that led up the sloping incline.

Zhou Guangming led the way, hobbling up the trail, crutches tucked under his arms. His atrophied right leg dangled awkwardly with every step, but it did not hinder his rapid pace. He traversed up and down worse inclines. He was a seasoned veteran, a trail-blazing itinerant evangelist, one who refused to flinch in the face of adversity. Guangming was not as handicapped as one might have imagined.

We arrived at the top-most home and paused to catch our breath. The sticky air stifled in typical tropical fashion. A layer of gray clouds blanketed the horizon, cloaking the mountaintops in a lazy haze. I surveyed the valley below. Verdant farmland wove between rising ranges and cascaded toward the Vietnam delta.

While we rested, Guangming and our Yao missionaries were inside the small home, greeting local residents. After a few minutes, they emerged from the miniature threshold and introduced us to the man of the house.

"This is Uncle Zhang," our Yao missionary smiled. "He became a Christian about one year ago."

I shook his hand and introduced myself. "I'm David. Hen gaoxing renshi ni!"

Uncle Zhang was in his mid-fifties, fit and graying with a cheery demeanor. As I spoke to the man, I immediately recognized his pastoral heart. He began telling us about recent salvations in his village.

"Twenty-six people gave their lives to the Lord in my home last year," he beamed. "A few of them were scared off from their new faith because of police warnings and cult activity, but there are still a handful of families that I am discipling now."

He told us about a group of women who met in his home every night. At eleven o'clock, Uncle Zhang and his wife secretly discipled them under candlelight because their husbands opposed their new Christian faith. Some of them beat and battered their wives because of their decision to follow Christ. The clandestine Bible study interrupted with occasional glances outside as the bruised women cautiously checked to make sure their husbands laid asleep in their homes.

Zhang Rong listened intently. He, too, spent many years sharing the Gospel among Yao communities and was blessed to hear testimonies of salvation. In the midst of ongoing persecution, the Yao were finally coming to Christ.

Zhang Rong sat forward on his small stool and placed his hand on my shoulder.

"See," he said, "I told you the harvest was in the seed!"

His eyes glimmered with joy. I sat silent, awed and overwhelmed that God used our small ministry to bring salvation to this unreached people group.

The wafting scent of garlic and smoke entered the room, and a table was set with porcelain bowls and chopsticks, fried greens, and steaming soup. We thanked Uncle Zhang's wife for the food and shared the meal with merriment. Afterward, we spent time praying with Uncle Zhang and his wife, encouraging them in their new faith.

We continued for two hours to the next village. We were greeted by more Yao Christians, who told us about nine new believers, each recently baptized at a nearby waterfall. This news encouraged me as I observed fruit blooming in the beclouded region. Years of missionary toil paid off as we witnessed people being delivered from their pagan rituals. We gave the new believers Bibles and Christian books, prayed for them, and headed to another village.

At the third village, we entered a little room where a crippled girl laid motionless on her bed. She had recently given her life to Jesus, and despite her limp, withered legs, her countenance radiated with newfound joy. There was a tenderness about her smile as she came to realize that she was a daughter of the Most High God. She was a princess awaiting a new, undamaged body. Someday, she would run across open fields in a glorious Kingdom, her hair dancing in the breeze as she turned to confirm that her Heavenly Father followed closely behind her.

I became overwhelmed with joy and stepped outside to hide my tears from the team. *Oh God, You have been at work in the hearts of the Yao all along,* I wept. *How could I have doubted You? You are the Author of salvation!*

I stood on the roadside, wiping the tears from my cheeks. My eyes fell upon a patch of wildflowers that blossomed at my feet. I thought of the description by William Wordsworth: "When all at once I saw a crowd, a host of golden daffodils." Orange petals fluttered in the gentle breeze, and beside them bloomed a bush of prickly purple flowers, a species I did not recognize.

With tears in my eyes, I stooped down and picked one of each flower. I planned to press the flowers for Lorna, to remind her that all was not lost. New life sprung up from the sordid soil, a spiritual harvest that we longed to see for so long. The flowers would serve as a remembrance of our many years of service among the Yao people.

A member of the short-term team, a muscly Hispanic man whose arms laced with tribal tattoos, carried the crippled girl outside and placed her in the front seat of the minivan. She would join the underground Christian training we planned for the following day. New Christians from villages in Yao Mountain arranged to travel to the city and join our fellowship. We expected the gathering to be a jubilant time of growing together in the faith.

Late that afternoon, we returned to Hekou City, celebrating God's goodness. But our plans were about to be altered.

After a two-hour drive, we entered the city. As we neared our hotel, three police cars with flashing cherry lights surrounded our vehicle. A megaphone sounded, and the gruff voice of a police officer demanded we remain in the van. The cops ordered Zhang

Rong to exit the vehicle alone, and moments later he returned to his seat.

"We're being detained," he told me. "They obtained outreach photos from one of our phones, and they want us to go to the police station."

My heart dropped. Zhang Rong and I had been interrogated countless times before, and it was never pleasant. Now, nearly all our local missionaries were in one place together, including their young children and new Yao believers. I braced myself for the worst.

The southern border of Yunnan Province was a hotbed of human trafficking. Vietnamese girls were traded into China and sold into the sex industry. Countless cults also made their way into the region, wreaking havoc on communities and scamming uneducated peasants. No wonder the authorities were on edge, dubious of outsiders, regardless of their purpose and intent.

We were escorted to the police station, and for the next six hours, we were questioned by the authorities, one-by-one. AK-47s slung over the shoulders of police officers. They spoke in forceful tones, hoping to extract information through manipulative means.

Where are you from?

Who do you work for?

What is the name of your church or organization?

The ten-month-old son and three-year-old daughter of our local missionaries cried in the sterile, dimly lit hall of the police precinct. I glanced outside the glass doors. Our crippled Yao sister sat still in the front seat of the van, frightened and unable to exit the vehicle. The orange and purple flowers that I planned to press for my wife wilted on the dashboard.

Hours passed and midnight grew closer. One of our local missionaries appeared from the interrogation room, bruised and bloodied. A father's heart ignited within me, and I became irate. I raised my voice to the police officers, demanding they adhere to the laws of the People's Republic of China.

"We have not violated a single regulation!" I shouted. "It's late, and we're tired. Let's get this over with."

Past midnight, the police escorted the short-term team and me back to our hotel. But they had yet to release our local missionaries. They shuffled us into a police car, and just before we left the precinct, I looked through the glass doors into the hallway. Inside the station sat the brothers and sisters I had raised over the years. Their worried countenance made my heart shudder.

Zhang Rong peered outside, and our eyes met. *Don't worry,* I motioned to him. *I am not leaving without you.* But the police car sped down the road. I turned around for one last glance at my detained friends.

The visiting team gathered in my hotel room and began interceding for our local missionary friends. The atmosphere filled with intensity, and we pleaded for God's favor. I bowed on the floor in anguish. I felt like a failure, like I had forsaken the ones so dear to me. I wrestled internally, wondering if this was all my fault. *Perhaps I should not have brought a foreign team to this area. What was I thinking? God, have mercy and set our local missionaries free!*

After forty-five minutes of intercessory prayer like those in the Book of Acts, there was a knock on my hotel door. I wondered if it was the police, returning to question us further. I turned the handle and cracked the door hesitantly. Zhang Rong stood in the hall with tears in his eyes. I was relieved to see that he had been released. But the emotional episode had taken a toll on both of us.

"They beat up our brother!" he wept in a hushed tone.

I placed my hand on his shoulder. "Wo zhidao," I replied tearfully. "I know."

We hugged each other tightly. I felt Zhang Rong's hot tears wet my back, and I was immediately reminded of his own experience of police brutality.

Six years earlier, he was arrested near Myanmar for preaching the Gospel among the Wa tribe. He disappeared for three days, and I was unable to contact him. When he arrived at my home in Kunming three days later, his face was covered with cigarette butt burns and bruises. I remember asking him if he wanted to lay low for a while, return home, and stay out of trouble. I will never forget his fervent reply.

"It is a joy to be persecuted for the sake of the Gospel," he said in New Testament manner. "I am honored to be counted worthy to suffer with Christ."

But today, he felt the blow of persecution for a brother he loved. This was an altogether different emotion. He felt as I had during his encounter with torture and affliction: powerless and paralyzed, unable to protect a loved one. Zhang Rong's very own apostolic father's heart swelled inside, and we wondered if this was the end of our ministry among the Yao tribe.

The visiting team sat in the hotel room, quiet and reverent, watching me and Zhang Rong weep for our persecuted brothers and sisters. I sensed their hearts grow for the plight of persecuted Christians. They experienced first-hand the risks involved with frontier missionary work in a hostile region. Persecution was real. It was no longer merely snarky remarks about Christian creeds or the rolling of eyes at the mention of faith. It came in the form of fists and made blood spill. I prayed they would carry this newfound passion back home to American churches.

The Western "Gospel" to which we have grown attached has become exceedingly absorbed with health and happiness, wealth and comfort. This erroneous perspective is directly opposed to the teachings of Jesus. No wonder that the suffering Church hardly ever crosses our minds; no wonder we so rarely pray for our persecuted brothers and sisters.

Nik Ripkin, a leading expert on the persecuted Church, goes so far as to say, "Rarely do sermons inform or inspire us about the suffering Church. We pray more for our military than we do for our brothers and sisters undergoing persecution. Even though Jesus said that He was sending us out as sheep in the midst of wolves, most Christians stay as sheep among the sheep."

The Apostle Paul reminds us to "Remember those who are in prison as if you were bound with them. Remember also those who are mistreated as if you felt their pain in your own bodies."

We are called to chase the heart of God; to join Him in His grand redemptive plan. His grace is upon those who suffer for His name's sake; His heart beats for those who have yet to hear the good news.

But the silence is deafening. Our prayers overflow with beseeching requests, rarely for a broken world, more for our own temporal trappings. While we are absorbed with material comfort and self-preservation, our response to God's heart is dreadfully lackluster.

But our visiting short-term team could no longer remain silent. They witnessed the unfolding of persecution before their own eyes; they heard the groaning of their suffering brothers and sisters. I prayed that they would cherish the meaningfully minuscule voices, like Horton did when he heard a Who call from a speck of dust, and vowed to protect it. I prayed that they would come to realize that "a person's a person, no matter how small."

The following day, I departed the city with our visiting team. We boarded a train back to Kunming, and our local missionaries returned to Within Reach Global outreach centers across Yunnan Province.

For the following months, our phones were tapped. Plainclothes police trailed local missionary movement. New Yao believers were startled at the sudden onset of persecution, and ministry efforts came to a halt.

But the blessedness of persecution would soon be realized. This promise from Jesus would not ensue without glorious outcome. Our team cast themselves completely into the arms of their Heavenly Father, believing that He was still in control.

Boldness came upon our local Yao missionary, who was beaten for preaching the Gospel. Not only did he return to neighboring villages to disciple his tribal brethren, but he also gathered the courage to propose to the girl of his dreams.

Six months after undergoing severe persecution on the Vietnam border, I returned with my wife and daughter to officiate the new couple's wedding. Our local missionaries traveled back to Hekou City with us to take part in the joyful occasion.

I was on edge that week, cautious and on yellow alert. I glanced over my shoulder a myriad times, scouring the sidewalks for plainclothes police. But Lorna was happy to be on the threshold of adventure. She had even gathered our daughter's outgrown clothing and shoes to give away to the poor.

One day after the wedding, our family strolled along the sidewalks of Hekou City in search for marginalized people to bless. At a curb perpendicular to the popular Vietnam Street, we spotted a small group of ethnic Yao mothers accompanied by their naked toddlers.

"Do you want to bless those kids?" Lorna asked Cara.

Our daughter's eyes lit with enthusiasm. She pulled a pair of outgrown shoes from her handbag and darted towards the naked children.

I watched my wife and daughter interact with the mothers and their young kids. They were touched by our small gesture of generosity. My heart filled with joy as I witnessed Lorna and Cara minister to marginalized families.

Meaningful missional moments like these materialized because of maltreatment. There could be no breakthrough without a battle. Triumph transpires only after severe trials.

I sensed the Holy Spirit remind me that there was yet hope for the Yao. The former glories would pale in comparison to His prospective plans. Orange and purple harvest blooms would grow bountifully across the countryside. Wilted flowers would return to the soil and germinate an expansive yield. Through the threshold of death, life would arise in the most unassuming spots. For God was ever in pursuit of unreached people groups and would cease at nothing to see their names written in the Lamb's Book of Life.

———◆———

When my family and I returned home to Chiang Mai, Thailand, the first thing we did was rest and reflect on God's goodness. We relaxed in quaint coffee shops and sipped hot Americanos. Lorna and I continued to read unfinished books while Cara played with Peppa Pig in a world of creative imagination. We decided to prepare a packed lunch and picnic at Buak Hard Public Park on the southwest corner of Chiang Mai's old city.

It was a cloudless day, moist and humid with moderate temperature. The park embellished with an array of fresh flowers and a series of small ponds. Cement sidewalks wound around the tailored grass and led up to Thai-style bridges that overlooked the water. Hundreds of catfish swam beneath the surface of the water, occasionally rising to dine on food pellets bestowed by generous visitors. Pigeons flocked on the lawn, awaiting a midday meal from passersby.

Cara and I fed the fish while Lorna watched us from our blanketed picnic spot. Reflections of an adjacent white bridge rippled on the water's edge like wet oil paint on canvas.

"Daddy, let's play hide-and-seek!" Cara said out of the blue.

"Okay! I'll hide first, and you try to find me."

She closed her eyes and began counting to ten while I found a tree trunk wide enough to hide behind.

"Ready or not, here I come!" Cara shouted.

After a short search, she found me peeking from behind the tree. A wide, girlish smile formed on her face, and she ran toward me, filled with delight.

"I found you!" she laughed and threw her arms around my neck. I spun her around until we both fell to the grass, dizzy and elated.

"Chase me, daddy," she said suddenly and took off across the lawn.

I watched her hair sway upon the gentle breath of the wind. The joy of life rippled through her muscles and coursed along her sinews with every step. It was a rapturous jaunt in expansive greens, a silly frolic over the verdant landscape. It was play without purpose, simple pleasure for pleasure's sake.

She turned to make sure I followed. "I'm going to get you!" I called, so she ran faster, giggling with glee. She felt my nearness, my outstretched hand brushing against her back. I caught her, and we tumbled on the ground together, panting heavily, trying to catch our breath.

Cara looked across the park and noticed the minuscule details: the blooming flowers, the rippling water, the playful catfish, and swooping pigeons. My miracle child filled with delight at the simple things. She could easily recognize the miracles of life and looked with wonderment at the world around her.

Oh, to possess such childlike awe! I thought to myself. *Oh, to see the mysteries of the world through an unblemished lens!*

King Solomon once said, "Do not say, 'Why were the former days better than these?' For it is not wise to ask such questions."

I often overlooked present splendor because I was so engrossed with former glories. I worried incessantly about the future. My nostalgic tendencies obscured the joy of the moment.

But I sensed the Holy Spirit say, *Don't dwell on the past. There are far, far better things ahead. Look around and see. This time, here and now, is the space between memories.*

CONNECT WITH US

CONNECT WITH DAVID JOANNES ONLINE:
www.davidjoannes.com

FACEBOOK: facebook.com/davidjoannesofficial
TWITTER: twitter.com/davidjoannes
EMAIL: david@withinreachglobal.org

TO LEARN MORE ABOUT WITHIN REACH GLOBAL
OR TO BECOME A MONTHLY VISION PARTNER, VISIT US ONLINE:
www.withinreachglobal.org

FACEBOOK: facebook.com/withinreachglobal
TWITTER: twitter.com/within_reach
NEWSLETTER: withinreachglobal.org/newsletter
EMAIL: info@withinreachglobal.org

⭕ **within reach global**

ABOUT THE AUTHOR

David Joannes is the founder and president of Within Reach Global, which serves the advance of the Gospel in some of Southeast Asia's most difficult places. David has a love for language, culture, and creative writing, and for the last 20 years, he has witnessed God's Kingdom established in forgotten parts of the globe. David lives in Chiang Mai, Thailand, with his wife, Lorna, and their daughter, Cara.

Made in the USA
Coppell, TX
15 January 2021